ROUGH MEN STAND READY

STANTON S. COERR

Armillary Press
Arlington, Virginia

Armillary Press
Arlington, Virginia

Printed in the United States of America and the United Kingdom

Book design and cover layout by Tara Mayberry, TeaBerryCreative.com

For Robin

Sonrisa de mi alma

Smile of my soul

I did not write this book for Marines.

The United States Marines with whom I served, in my twenty-five years in the world's most heavily-armed gang, already know everything here. The ones who were with me in Iraq you will soon meet. The others know who they are, and they know that this book is a look inside a tribe fierce in its ways, loyal to its members, ferocious in battle, and full of a deep love for one another and for the honor of their Corps.

This book is for everyone else.

Because it is *you*—*you*, the reader; *you* the taxpayer; *you* the American—who pays the bills. We work for you. You deserve to know what we do. And why.

It is for all of you that I wrote it down.

———•••———

Everything in this book happened.

I kept a journal in my right leg cargo pocket and I wrote in it hour by hour from January to July 2003.

The men with whom I went to The Show—Marines, soldiers and even one sailor—saw it all with me. I brought my five teams of Marines to work for a different warrior tribe, the proud men carrying the colors of the centuries-old Royal Irish. I was learning as fast as I could their regimental system and its nuances and I wrote it all down. Any mistakes in that transcription are mine alone.

———•••———

I want to recognize the two men who made me who I am today.

I went through Duke University on a Naval ROTC scholarship. Those of us who choose the Marine Corps as their future are handed to a young officer on the staff called an MOI: Marine Officer Instructor. I had two of those.

Ken Schwenke was a handsome young Captain with a charming young wife, a tanker on the way up and out of the Marine Corps to enormous success in the business world. Ken was a strikingly intelligent officer and a gifted, natural leader, smooth and calm, the sort of guy who always seemed to have the right answer. He was precisely the sort of guy an 18-year-old kid will gravitate to and emulate. His motto for all things was *it's easier to ask forgiveness than permission,* and my ability to make things happen in a combat environment are due to a certain ethically casual attitude about stupid rules written by those who don't fight...an attitude learned at his knee.

Ken Schwenke taught me how to win.

Ken was replaced by Mike Dossett. Mike is simply this: the finest United States Marine with whom I have ever served. He was polar opposite to Schwenke: a by-the-book, clean-cut prior-enlisted Marine infantry officer who finished first in *every single thing he did,* devoted husband and father of teenagers, and by the force of his example he showed us how Marine officers should be. Mike Dossett made us tough and hard, men of strength, men who always hear his voice in our heads insisting *you must be competitive.* His character and guidance were perfect counterpoise to Schwenke's.

Mike Dossett taught me how to lead.

———•••———

Thank you to Tim Collins, commander of the I Royal Irish, SAS OBE and Colonel, British Army, the finest small unit leader I have ever seen. Tim Collins taught me how to fight.

Thank you to Sid Heal, Glenn Walsh and Brian Borlet, seasoned combat veterans all, my confidants, who kept me sane while I was doing just that. You are my brothers for life.

Thank you to the men on whom I imprinted while learning how to write narrative nonfiction: James Webb (Marine); Karl Marlantes (Marine); Phil Caputo (Marine);Michael Herr (journalist);Hunter Thompson (crazed genius); George Christie (Hell's Angel...*and Marine*); Tim O'Brien (soldier); and Anthony Bourdain (chef).

And to the woman who is above them all in her literary gifts: Annie Dillard.

———•••———

Thank you to my wife and partner, Robin: biographer and writer and historian and thinker and my LoveChicken. You are the center of me.

And a special thank you to my sons: Tanner, Collin and Jackson.

The three of you will carry on my name, and with my grandchildren someday you will know the special love only a father can understand.

This book is my past; you guys are my future.

This book will help you understand Dad a little better.

May you never know the hard hand of war.

WHAT'S IT LIKE IN THE SHOW, CRASH?

—*Bull Durham*

Six hours before I heard my first shot fired in anger and saw my first dead body I awoke in the dark crystal of desert night, looking straight up from my hole on the Kuwait-Iraq border. Bombers were flying north, hundreds of them, too high for me to hear them and heading for Baghdad, and when they got right above me their rotating red lights winked off and they went black and silent when they crossed into war.

THE TRIBE

Listen to me, boy. Only gods and heroes can be brave in isolation. A man may call upon courage only one way, in the ranks with his brothers-in-arms, the line of his tribe.
—Steven Pressfield, *Gates of Fire*

A tribe requires young men to undergo a rite of passage, a time in the wilderness overseen by the elders. This rite for Marines is Officer Candidate School or boot camp. The elders are drill instructors and they are feared, and at their hand is the next generation shaped.

A tribe requires veneration of elders. These elders wear their status on their collars and their history on their chests.

A tribe requires its warriors to cut their hair all the same distinctive way.

A tribe allows you to mark yourself once you have been accepted. Those markings on biceps and triceps and chests are burned in with needles and ink and celebrate the tribe above self.

A tribe requires blood oath.

A tribe venerates its past in song and story. Marines sing of the Halls of Montezuma and stand straight and celebrate those who fell.

A tribe has a defined path to rule, overseen by the chieftains. These Marine chieftains are generals and Sergeants Major and their word is handed from on high by oral and written tradition, and it is followed without hesitation, and that path to rule is beset by strife and fear and blood.

A tribe has its own language, impossible by design for the uninitiated to understand. Only members of the tribe may speak that language. It is stripped down from normal speech into a patois of slang, insult, shorthand and icon, and refers constantly to rites and shared past an outsider has not experienced and never could.

A tribe celebrates the drawing of blood and the defense of its warriors, and there is no individual veneration without his trial benefitting the group.

A tribe is swift in excommunication of those who cannot compete.

A tribe exists to continue itself and that which it finds true, exports violence, and rewards death.

A tribe does not care about the individual warrior. The tribe protects itself. The warriors will die without hesitation for one another, and for the tribe. Those who do so are the basis of the songs and stories and the sacred text.

———•••———

George Christie was a Marine during Vietnam. He wrote a book called *Exile on Front Street*, and he discussed life in a tribe. Closed communities, he called them, and asserted the most important rule: you wear the same uniform, you're family.

After leaving the Marines, he was national president of the Hells Angels.

———•••———

JANUARY 2003 ▶ OCEANSIDE, CALIFORNIA
On the day before I left for war I went for my tribal markings.

Ten years seemed like an adequate cooling-off period for the tattoo I had always wanted, so I snuck off the base. This was in direct violation of the CO's directive that NO ONE was to leave Camp Pendleton for any reason. Well, fuck that...if I got killed, I wanted a Marine Corps tattoo on my body when I went into the grave.

I went into About Face, on the infamous Hill Street in Oceanside, on the recommendation of a heavily-tattooed friend. I was the only customer in there, and I had a sudden junior-high-kid-trying-to-buy-a-Playboy feeling. The guy at the counter came over to talk to me; he of course was tattooed up and down both arms and all over his neck. A wry, hand-lettered sign next to the cash register said Tattoo Removal Kit, and had an arrow pointed to a straight razor and bottle of rubbing alcohol taped below.

I started to have second thoughts. He showed me a huge book of designs, and I had a sudden light-headed feeling of being a woman looking at bridal patterns.

I knew I didn't want our Marine Corps symbol—the eagle, globe and anchor—because someone who is not a Marine would think it was just a cool design. I wanted the word Marines, and I had wanted it on the top of my left shoulder. The female Navy doctor who gave me my smallpox vaccine had put the kibosh on that idea, as my smallpox blister was beginning to form on my left arm. She made it clear that unless I wanted a burning infection I would have to get it elsewhere.

Well, OK...high on the right arm. My theory was that if you are in a group in which you are comfortable enough to take off your shirt, having a tattoo isn't going to matter.

The tattoo artist traced the letters from an obscure typeface book way in the back. He drew the design onto paper, which he then rubbed onto my arm. He did it four times, my heartbeat increasing the longer I sat in the chair. Finally he was ready, and pulled out a fearsome-looking needle gun and ink bottles. I tried to be cool and tough.

The needle jumped into my arm, and there was no turning back.

Marines.

The guy mentioned that a lot of my tribesmen had come in before they deployed, kids, mostly, and had gone heavily for the skulls and crossbones and bright colors and dripping blood.

The Marine Corps would be with them forever.

Now it was forever part of me, even after I was dead. Especially then.

———•••———

Where you been? We ain't seen you, said a soldier in Vietnam to writer Michael Herr.

Up in I Corps, Herr replied.

With the *Marines?*

That's what's up there.

Well, all I got to say is Good Luck! Marines. Fuck that.

RISE

Men must do or risk something to become men.
—Camille Paglia

Of the first 23 American astronauts, 20 were first-born sons.

———•••———

1987

I came home from college my sophomore year and announced to everyone that I had joined the Marines' officer program.

The man next door to my boyhood home sold insurance. He was the sort of man whose kids called him sir and who yelled sweaty from behind the mower on hot summer days for one of his daughters to bring him a beer.

I went over to visit and told him what I was going to do.

He said you know they teach those Marines to eat snakes.

———•••———

AUGUST 1990 ▶ FIRST DAY OF FLIGHT SCHOOL, PENSACOLA, FLORIDA

I walked into our new apartment and as I stepped in my roommate handed me the phone. On the other end was our buddy, a Marine tank officer with whom I had gone through Duke.

Desert Shield was kicking off, and all of us who had selected flight school were not the BMOCs anymore of whom everyone was jealous. Now, *we* were jealous of those who had gone into ground combat jobs and were preparing to go the Gulf and fight and kill bad guys while we memorized things from books in Florida.

Hey Stan! We are spinning up like you read about.

Wait...you guys are going?

Yes, I'm going. *The whole Marine Corps is going.*

And that said it all.

The whole Marine Corps, that is, except me.

———•••———

So I tried to quit.

As Desert Shield built toward Desert Storm, the Marines in flight school grew more and more agitated. Our brothers were deployed in the desert, preparing to get into the fight.

We were buried in books, sitting in classrooms, chasing girls in the Pensacola bars, sweating in the Florida summer, missing the action. We felt like an NFL practice squad sitting in our street clothes while guys we knew played the game.

We wanted into the fight.

So as a group we formulated a really great plan.

On a Monday morning a baker's dozen of us Second Lieutenants showed up at the training command headquarters, to the building that owned all of us. We wore our service uniforms and walked down the long corridor to the suite of offices supporting the commander.

On the way we passed the usual row of photographs, former commanders going back decades, each stern and formal in his service uniform for his command photo in front of American and Marine Corps flags.

Except one. One Colonel from the 1960s glared at us from behind his glass, but he was wearing wrinkled field utilities. A big, stern bulldog of a man.

Colonel Donald Conroy, U.S. Marine Corps. The Great Santini.

We marched en masse into the front office. A sweet lady asked us what we needed and we told her: we need to see the CO.

Right now?

Yes, ma'am.

She swept the group and looked alarmed.

All of you?

Yep.

She disappeared into the Colonel's office. A male voice boomed out: get in here!

She fled. We entered.

We stood at attention, fresh-faced and clean-shirted, our uniforms but for the CNN ribbon we each wore but had not earned bare of decoration. Even our brown lieutenant bars blended into our brown shirts.

The Colonel rocked back in his chair, bemused, wondering the source of this mutiny. *His* chest was a block of color, row upon row of combat decorations, air medals and awards for heroism and leadership and command and war, topped with gleaming gold naval flight officer wings. On each collar perched a silver eagle.

Now he stared at us and did not smile. This was Spider Nyland, an up-and-comer, veteran of hundreds of fighter missions in Vietnam, former fighter squadron commander, future four-star general.

We had a spokesman. He took a half step forward.

Sir, we want to quit.

Spider iced over.

You what?

We want to quit. There is a war in Saudi Arabia. We want to go to the infantry. We can do more good there than here.

All of you?

Yes, sir, all of us.

Spider glared at us. He rocked forward in his chair and put his arms on the desk. The moment hung in the air.

He pointed at us. You motherfuckers! Get out of my office and get back in your fucking books!

That answered that.

We scurried out. I whispered to the guy trotting next to me That went well. He said shut up.

We ran, whipped, back down the corridor.

Santini glared, unimpressed.

As we fled, Spider's voice echoed down the hall after us: IF *I* CAN'T GO...*YOU* CAN'T GO!

———••———

One of the guys with me that day was a big, handsome BMOC type guy, all muscle and knowledge and confidence, the kind of guy we hung around in the bars, to pick up the castoffs from the girls who were throwing themselves at him.

We hadn't even started flight school yet but we knew how hard it was, through dark rumors and gossip and the pipeline of older members of the tribe, discussions with guys ahead of us.

Not this guy. He feared nothing. He had the mandatory convertible sports car and he even went out and got a new license plate for it that read GETJETS.

He washed out.

———••———

On the day I was accepted to graduate school at Harvard, I walked through a canyon on Camp Pendleton. A hawk flew directly across my path. It was carrying in its talons a writhing rattlesnake.

———••———

Shiloh

He walked away with only his clothes and his only shoes
And our only rifle
The men waited at the fence for him, quiet and still
Staring hard at me
As if they would never see me again
Their hats were pulled down low over their eyes so they were
    looking at me from the mouths of caves
Which was just fine cause I did not want to see their eyes and
The lying in them

They knew better than to speak to him, or to me
Or to the children

Jacob crawled along the first row of corn and wove in and out of
The stalks like the snake we saw
Last summer
Sarah stood next to me and watched her father walk away
She held very tight to my skirt
She did not cry

The men watched him come and I could not hear a thing
Nothing, just dead silence
No marching feet or drums or horses like I had heard
The last time

This time just nothing

These were sent for him, only for him
I knew they needed men, or that is what I heard
I wish a bird had sung, or one of the dogs had howled because
This silence made it harder

I was alone now, alone before he even left, alone when they
Came
Those days ago to speak with him
Heavy voices by the fire
He had left me then, now they were here to take him

Then quick now one sound
Abraham age seven ran from behind the house with a long stick
    against his cheek and with his one eye closed just like daddy
He fired

VIGILS

Caminante, no hay camino,
se hace camino al andar.

Traveler, there is no road; you make
your own path as you walk.
—Antonio Machado

JANUARY 2003 ▶ CAMP PENDLETON, CALIFORNIA

We had our farewell dinner at the run-down Subway next to my run-down barracks. Very romantic.

I was a mess.

I had a sinus infection, yellow fever and anthrax, all running through my system from yesterday's inoculations. I had no sleep last night, my left arm burned and itched from my smallpox scratch, my right arm burned and itched from my now-four-hour old tattoo covered in Vaseline, and I was an emotional wreck as I prepared to say goodbye to my three-year-old son.

Little Jackson didn't comprehend what was happening, or why everyone kept crying. We poked around the base a bit, Jackson wanting to climb and explore. I showed him an owl nest in the queen palm above our barracks, with two chicks in it who peered over the edge at dusk each night and cheeped at us.

In his tiny orange Izod shirt, he looked so small and helpless. He needed his daddy, and I needed him.

Then just like that, it was time to say goodbye.

I knelt down and held Jackson by the shoulders in the parking lot. I looked him in the eye.

Buddy, you know that Daddy loves you very much.

Jackson looked at me and then at the ground. Yeah, Daddy.

Daddy is going away, just for a little while. I am going to be back very, very soon. You be a good boy, OK?

At that, I held him close, and he threw his little arms around my neck. He said, I love you, Daddy, and he suddenly grasped that I was leaving for a long time and we both started to cry.

I couldn't breathe.

I buckled Jackson into his seat, kissed him and stroked his hair.

I was dizzy, woozy from the vaccine in one arm and new ink on the other, sick and tense from excitement and anger and frustration and sadness, drained and drawn. I hadn't even done anything yet, and I was already exhausted.

Hiding the tears from my little boy, I turned and I walked away and I did not lookback.

Alpha Company I/7 was sharing the hangar with us. Real Marines: straight-up infantry, and a desert battalion to boot. If there was going to be a fight, these guys would be in it. Their CO was a few rows down from me, another of the million or so officers whom I knew from somewhere but couldn't quite place. He was a good man: these kids would be in good hands.

And that's what they were: kids. When you strip away the huge, fearsome weapons and ammo belts and beefy flak jackets and helmets and gloves and sunglasses, these Marines look no different than the high school kid who just handed you a burger through the drive-through window: skinny and pale and with their shaved heads somehow even more innocent. Every time I see a bunch of Marines in one place, I am slapped in the face by how they look. I heard a woman once say My God...they're just babies! and she was right.

They were all scared to death of me. Their Staff NCOs put the fear of God into them about officers to start with, so even Second Lieutenants were basically immortal in the eyes of these kids. A Major may as well have just walked down from Olympus, as far as they were concerned. In addition to my Major's gold oak leaves, I wore two sets of wings on my left breast- gold jump wings and gold aviator wings—so I was even more intimidating. They could see from across the room that I was Someone Important and the crowd opened when I passed and then closed behind me.

———•••———

I loved these kids. They piled up together like puppies, sprawled on the floor, sharing their chewing tobacco and magazines and telling each other to shut up and fuck off. Some of them were the same age I was as a high school senior.

One young Marine was sound asleep right on the concrete, lying on his right side, both arms and both legs wrapped around his rifle and a water bottle for a pillow.

Hip-hop music blasted from one corner, and U.S. Marines heading to war watched *Born On The Fourth Of July* on a TV in the center of the room, nonplussed at the scenes of Tom Cruise as Ron Kovic, U.S. Marine in a war, vomiting and shitting himself in a VA hospital after being shot through the spine.

Irony died a quick death in that hangar and stayed dead.

———•••———

Three hundred men were sharing one head, trying to piss and shit and shave and bathe and brush their teeth in ten sinks.

All of us had oozing smallpox vaccine blisters, which we had been Ordered Not To Touch for fear of spreading the infection. My thought: if every one of us already has the infection, which you assholes gave us in the first place and without which we can't even get into Kuwait, who were we afraid of spreading it *to*?

But we all kept our mouths shut and dealt with the blisters, which were at first beneath bandages. We were told that once the blister pops on its own, we were to take the bandage off to let it heal.

Some guys were inoculated before others, and thus decided that this filthy bathroom crammed with guys was the place to take their bandages off. The trash cans overflowed and bandages soaked with pus and disease and blood fell in drifts around the cans and we left them there.

I FEBRUARY 2003 ▶ 0700
Third Air-Naval Gunfire Liaison Company was 26 hours on the move.

I let the troops shuttle through the 747 cockpit. The pilots saw my aviator wings and so I went last.

I sat facing directly forward on a sheepskin-covered jumpseat, like in a Volkswagen Beetle, and watched the pilots doing their thing. That marked the first and last time I have walked into the cockpit of an airliner in flight while carrying a weapon. There was a lot less actual flying than I expected...the two pilots took turns getting up to pee and getting coffee and talking to me while the autopilot guided us over the Alps.

Overwater airliners, I discovered, all had a fax machine, like a teletype machine from the old movies. The airlines had centers in the States from which they received guidance via satellite link... where the crew will stay overnight, times of departure for the following day, messages from family to the pilots, and so forth.

The lead stewardess on our flight was terrified about staying overnight in Kuwait City, convinced that terrorists would attack anyone delivering the American military into the Persian Gulf, and was thus relieved that this crew was scheduled to turn straight around back to the States after dropping us. The pilot in command therefore impishly invented a letter from Delta center to the plane, informing the crew that they would be staying only a few days in Kuwait and even giving hotel reservation instructions. The three pilots gathered at the front of the plane while that stewardess was summoned and, with serious faces and heavy tones, handed the memo with the information they had created. All shouted with laughter when she reacted with horror and then saw through their gag.

———•••———

I watched the sun slowly setting over Italy.

Over Milan, the teletype came alive.

It faced me so I watched the letters clacking across the page:

Space Shuttle Columbia has broken up over Texas while on final approach. Tell everyone before they leave the plane.

All aboard are dead.

———•••———

The stewardesses were taking photos with our Marines; they held our rifles, one in each arm, and the Marines cheerfully draped arms over their shoulders.

The pain of missing my son grew as a linear function with our distance from home.

On our long descent into Aviano, Sid joined me up front to watch a gorgeous sunset over the snowy Italian Alps. Breathtaking from this altitude. Small, tidy houses dotted the small villages in the farmland at the base of the Alps over which we descended, into orange glow from the sun on snow. The houses were quiet and innocent and unknowing in the gloaming.

———•••———

Aviano.

This was a smooth, most cheerful and efficient operation ...the American Red Cross in action again. Nice ladies, young...Air Force wife volunteers smiled and greeted us as we rolled in. Everyone piled into the heads, again, which naturally and promptly run out of toilet paper and hot water. Juice, coffee, cookies, goodie bags, nice people, warmth.

A clean, smiling officer in civilian clothes gathered us together to greet us. This was Lieutenant Colonel Romano, the Air Force guy given the task, I guess, of taking care of this cranky skinheaded group of Californians for our few hours here. He was a brash and good-natured New Yorker and keeps insisting if you need anything, you let me know. Me, personally! I will get it for you guys! Beer, pizza, women—except that one over there in the red... she's my daughter!

We fanned out and ratfucked the goodie bags: sunscreen, lotion, shaving cream, pens. One table had a husband-and-wife team with a digital camera and clipboard; they took photos of each of us and had us write out an e-mail address to send it to and the message was your husband is safe so far.

I ate a cookie and sat by myself in a plastic molded chair, just watching the boys. I realized with a start that though our bodies thought it was dawn, it was actually a Friday night, and all these Air Force folks seem to have no other goal than getting us what we need. On a Friday night. I was impressed.

Air Force F-117 guys in here with us, the 8th Fighter Squadron. F-117s. If *those* guys are here, that means this thing is *on*.

Aviano was beautiful and freezing, below zero. We were surrounded by snow-covered peaks, and the word picturesque kept coming to mind. We were now through two sunrises and two sunsets on our journey...chasing the sun around the globe.

The pilots and stewardesses were in the hangar with us, chatting and drinking coffee. They seemed worried for us, as did all the volunteers here.

Jet lag hit. I remembered Officer Candidate School...the more tired you get, the more sorry for yourself you feel. The troops gave me energy.

As we stood up to troop back to the plane, Sid put it perfectly: This is the end of luxury for a long time.

———•••———

Aggressive, controlling Type A personalities like mine were precisely the kind that get ground down by the Marine Corps system if you take things too seriously.

I was content to just look out the window, wait for someone to tell me what to do, letting life roll along with me adrift on top.

———•••———

Mark Twain said wars were invented to force Americans to learn geography, and our 747's route of flight took us over Europe, over two oceans, across the Persian Gulf. We now flew with windows closed and lights off.

We passed over Luxor, a beautifully lit city arcing around a bend in the river. I only knew the city by looking at the map the pilot showed me and snuck quick peeks below the shade. The night was crystalline, sparkling, gorgeous.

We crossed Saudi Arabia and headed out over the Red Sea toward Kuwait.

Off each wing was an American fighter plane.

———•••———

0242 KUWAIT TIME ▶ 2 FEBRUARY 2003

We were on the ground in the Persian Gulf. It was the first time in this part of the world for most of us; I wouldn't be a bit surprised if it was the first time on an airplane for some of these guys.

On the way in, one of the pilots got up and disappeared into the cabin. He came back to me and said I need you to hold this for me. It was a tiny bottle of Jack Daniel's. I was touched and told him so.

The lead stewardess, she of the fear of staying in Kuwait, made the final announcements over the PA...fasten your seat belt, tray tables upright and locked.

She continued her usual patter and then her voice hitched and she unkeyed the mike.

She took a deep breath and came back on and wished us all good luck and then she started to cry.

LAUDS

We are not briefcase-carrying guys.
Our job is to make widows and orphans.
—Colonel J.P. Sexton
Commanding Officer Marine Aircraft Group 39
to his attack pilots, 1992

Sid Heal stood in the middle of the squad bay at dusk, the entire tent gathered around him. He was the oldest among us, by far, and this would be his fourth war.

Sid was a radio operator in Vietnam. His unit was eight-inch guns, enormous artillery. They were firing in support of the infantry and they fired so many rounds everyone was worried that the last round in the gun would simply explode in the burning-hot tube, cooking off, killing everyone around it.

The muzzle blast of that gun is so powerful that it had cut the communication wires, so young Sid was holding the wires together in his hands, to get the data to the guns so they could get the round out of the tube. He was directly beneath it when the gun fired.

When a round is coming in—or, in this case, going out—young Marines are taught to scream for as long as they can. Screaming equalizes the pressure in the inner ear, and helps counteract the violence of the enormous noise and pressure wave from exploding ordnance.

Sid did that. He was knocked flat, unconscious, by the concussion of the blast, and then got up, walked across the LZ in a daze, made it to the CP. He sat in a chair and then fell over and didn't stand up again for weeks. His left eardrum was blown out and he had a traumatic brain injury: he ended up in Guam.

He was in Somalia during United Shield, General Zinni's withdrawal, and fought in Desert Storm as a member of 3d ANGLICO. On top of all this, he had been in more street fights than the rest of us put together, and these things combined to give him an air of authority and weight.

A Marine asked him Sir why are we doing this?

He said in Desert Storm women...and now he choked up...women were coming out of their houses screaming USA! USA! USA! They were holding up their babies to us, the only thing of any value they had to show us. They were crying.

He was choking up and then he too was crying, and he said that's the reason we're doing this.

———◆◆◆———

Sid later told me more, about the fight he was in on Firebase Ross months before he was wounded.

They were trapped, cut off, surrounded, overrun, the Viet Cong using the January monsoon rain in the middle of the night to cover their approach. It was the end.

It was so bad that the artillerymen of 3/11, India Battery, shooting right next to Sid's unit, was doing a direct-lay of the 155-millimeter guns, shooting a truly nasty round called the flechette flat into the trees around them. The flechette is a round full of thousands of fin-stabilized nails, and going out faster than the speed of sound they simply vaporize anything in front of them in a monstrous blast of fire and heat and sound and steel.

His own unit's eight-inch guns had boresighted their tubes flat into the treeline as well. They didn't have flechette so they got down to the last option: putting the bags of gunpowder one after the other into the gun without any rounds and just blasting away with that, making an enormous flamethrower. When even that didn't work they got to the end of the line, and were preparing for It, The End, the last full measure in which they would take their rounds apart, pull out the eyebolts, load *those* into the tubes, and destroy the tubes with one last horrifying blast of scything shot and then fight by hand and rifle and knife anyone who kept coming.

But then into the fight and up onto Ross came other men from Seventh Marines, Bravo Company I/7, men he didn't even know, running into their lines in the howling dark, running with crates of ammunition and pulling it into the holes with them, firing heavy weapons and sprinting into a hopeless fight they knew was to the death, running to the sound of the guns to save their brothers. And Sid teared up and told me that he loved that unit and those men and their descendants now, from that moment to this.

The tribe.

⎯⎯⎯•••⎯⎯⎯

Tim Collins, Lieutenant Colonel British Army, Special Air Service and Commanding Officer, I Royal Irish Regiment turned to greet me with a smile and tilted head, a handsome, powerful man with grey hair and bright blue eyes.

He sized me up as my boss introduced us, and seemed pleased that the Marines had given him a field grade officer, an attack helicopter pilot no less, and four teams of highly-trained fire support experts to make his job easier.

Good to have you, Stan. I must take you over to meet the lads-after this meeting? he said in a marvelous Belfast brogue. Purebred Irishmen somehow seem to sound exactly as Americans *think* they should sound, and Collins was no different. His educated, singsong Irish accent made listening to him a pleasure.

We had all heard of the SAS, legendary operators who were the unit on which the American's Delta Force was based. Anyone who came from one of those units would be a fighter of the first order. I was going to like this guy.

———••———

The Royal Irish Regiment was raised in 1688, in Enniskillen in what is now Northern Ireland.

They are closely aligned with the people of that country, and the Regiment has a shrine to their exploits in St. Anne's Church in Belfast. The two battalions then were the Enniskillen Fusiliers and Enniskillen Rifles. Numerous combinations and changes ensued over three hundred years of history, culminating in these battalions' merging with the Ulster Defense Battalion to form the 1 Royal Irish Rangers, later renamed the 1 Royal Irish Regiment.

The officers with whom I deployed to the desert still referred to their soldiers, fondly, as rangers, not soldiers, to distinguish them from the Royal Irish Guards, a 9-to-5-type unit of the Royal Irish which performed day-today police duties in Belfast and went home to their families at night. These men wanted no confusion between their combat-tested trigger-pullers and their brothers back home.

The British Army uses a regimental system: your identification is with your regiment above all else. The men know and take care of each other throughout their careers, and the regiment is your home. If your father was in 1 Parachute Battalion, you too will be in that unit. So will your son, and his after him. It is not uncommon to meet officers who were the third or fourth generation in that very same unit of 600 or so men. This is a tribal brotherhood.

The United States Marines are different. Our loyalty is clear: to the Corps itself. That is our tribe. It is very unusual for an officer to go to the same battalion twice, still more unusual for someone to be raised in a unit and then command it. Loyalty in the Marines is to Corps, then country, with unit somewhere down the list. We all know we will be with one battalion for only a few years, and then likely never again.

Collins himself had started as a Lieutenant with the Royal Irish, as had many of the Captains and Majors we had with us now. It was not uncommon for enlisted men to serve their entire enlistments with the battalion. The father of our intelligence officer had been a Sergeant Major with the Royal Irish, and several of our Sergeants Major had actually babysat for this officer when he was a *just a fat little toad*, as the Regimental Sergeant Major, the RSM, delicately put it.

Sergeants Major run things in the British Army as they do in my Marine Corps, but with a twist.

First, there are several Sergeants Major in a British battalion. By contrast, a Marine rifle battalion (and all other units of that size) has only one Sergeant Major. For us, he is the unquestioned king, and by tradition is even called sir by enlisted men, the only enlisted Marine so honored.

Second, for us Sergeant Major is as high as an enlisted man goes, and is very high indeed. The British Army, in what I think is a much more intelligent use of these men, allows them to move laterally into the officer ranks, directly from Sergeant Major to Major, with the understanding that they will almost certainly go no higher. This made sense to me: while allow that much infantry experience to walk out the door due to a man reaching an arbitrary number of years of service?

Because of this quirk of the British system, we not only had several Sergeants Major in the Royal Irish, we also had some *very* senior Majors. These men were my peers in rank, but I was certainly no equal to them in the field of infantry.

This tribal knowledge, honored and retained within one battalion, made for a very strong unit.

I was proud to be with them.

————•••————

Collins took me over to the 16th UK Air Assault Brigade briefing tent to introduce me to the lads.

The British Army is actually an army of the entire UK; the Royal Irish alone had men from seventeen different countries. Our officer cadre alone held men from England, Scotland, Wales, Northern Ireland and the Republic of Ireland to the south, Canadians, even an Australian and a South African. Brian and I added American to the officers' list, and our Marines added Mexicans to the Royal Irish stew.

I was charmed and impressed immediately. 1 Royal Irish had four rifle companies, all commanded by Majors. The British treat rifle company commands as a much more senior billet than do the Marines, who usually assign midrange Captains, even sometimes First Lieutenants in a pinch, to these positions. When I thought about it, it made sense: rather than using company command as a proving ground, a stepping stone for higher rank and billet, the British Army treated that job as an end in itself.

Like my Marine brethren, all these guys had spent their careers to this point gunning for this, the most desirable of jobs. The British Army is very small and battalion commands are few; these guys knew that once they finished this job it was years of staff work ahead of them. They were also contending with another quirk of their system: men are given billets based on their age, not their time in grade. When they referred to a guy as being *too young* or *too old* for a billet, they meant not that he had too few or too many years in his current rank, but that he was literally the wrong age for the job. Weird.

Robby Boyd, a balding, cheerful Brit with a broad and open face, commanded A Company. Robby was welcoming and open, the sort of guy who would lean in conspiratorially, standing toe-to-toe with you to make a point. Robby always had a smile on his face, but had the core of steel that all infantry officers have and I was glad he was on our team. Like all Brits, he was a marvelous storyteller, and as the infantry provides no shortage of terrible—and therefore funny—situations Robby was a good man to have around. He was also the senior man among the company commanders; should anything have happened to Collins or to his second in command, the 2IC, Robby was next in line.

Mike Murdock commanded Bravo. Mike was lean and angular, black-haired and pasty-skinned, almost a parody of a British gent in appearance but a full-blooded Irishman in accent and temperament. Mike wore on his right shoulder the red dagger patch of the Royal Marines, indicating that he had completed the Royal Marines' commando course. Mike didn't strike me as a badass, but had a methodical, patient air to him. I could see immediately that could probably go days without sleep, and was a dogged, determined sort. He was very quiet and polite, not in any way the hard-driving infantrymen, but enormously capable.

Colin Marks commanded C Company. Colin was from Northern Ireland, and had the impenetrable accent to go with his heritage. He was short and tough, pugnacious and very intense, prone to long soaring wonderful episodes of profanity. I never saw him smile during my entire time knowing him, and he was very tough on his soldiers. He had an air of ambition, and most certainly wanted to perform well during this campaign. A warrior.

Marcus Readman commanded D Company of the Royal Gurkha Rifles. Marcus was a towering, serious man, the proper London gent with an educated, upper-crust accent but an easy rapport with junior soldiers. He had the long, loping stride and the easy walk of the career infantryman, which covers great gulps of ground without effort while normal-sized people like me scurry and hop along beside. His long legs ended in huge feet holding him up, and he complained constantly about not being able to find boots that fit, and about the British Army's insistence that their soldiers wear boots made for jungle warfare into a desert war. I became his favorite person when I scrounged up a pair of Marine Corps desert boots for him. I liked him immediately.

The man I would be working with most, though, was Richard Wallwork. Like me, he was *attached to*—not a member of—the Royal Irish. Richard commanded the artillery battery we would be using, 105-millimeter guns and radar systems to support them, and between us we would be in charge of the fire support planning. His guns, other British artillery, and my Marine Corps artillery would be indirect fire assets (indirect fire: big heavy rounds that go up and come down in a big arc. Direct fire: rifles and machine guns that shoot straight) while the biggest punch of all would be the British and American aircraft I controlled with my radio. Richard and I could summon enormous death and destruction by speaking into radios.

Richard was handsome and square-jawed and black-haired and *young*: the youngest battery commander in the British Army. He was the prototypical and perfect artilleryman: organized, efficient, highly disciplined, intense, focused, all maps and matrixes and frequency cards and timelines. I liked him right away and liked him more once we got into the fight.

———•••———

My entire reason for our being there was to be right in the seam between U.S. and British forces, ensuring that we were coordinated. Getting killed is one thing. Getting killed by your own guys is something else entirely.

———•••———

We also had the Gurkhas, the ultimate tribe.

The Gurkha Rifles are Nepalese soldiers with a legend that precedes them, remnants of the days when the sun never set on Brittania.

They are tough and ferocious and fearless in battle, their reputation cemented during the campaigns against the Japanese during the Second World War. Each man carried a Gurkha fighting knife, called a kukri, which is a curved, heavy blade adapted from their tribal agricultural tools.

In an ancient tradition of duels, young men from warring Nepali tribes run along a mountain path toward one another from their villages, carrying only this knife in one hand and a handful of stones in the other. They throw the stones at their opponent until they get within arm's reach, then it is kill or be killed. Only one man walks away from these duels.

In October of each year, the Nepalese mountain villagers have a festival. The youngest member of the tribe spends ten days sharpening his kukri prior to this event. On the last night of the festival, villagers tie a goat to a tree. One man holds the animal's hind legs, while another pulls on a lead and sprinkles water on the goat's neck, matting down the hair and exposing the vertebrae. One small, short chop, and the goat's head rolls away.

The martial backbone of these tribes extends naturally to the profession of arms; killing an enemy soldier with this knife is highly desirable, and the Gurkha legend grew from their World War II habit of dropping their rifles and charging Japanese positions with only their knives. The Japanese were terrified of them, and would retreat when they knew a Gurkha unit was preparing to attack.

Marcus told me that each Gurkha before me represented at least a hundred other men who had tried to get into the Army, and thus they were truly the cream of Nepalese manhood. The Gurkha selection process begins in the mountain villages with competitions of hiking and fighting and sports, culminating in a run up the side of a mountain wearing a full pack. Winners of these local competitions then went to a nationwide winnowing process which was similarly grueling; only the best men in the country are selected for the Army.

These men are then flown straight into Heathrow and thrown into Army training. The usual fear and stress of boot camp is combined with the culture shock of a tribal, rural people, most of whom had grown up without electricity or running water, thrown into the center of Europe. These are men who had never seen a car, never seen a light switch or a doorknob or a paved road or the written word, learning how to be a soldier in a new language.

In order to command the Gurkhas, a young officer must choose, fresh from Sandhurst, a completely different career path than that of his mates. Current and former Gurkha officers meet during the selection process at the end of each Sandhurst class, and young officers who have applied for the Gurkhas are screened and interviewed. Very few are chosen (Marcus was one of only three from his class) and I had the impression that success in this competition goes not always to the man with the highest grades or test scores. The panel looks for an inner strength and compassion and aptitude and a man's fitness for commanding those very unlike himself.

After being selected, Gurkha officers undergo intensive training in speaking Nepali, in order to communicate with their troops. The Gurkha soldiers are similarly trained in English, but most did not speak it well and spoke to one another in their native tongue. These young British Lieutenants are then posted to Nepal, where they go on walkabout for months through the high mountains villages, carrying only the packs on their backs. They check on British public works projects- dams, bridges, electrical plants and so forth—and make their way across the country. Such immersion results in total fluency.

After finishing this tour, a young Lieutenant is then assigned a platoon of Gurkhas in a Gurkha rifle company, which in turn usually works for a British Army rifle battalion. These companies therefore have two British officers: one rifle platoon commander, and the company commander. Gurkha officers commanded the other platoons, and the company number two man, the 2IC, was likewise a Gurkha. All the enlisted soldiers, up to and including the Sergeant Major, were Nepalese.

Their appearance and demeanor belied their ferocity. They were *tiny* guys, short and strong, most of them barely over five feet tall. Walking behind them was to wonder why someone had brought his little brothers to a war. Every single one of them had a huge smile on his face at all times, the most cheerful men I had ever met. They simply did not experience physical discomfort of any kind: no hike was too long, no day too hot, no night too cold, no hole too deep to dig it deeper.

They were in astounding physical condition. During a training exercise in the Kuwaiti desert, I watched the Gurkhas running through a live-fire range by squads. They were in such amazing shape that they, *running in sand with full packs*, could drop the controllers, who were wearing only field trousers and T-shirts and carrying only clipboards. The British had to stage their evaluators in relays to keep up with them.

Perhaps it was their brutal upbringing but they were gloriously happy at their lot in life. They were deeply devoted to one another: every meal was a shared stew, every fighting hole was not for two men (as Western armies do it) but for eight or ten or a dozen, enormous craters in which they piled like puppies.

Think of the Sherpas who work on Mount Everest: these are neighboring tribes. All the Gurkhas in I Royal Irish were named either Limbu or Rae. Those were the tribes who sourced our regiment. *Real* tribes.

We all loved them.

The favorite story among the officers came from the preceding Christmas. There were nineteen Royal Irish soldiers from

Fiji, huge, muscular black men with the lovely lilt of their mother island, sweet-natured gentle giants who loved to sing.

During the Christmas leave period, while the rest of the lads scattered across Britain and the neighboring islands, the Fijians and Gurkhas were left in the Royal Irish barracks in Canterbury for nearly two weeks, unable to take the time to make it back to their respective countries even had they been able to afford it. The two tribes were stranded in the bitter English winter.

Bored soldiers always get into trouble. One night, the Fijians started in on the Gurkhas, harassing them and picking fights. This was not a good idea. The Gurkhas, 120 pounds soaking wet, had banded together and gone through the NFL-sized Fijians like a scythe. The Fijians had moved out en masse and begged Collins not to have to live with the Gurkhas ever again.

For some reason, the Gurkha soldiers were paid only half what other British Army troops of the same rank and time in service earned. Cherie Blair, the annoying and ambitious wife of the Prime Minister, had adopted these soldiers and the unfairness of their pay as one of her missions to fix in British Parliament, thus ensuring that along with the usual stresses and difficulties of taking men into combat Tim Collins had to deal with 10 Downing Street looking over his shoulder.

<hr>

Americans were not allowed to take military vehicles into Kuwait, so I hitchhiked with my new British friends over to Camp Doha, an immense U.S. Army logistics base on the outskirts of Kuwait City. We in the infantry were already becoming country cousins, living far north of the city in tents while the Americans built hulking, hideous bases in its own image.

The Brits had their own cars, assigned to the Brigade and handed out case-by-case, and I certainly wasn't getting off the base any other way. Doha was a dump and highly restrictive, with endless checking of ID, but it was the closest thing to civilization we could find.

In the absence of women and beer, soldiers and Marines need two things: a telephone and junk food. Telephones were in a little building with pay phones lining the walls; AT&T must have had some great lobbyists, because every time I had been overseas the only phone option was through their overpriced calling cards. No worries, though: nowhere else to spend our money. We all trooped in there and figured out the system. Get in line, draw a number like at the barber shop, and then come back because it's going to be a while. You draw a number forty or fifty behind the one just called, so you head over to meet need #2.

Doha had a huge indoor walking mall, with everything an American teenager could want to buy with the money burning a hole in his pocket. A PX carried the latest hip-hop and heavy metal. Little shops run by Kuwaitis would stitch your name on anything you could think of, including the peculiar option of having your name written in Arabic. Why you would want the bad guys to know your name was beyond me. It was also beyond Lieutenant General Conway, the commander of all Marines in theater: he put out the word that no one in First Marine Expeditionary Force, I MEF, would have Arabic anywhere on his person.

The back of the building was devoted to calories: Burger King, Pizza Hut, KFC, Baskin Robbins. Each had a counter behind which with harried employees bumped into one another to deal with the 60- to 90-minute line stretching before them, and the unlucky ones worked the cash registers and dealt with angry, frustrated

Type-A personalities one after the other. The Brits, for some reason, loved KFC above all else, and would wait for that line almost indefinitely.

The phone room was a rectangular box with phones every five feet, each with a tiny cubicle built around it for physical (but not auditory) privacy. Men in desert camouflage hunched over, their heads almost resting on their desks, and whispered sweet nothings to their sweethearts, trying to be romantic and quiet at the same time.

An endless stream of soldiers left a fascinating collage of graffiti in the wood dividers, ground in with ballpoint pen.

———— •••• ————

Prior to coming to Kuwait and preparing for this war, the Royal Irish had been on deployment into Northern Ireland, where they did a five-month rotation as part of the normal cycle of British Army battalions through that difficult environment.

I thought for a quick second about this: some of these lads were from Northern Ireland and therefore patrolling *their own* neighborhoods, wearing the uniform of the hated colonizers. I took it another step: they were probably kicking in doors and arresting people they actually knew.

This rotation, combined with tours in Cyprus and Sierra Leone and other sketchy parts of the world, made for wonderful stories and a broad, deep understanding of the hostility of foreign lands. This experience made them experts in urban warfare and tactics, and driving with them was a learning event for me.

Seeing an intersection ahead on our return from Doha, Mike Murdock slowed to walking speed nearly 200 yards short and drifted slowly toward the red light in high first gear, leaving himself torque in the engine and room to maneuver should he spot anything dangerous. I thought this was somewhat needlessly prudent, with my frame of reference the typically American habit of roaring up to a stop and then hitting the brakes to within four feet of the bumper in front.

I mentioned this, and Mike pointed out the spot where, just last month, an American contractor had been ambushed and killed. I rechecked the loaded pistol strapped to my leg and thought about that.

We started the campaign at Camp Commando, at the base of Mutla Ridge.

Twelve years earlier our brothers in Desert Storm had stopped where we now began.

We were to head out in the dark of morning to Udairi Range complex, a vast wasteland of open desert with the amenities of the Empty Quarter and charm of Death Valley, put there by Allah for live fire.

I found another ANGLICO officer, Milo Kaufman, in the tent, standing behind a long row of computer screens.

The British held another of their endless staff meetings at the rectangular table dominating the center of the huge tent structure. I walked over to Milo.

Hey, dude. Do you have any scoop on our airplanes for tomorrow? Everything set?

Milo spit a wad of tobacco juice from the ever-present Copenhagen in his lip, and smiled at me.

No, that thing got cancelled.

You're shitting me.

No. I am not shitting you. They canked it a couple of hours ago.

I felt my gorge rising.

Milo, I scheduled this thing two weeks ago. I cleared it through the MEF Three shop this morning, and double-checked it this afternoon. And now, at midnight the day of, you're telling me someone canked it? Who?

I knew it wasn't Milo's fault, but I vented at him anyway. I was also angry that Milo, an artillery officer, had been made the Air Officer for the Division staff. Wrong guy in the wrong billet.

Another U.S Marine officer walked up behind me out of the dark. He was from First Force Reconnaissance.

No, man, that is our range. My guys are out there sleeping in the rain right now. We have the range for tomorrow.

I was ready to start screaming, but mindful of the British general across the room.

Well, that was a stupid decision on someone's part. If your guys are in the rain, that's your problem. I have the range, I reserved it, I went through all the channels, I hissed. You guys can work in with us, and we will try to get your people qualified, but you should have done the paperwork.

The Recon guy flamed right back at me. Hey, listen. I don't know who you think you are, but we have been out there for over a day waiting for this fucked-up MEF to figure out who owns the range. I am not giving it back. *You* can work in with *us*, but that's the best I can do.

Fuck you. It's not yours to give back. It's mine.

Milo stepped in. Listen, let's figure it out in the morning. I'll go over to MEF and see what they say.

Milo, that's great, I said, except that we are supposed to be out there before daybreak. Think the MEF guys will make a decision before we leave out of here at 0500?

No, but what else do you propose?'

I thought for a minute. I saw where this was going. We would run around in the dark tomorrow morning, for hours, and something would happen to fuck it up. We would sit all day in the rain and never get any airplanes. Fuck it.

You know what? Forget it. Let Force have it.

The Force guy, vindicated, nodded in triumph and walked out.

Then spake Pyrrhus. His guys didn't get trained after all. No planes. Bad weather. They just sat for two more days in the rain.

———•••———

Sergeant Glenn Walsh sidled up between the racks, conspiratorial and grinning. He leaned in quietly.

Sir, do you drink?

I looked up from my book, startled.

Yeah. Why?

Well, sir, Shofani gave us a little present...Carlos and I thought you might enjoy helping us out with it.

I thought for about two seconds about the stern edicts against drinking on the camp. Fuck it. What are they going to do: activate me, take me from my son, shave my head and send me to Iraq?

I went outside the tent with the boys, feeling like I was playing hooky from school. The tents were like a wedding tent, with every ten feet or so a seam which could be unlaced and opened, and through one of these seams we were birthed into the cold dark.

Walsh handed me the bottle. It burned going down and tasted great, and I suddenly realized that none of us had had a drink in at least two weeks. It would suck to be an alcoholic in a war, I bet.

Lopez took a sip and passed the bottle to Walsh, who passed it back to me. High school all over again. Walsh looked hard at me.

Sir, you doing OK?

Yeah, sure, I said, not knowing what he was getting at.

OK. No biggie. I know that you were pretty bummed out when we all had to go over to a different platoon, but you seem to be your old self again.

Well, I said, I wasn't worried about me. I was worried about them fucking with you guys.

Carlos Lopez spoke up. Yes, sir, we were all pretty worried about that, too. I guess the Gunny got yelled at by somebody, and he is leaving everybody alone.

Right you are I said. He got fired, actually. Bad for him, good for us.

Walsh smiled and took another sip, then kept the bottle moving. I looked up at the stars, crystalline and cold. The night was jet black, the way that night can be only over the desert and the ocean. The lights of Kuwait City sparkled against the bay, and it was actually quite a pleasant scene.

Our living conditions were going to start heading downhill, soon and fast. They always do, the closer you get to war.

———•••———

The Marine enlisted chow tent had added a television so at the end of every meal rows of senior officers stood in the back of the troops' tent, sneaking an unauthorized peek at the real world, while the enlisted boys sat and ate slowly and with unusual satisfaction given the august company.

Hans Blix testified before the United Nations and said that Iraq is cooperating. The comments around the tent ran to Yeah...

no shit...I would too, with 150,000 guys on my border. No one at the UN (or on CNN for that matter) seemed to register that Saddam had been uncooperating since 1990, and that he was undoubtedly trying to buy time to get his folks ready before the ass-kicking came.

Two million people protested in Hyde Park, downtown London. The television cameras were the center of it all, of course. So many people so vociferously opposed to the war were quite convincing.

A young Marine I had never seen before took it all in, and then turned around, looking for someone with an answer and assuming officers knew it all. Actually not unreasonable, in this camp.

Seeing all the gold on my collar and chest, he assumed I would know: Sir, they won't make us wait here all summer, will they?

No, don't worry, I told him. General Conway and General Mattis knew we have to kick this thing off before it gets too hot.

I tried to sound convincing, but I couldn't even convince myself. Holy shit...what if they *do* go wobbly and slam on the brakes? I could very easily picture all of us training here for six more months until they decided what to do. It happened to the guys waiting to jump into Normandy. We *had* to go in the cool weather, but it's just as cool in October as it is in February...and it gets cooler, not hotter, if you kick off in fall. My mind ran wild...we will stay right here...in these tents...the British will go home...we will have to train at night in the summer...out in the desert...I would miss another war just like Desert Storm and Mogadishu...

I got hold of myself and walked back to my tent to worry in peace.

---

19 FEBRUARY 2003 ▶ CAMP COYOTE, UK
TRANSIT CAMP, NORTHERN KUWAIT

The Road Warrior came to life.

Vehicles bombed across the desert, trailing huge plumes of dust, skeleton vehicles, stripped-down Land Rovers and tracked vehicles with trailers like something invented by NASA. Exoskeleton vehicles, too, with fuel lashed to the side and evil guns with monstrous barrels like snouts drooping from ring mounts on top. The men driving them and manning the weapons look like they came from the *Mad Max* set, too: masks over their faces and tinted goggles over their eyes, angry nomads glaring down at the pedestrian. The tiny bits of skin—cheekbones and ears- which remained exposed sunburned instantly. At the end of each day a strange race of Raccoon Men had invaded the Arabian Desert.

Natural gas flares burned in the distance, from the gas-oil separation platforms, GOSPs, on the Iraqi side of the border, and at night these orange beacons added an otherworldly glow to the bare sand and lend a faint roar to the background. From the standing position, you felt like you could see the curvature of the earth.

Dominating our landscape was something out of Kubrick: two behemoth satellite tracking dishes, each over 100 feet across. They sat astride an enigmatically fenced-off enclosure as if patiently waiting for a message from outer space...which, of course, they once did. One looked at the sky, the other on its side, intact, blown up by the Special Operations boys during Desert Storm twelve years earlier, two mastodons, trapped forever in the sand, their La Brea, baking in the sun.

———••———

I took five teams to the Irish and into the war.

ANGLICO is designed to break into small teams, purpose-built top-heavy with officers and SNCOs so teams can go overseas without any support and run on their own. Each team had to be self-sufficient, each had to be balanced, each had to work without being able to talk to me.

My own team was Lance Corporal Conde, my driver; Staff Sergeant Scull, my communications chief; Staff Sergeant Arreola, my platoon sergeant, and me. We were a family. A combat family.

Commander Brian Borlet was my right-hand man for the entire war, and commanded a second team. Brian was a Navy officer, a ship driver (minesweepers: *wooden ships and iron men*) turned infantry and fires expert. He was fire-and-forget and actually outranked me, but as a Navy officer he preferred me in command. Brian had been in Desert Storm and knew his shit, and was besides an avid outdoorsman.

We slept side by side each night in the field, and Brian slept the same way every time: flat on his back, hands at his sides, so I woke each morning next to a corpse.

———••———

Chief Warrant Officer-5 Sid Heal commanded a third team. He had forgotten more about combat than I would ever know, and was a straight-arrow, teetotaling family man from Michigan. I could not believe a guy who had been in Vietnam was working for me. *He is older than 50* the Marines said with awe and he was a grandfather and could run faster than anyone on the teams. A CWO-5 ranks somewhere between the Commandant and God in the Marine Corps, and I was taking him into his fourth war.

Sergeant Gavin Wilson took four men with him to make my fourth team. Tall, bright, wry humor, deeply committed to his people, he would do well.

Sergeant Glenn Walsh was team five. He had also been in Desert Storm, and had joined back up with 3d ANGLICO a few months earlier only to go to this war. He was the same age as men far senior to him...and smarter. Glenn was a Los Angeles street cop and former prison guard (as all Los Angeles Sheriff's Department cops are when they begin), feared no man, and knew his shit backwards and forwards.

I knew he was one of the strongest NCOs in the unit, but with a twist: other officers didn't want him.

They didn't want Sid, Brian or Wilson, either. I couldn't understand it.

When we carved up the unit months earlier back in California, these men were mine for the taking. It took me a while but I then understood. Simple: most officers do not like having people beneath them who are smarter than they are.

Didn't bother me. I grabbed these superstars and never looked back.

I also had four British Royal Air Force men seconded to me and I spread them and their radios across my teams. Their senior man was a Lieutenant (*Leftenant*) named Davidson...and I didn't like him. He was arrogant and abrasive and something in me knew he would not do well. I talked myself out of doing what I knew was right (sending him back) by convincing myself that I was making a snap judgment.

I could not put an officer beneath one of my Sergeants, so I gave him a team. This would prove to be a mistake.

Each team was a combat family, all in one vehicle. These men would live and fight together and they had to mesh. They had to become family, in a hurry.

———•••———

Word came down from the generals.

Some congressman had had a worried mother call him and say I am so worried about my son, what if he gets killed? *He is only seventeen.*

Our response: a shrug, Yeah, *it's the fucking Marines,* you sign up to get shot at.

The generals' response: pull all seventeen-year-olds out of their units.

So a parade of teenage kids showed up in the rear camp. A very unhappy parade of kids, who just wanted to be with their units, terrified they would miss the war.

They were told they would stay in Commando until they turn eighteen, when it would be OK to get them killed.

———•••———

I only yelled at my Marines once in six months.

I was trying to do a close air support exercise, brushing them up on their air control procedures with real airplanes simulating dropping bombs. I planned to set us up on a little OP near the camp, a little hill, and spread the teams out across the desert where I could see them.

We were supposed to leave at 1530. At 1550, they were still messing around with gear and vehicles. It is cold in the desert in winter. Everyone was in fleece pullovers and gloves and hats, and they were complaining and dragging.

I flamed.

Everyone over here, right now I yelled from beside our tent.

Laughter stopped and smiles disappeared. They looked startled: Major Coerr doesn't raise his voice, ever. This must be serious.

The boys slunk over and gathered around. We were now half an hour behind schedule, and it didn't look like we were heading anywhere soon. The weak winter sun was already getting low in the sky. I stood with the tent to my back, facing their semicircle.

Chief Warrant Officer Heal. Is your team ready to go? I demanded.

Yes, sir, Sid replied.

Commander Borlet, sir? I asked.

Yep.

Sergeant Walsh?

No, sir. Walsh looked right at me, taking it like a man.

Sergeant Wilson?

No, sir.

Leftenant Davidson?

No, sir, replied Davidson.

Gents, do we have a problem? I asked rhetorically. Was there any confusion about the time we were to leave?

Eyes on bootlaces and sand.

Does anyone not want to do this? Because I will happily leave any one of you here when it is time to go across the border. We all know that Colonel Collins is not a patient man. Does anyone think he is going wait for his Americans to get their shit together when we go do this for real? Let's ask Conde, shall we? When Collins goes somewhere, he walks to his Rover and they drive off without looking back. Right, Lance Corporal Conde?

Yes, sir. That's what he does, Conde affirmed.

You guys want to stay here when the fight starts?

No, sir, replied Walsh on behalf of everyone.

Get your shit together. Right now. You guys know that I keep as much bullshit off of you as I can. I am doing my part. But you are not doing yours. This, this right here, is not bullshit. This is serious, and important. This is what we do.

You have had all day to get gear ready. We are going to the field for two hours. That's it.

Calling in air is going to be our bread and butter when this thing starts, and we are not ready. If you guys want to have inspections and tests and 0530 reveille and all the shit that other platoons are doing, Staff Sergeant Arreola can make that happen.

Damn right, sir, said Arreola.

Anybody want to do that?

Lance Corporal Macis piped up. No sir.

Good. You have five minutes. I stormed off, angry and triumphant, my point made.

Three minutes later, they were lined up and ready.

We drove out to our little OP, where the radios all died.

When people spoke to my son about where his daddy was, they expected a sad little face and a lament about separation from his father. Instead he would square his little shoulders and say that he was doing OK because daddy is in Iraq killing Saddam Hussein.

An adult asked him where Iraq was and he told her, duh, it is right behind the PX at Miramar Air Station.

0300 ▶ CHECKPOINT GRYPHON, OPEN DESERT, NORTHERN KUWAIT

Several hundred vehicles were front to back on the desert floor, each a segment in a centipede of creeping approaching death. Tactic: just follow the guy in front; guy behind follows you. Simple.

Two days in the desert without sleep caught up to us, and I found myself falling asleep sitting up. There was nothing happening, nothing whatsoever, so I put us on a watch schedule.

Scull was driving and took the first watch. He was to simply move out when the vehicle in front of us moved: follow the leader. Simple as that.

One man awake, everyone else asleep.

The radio hissed softly and our engine idled in the freezing indigo night. The red brake lights of the Rover in front of us, tactical lighting, duct-taped over with just a slit letting out a sliver of light, were soft and muted in the sandy dark. It was warm in the Humvee.

Arreola slept in his seat.

Conde and I crawled in the back of the Humvee to rack out. So nice and warm. We smashed in back there, lying on top of all our gear, and both fell into REM sleep instantly.

So warm. So cozy. I dreamed.

I startled awake.

Had I been asleep ten minutes? Two hours? The engine still idled.

I flipped over and looked out our windshield into the black where the brake lights had been.

Nothing.

I looked behind us. More than one hundred vehicles waited to follow us, faint lights haloed in dust, engines idling gently.

I looked forward again, and this time noticed Scull, behind the wheel, head rocked back and at an angle. He snored happily.

Bad.

I yelled to Scull Staff Sergeant! Wake up! What time is it?

Scull startled with a sharp snort, his mind caging and orienting as he put the Humvee in gear, still asleep, ready to drive. Conde and I scrambled forward over sleeping bags, packs, radios, MRE cases, Arreola. I jumped into the front seat.

Where is the rest of the convoy? I asked.

Fuck if I know, sir, said Scull, as he floored it from our parking place, driving confidently out across the desert floor, lights out, on NVGs.

Where are you going?

Don't know, sir! This way!

I got ready to start yelling at him, and then realized that I didn't have a better plan. I didn't have a better direction, either. We were headed generally east, which would eventually run us into the four-lane highway back to the camp. I very much did not want to lead the second half of the convoy in a circle back whence we had just come. So off we trundled across the sand.

Dozens after dozens of vehicles, their drivers awake, ground along behind us, following our blacked-out taillights and oblivious to the fact that we had no idea where we were or where we were going. We ended up heading perpendicular to long lines of vehicles from other battalions, thousands of men on the desert floor, us zooming jauntily along across their direction of travel. I giggled at the absurdity.

A road guard materialized, a poor British soldier standing with a Kuwaiti counterpart, both of whom floated up out of the gloom at a forlorn intersection of dirt roads. We pulled up in a cloud of sand, everyone behind us slamming on their brakes, and asked for directions as if stopping at the gas station. I was afflicted now with a serious case of the giggles, which did not help Scull's concentration as the poor trooper tried to remember the direction the Irish had gone almost twenty minutes before.

By some miracle, like hitting a bullet with a bullet, we saw a long row of faint lights off in the desert distance and floored it and joined right up where we belonged, behind Richard's Rover.

Two men awake from now on.

—————•••—————

Arreola's father died, in Mexico.

An ANGLICO message flashed across our radios and I went to tell him.

Collins insisted that Arreola go back for the funeral. I agreed.

Arreola did not.

He said Sir that is going to take at least a week and we are going to be over the border before then. I can't be gone when that happens.

————•••————

Major General Jim Mattis was commanding general of 1st Marine Division, in charge of the riflemen who were going to bear the brunt of George Bush's decision to go to war.

He was small, wiry, and feisty, a lifelong bachelor married to the Marine Corps. He had a reputation as an ass-kicking, ferocious leader, an officer who took shit from no man, but was the most caring and gentle of men who would do anything for his Marines, a scholar and thinker.

He was a tribal elder, and we revered him.

————•••————

Mattis had led Task Force Ripper during Desert Storm and there had cemented his reputation as a man on the way up.

This reputation, well-earned even then, was solidified when as a one-star he took Task Force 58, thousands of Marines afloat that he merged into one combat force, 400 miles over Pakistan and into Afghanistan late in 2001 to retaliate on behalf of us all against Al-Qaeda's attacks on September 11th.

He had sent some of his men onboard aircraft, refueling in Pakistan, the first combat forces into the country. The rest of the task force went overland, across Pakistan, led by a young

Lieutenant Colonel. This sort of multipronged attack was signature Mattis: swift, decisive, relying upon mission-type orders in which his officers, spread across two countries and a dozen ships at sea, got the job done without consulting him.

My close friend was in the first section of Cobras into Afghanistan that night, and he met up with Brigadier General Mattis to get his orders for the first engagement. It was a pretty short brief: Mattis said Hoss I want you to go out and kill those fuckers.

———•••———

I checked in to Third Battalion, Seventh Marines in Twentynine Palms, California in 1994. Then-Colonel Jim Mattis, the Seventh Marines regimental commander, called for me to come see him.

I was not only just a brand-new Captain, but I was an aviator in an infantry regiment: I was *not* a key player. Colonel Mattis took his phone off the hook, closed his office door and spent over an hour, just me and him, telling me his warfighting philosophy, vision, goals and expectations. He told me how he saw us fighting—and where—and how he was getting us ready to do just that.

Mattis's callsign was Chaos. He created chaos for the enemy-cycling too fast for them to follow, getting inside their decision loops and forcing them into decisions they didn't want to make. He was a blunt, smart warfighter, just the sort of man our bulldog General Al Gray had started pulling up the ladder behind him when he was Commandant in the late 1980s.

The entire Marine Corps loved him: a walking legend in his time.

———•••———

Blair "Paddy" Mayne was a founder of the Special Air Service and its commanding officer in combat, a pioneering, fearless, asskicking desert fighter in World War II and an icon of the British Army.

Collins named our camp for him. He viewed him as a venerated tribal elder and now so did I.

---

5 MARCH 2003 ▶ FORT BLAIR MAYNE, NORTHERN KUWAIT

Barossa Day.

Barossa is a small village in Spain, and is the site on which the Irish kicked the shit out of the French Army in 1811 and took the French unit battle colors, their *eagle*. Since that day, the Irish Rangers have celebrated Barossa Day each year.

This year gave us particular pleasure, as we were in a combat zone, and since the French had been so difficult in the past few months in the United Nations, anything celebrating a French military defeat was especially rewarding.

A British officer stopped me walking across camp in mid-afternoon. He looked me right in the eyes, and said Stan word has it that you perhaps have a wee nip of the strong stuff hidden away somewhere? Like all Irishmen, he phrased his statement as a question.

I sure do, Jackie. I replied. The airline pilot on the way over gave it to me. Why do you ask?

Oh, well, he said, as if he had just thought of this, The officers have been known to knock back a few from time to time during

Barossa Night. Tradition is that if we are deployed, we gather whatever we can find in the camp and mix it into the punch. Would the Marines be interested in adding to the mix?

I smiled at him. You bet. What's in it for me?

Oh, mate, don't worry. We'll take care of you.

So I gave up my only stash of booze. For the greater good, of course.

Barossa Night started with social hour. The RSM had scrounged up non-alcoholic beer from somewhere, so we all filled our mugs to the top and pretended. Robby Boyd kept everyone in stitches with stories, and Sid, Brian and I joined right in. The Gurkha senior officer, Tika-sabh, insisted that I sit next to him for the festivities.

The ceremony reminded me of a Marine Corps mess night, a celebration of tribal bonds. Formal presentations of the beef and drink, speeches read and toasts exchanged. General Jacko Page, the commander of the 16th UK Air Assault Brigade, was the guest of honor.

The Barossa punch was served up in a centuries-old silver tureen, part of the regimental silver and brought from Canterbury for this occasion, and each officer raised it to his lips, shouted Barossa! and drank heartily. The lieutenants performed skits, imitating the RSM and Collins himself; one dressed as an Arab and was the butt of the rest of the officers' jokes. Cigars appeared.

The unit colors were displayed, the first time I had seen them since attaching to the Irish. The colors themselves were heavy brocade, thick and deep and gorgeous, with each campaign sewn directly onto the flag itself, rather than hung as a streamer as the Marines do it.

The colors are kept in a locked, specially-made steel box, and only an officer may handle the flag. Anyone who touches it must wear gloves.

Every 25 years, the colors are retired and hung at St. Anne's Church in Belfast, in the shrine to the Irish Rangers.

Gold thread and silver in the sand.

———— •••• ————

Al-Jaber Airfield, Kuwait City

The Fires Summit.

Pilots in tan flight suits sat in metal folding chairs at the back of the cavernous auditorium, a room the size of a high school gym. Pistols hung across their chests in shoulder holsters.

The senior aviators, squadron and group commanders, sat near the front, with their counterpart battalion and regimental infantry commanders.

Younger infantry officers, healthier of back and knee, thinner of waist and thicker of hair, sat towards the back. These were battalion fire support coordinators, Majors who commanded a rifle battalion's weapons company (heavy guns, 81mm mortars, rockets and TOW missiles) and were therefore the key men in a battalion's fire support planning. These guys were firsts among equals, and were almost always the best and usually most senior of the young officers in a battalion.

Most had with him his battalion air officer, an aviator serving with a rifle battalion (as I had with 3/7) responsible for coordinating air strikes with the infantry's scheme of maneuver and the indirect fire of both mortars and artillery.

Richard and I—the artillery and aviation experts—were the equivalent for our battalion. We needed to know the big picture.

———— •••• ————

Logistics was going to be an issue. It was a fuck of a long way to Baghdad from here, and there were a hell of a lot of bad guys massing on the border who knew we were coming.

Good generals study history.

Great generals—Genghis Khan, Caesar, Napoleon, Grant, Eisenhower—study logistics.

Mattis studied both.

When Chaos Mattis took the boys into Afghanistan, it took him 0.5 short tons (a short ton is 2000 pounds even, versus a ton which is closer to 2200 pounds) per Marine deployed. *That* is what light and fast looks like.

They were expecting that it would be 2.5 short tons per Marine to get a guy to Baghdad: five times the weight in the fight fifteen months earlier. If the logistics guys didn't have their shit together, we would all run out of ammo and chow and water 300 miles into Indian country.

Hair atop heads grew noticeably sparser the further forward you looked. Heads gleamed in the fluorescent light. Jaws were set.

Showtime.

Major General Mattis stood to address us. As always, he spoke without notes, having long ago memorized everything.

———•••———

Gentlemen, this is going to be the most air-centric division in the history of warfare. Don't you worry about the lack of shaping; if we need to kill something, it is going to get killed. I would storm the gates of hell if 3d Marine Air Wing was overhead.

He looked toward the back of the room, and spoke very clearly, hands on hips.

There is one way to have a short—but exciting!—conversation with me, and that is to move too slow.

This is not a marathon, this is a sprint. This is Log Light: if you can't eat it, shoot it or wear it, leave it behind.

In about a month, I am going to go forward of our Marines up to the border between Iraq and Kuwait. And when I get there, one of two things is going to happen.

Either the commander of the Iraqi 51st Mechanized Division is going to surrender his army in the field to me.

Or he and all his guys are going to die.

———•••———

We wandered over to the chow hall before heading back to Commando. By far, the best chow I have ever had in any chow hall, ever. They even had a little Filipino man standing behind a three-sided table covered with ice creams of any flavor and combination imaginable. *Fucking Air Force.*

On the way back, exhausted from worrying and fretting and being generally pissed off and unhappy and missing my son, I stretched out in the dark in the bed of the Humvee and fell asleep.

I woke with a start when the vehicle slammed to a stop and I kept going and slammed into the truck bed.

I heard people yelling and running, doors slamming, rounds being racked into pistol chambers.

I poked my head over the dashboard to see what the commotion was about, and there was an infantry officer, crouched in the dark behind one side of the Hummer, his pistol pointed out into the scrub next to the highway. Cars flew past at eighty miles an hour five feet away.

Hey Dave, I yelled, what the fuck?

We just took rounds from those trees he said, his eyes never leaving the darkness across the hood. Don't know where the guy went.

OK...so why are we sitting here waiting for him to shoot at us again?

Just gotta make sure he's gone.

With this kind of stupidity, it was going to be a long war. I went back to sleep.

————◆◆————

This was my first foray out into the open desert, and it was a National Geographic special come to life.

British and American officers loaded up and headed across the desert to the marvelously-named Camp Matilda, a Marine Corps base camp far north towards Iraq.

Camels ambled along next to the road or stood and stared stupidly at the cars whizzing by feet away. I assumed they would be herded by men in flowing robes on camels, like in *Lawrence of Arabia*...the men indeed wore robes and flowing headdresses, but herded their beasts in pickup trucks. Wealthier Kuwaitis zoomed by in red-checked caftans driving the ubiquitous Mercedes sedan.

First Marine Division was holding their first ROC drill: a Rehearsal of Concept, a walkthrough of what we would be doing.

Intelligence Marines had spent days building an enormous reproduction of southern Iraq in a bowl formed by a huge, semicircular sand dune. Each road, each river, each canal, each oil field was built to scale and even in proper color (water was blue dye poured into a ditch; roads were black sand). The layout was enormous, roughly the size of a football field.

One of my British officers asked if this terrain model of Iraq was meant to be life-sized.

Each Marine unit wore football jerseys in different colors...and with proper numbers. 1st Battalion, 5th Marines, known as 1/5, wore blue jerseys with 15 on the back, and other units were similarly identified. Principal staff from those units stood on the border drawn in the sand.

About 300 officers stood and sat on the dune above. It was the perfect way to visualize what was about to happen.

Mattis stood up and took a handheld microphone. Without referencing a single piece of paper, he spoke for over an hour. He dictated what each unit would do and in what sequence, and outlined his end state for each phase of the early war.

Log Light: hard and fast.

Mattis's complete mastery of every nuance of the battle forthcoming was truly impressive.

A narrator then took over and spoke through each day of the early war in sequence. As each movement was described, the officers from that unit walked to the proper place on their terrain model, and by the end of an hour the colored jerseys were spread over a football field's worth of sand. What a show.

At the end of the drill, questions were taken and then Mattis dismissed everyone. No messing around with this guy.

As everyone rose to leave, Mattis took the microphone

He said Men, you've got about thirty days.

———•••———

As we walked back to the vehicles my British officers were wide-eyed. Marcus said Mate, are all your generals that good?

I told him the truth. No. Mattis is the best we have.

———•••———

We had bailed Kuwait's fat out of the fire twelve years before. Were it not for U.S. and British forces, Saddam would have had a palace in Kuwait City.

We had 150,000 guys in Kuwait now, preparing to get rid of these assholes to the north *again*, and once and for all. In return, Kuwaitis gave us one range to work on. One. Their entire fucking *country* was a range, a vast, wind-whipped wasteland, and they wouldn't let our boys, putting their lives on the line for this shitty country, practice shooting.

Well, they could either let us train like we needed to, or bring their own rich pansy pussy men back from Paris and London and give them rifles, but they wanted it both ways: national sovereignty that someone else defended.

As far as I was concerned, we should just have just turned this whole force around and taken over Kuwait City, and then hooked a right and taken Saudi Arabia while we were at it.

Fuckers. That would fix their little red wagons.

————•••————

I went to that one range, called Udairi, one week before we went over the border, to supervise air and fires as the Gurkhas worked that live-fire exercise.

On the way there we drove due west through U.S. Army V Corps, based around the Third Infantry Division, our brothers from another warrior tribe, who would be side by side with us as we pushed into Iraq. V Corps was fully mechanized, ready for the fight, soldiers and vehicles in the wasteland.

I had never seen this many combat soldiers in one place.

I just couldn't believe how many of them there were: they stretched north farther than I could see, and in an unending mass east and west from far behind me to the horizon in front. As far as I could see in every direction, for over an hour traveling at 25 to 30 miles per hour, troops and trucks and Humvees and tents and tanks and fighting vehicles stretched away to the horizon.

Soldiers sprawled across the tops of the behemoth MIAI main battle tanks and Bradleys, sound asleep. Many of them had rigged little shelters with their ponchos, stretching the fabric from the top of the vertical armor to poles sunk in the sand which provided them shade as the day progressed. These little roofs also gave the perfect rows of tanks the appearance of a cheerful little small-town street, verandas lined in neat little rows.

The soldiers were beyond filthy; these boys had been in theater much longer than we had, since before Christmas, and there were no tents and showers for them. They just slept on the ground or on top of their machines.

From several hundred yards, I could see the V of dirt and sweat, front and back of their tanker jumpsuits, and I could actually tell from that distance that some of them hadn't shaved in days.

American flags flew high and proud, but a bit forlorn, providing a tiny splash of color against an unending backdrop of cold-rolled green steel and filth and sand and dirt.

———◆•◆———

Rick Atkinson wrote about our lads, our grandfathers from these same units, who pushed across the sea and through a desert and across river after river and then through defended countries and into the belly of the Nazi beast and he used a lovely and perfect phrase that theirs was uniquely American because it was *a war of movement, distance and horsepower.*

———•••———

As would be, soon, ours.

Those three things required fuel. Lots of it.

Just so, on my left was the supply chain for these soldiers in these vehicles. Hubcap to hubcap were parked full eighteen-wheeler fuel tankers, and as we drove for that hour those tanker trucks were a wall of chrome, flashing by without gap or surcease.

———•••———

In 1950, in Korea, the First Marine Division was side-by-side with the US Army Third Infantry Division.

In 2003, in Iraq, the First Marine Division was side-by-side with the US Army Third Infantry Division.

———•••———

Thunderstorm over the Gulf. The rain sheeted down onto our tents, which felt cozy and dry. I felt for all the infantry guys up north of us, my tribesmen, living out in the dirt, filthy and soaked. I snuggled farther into my sleeping bag and thought of flowers and fireflies and warm North Carolina summer rain.

———•••———

Desert navigation is much more difficult than it would seem.

In theory, you would just shoot an azimuth out across the waste-land and drive (or walk) in a straight line. There is nothing out here...we just walk straight...

This works fine if you have a level path, or if you can see what you are looking for, but once you start stumbling into washes and deal with a sandstorm or two, it is easy to get lost without a GPS.

In the desert, as in snow, things which have sharp outlines appear closer than they really are. This is why crisp, steep mountains seem as if they are looming right over you when in fact they are thirty or forty miles away. Distances are extraordinarily difficult to gauge without any intermediate references, and in the absence of a tree or hill or structure to latch onto, the brain simply gives up and starts guessing.

Americans, in particular, have a habit of looking at distances as *football fields* laid end-to-end, splitting miles into a more-com-fortable base-10 system.

Fortunately, Desert Storm lit a fire under both the American mil-itary and the outdoors industry, and GPS systems progressed and shrank while becoming more affordable. GPS is brilliantly simple: if two points can put you on a line, and three references can triangulate, then six or eight or ten references, all constantly updating, will pinpoint you down to the inch.

GPS satellites are used by both civilians and the military, and there were dire predictions that the Defense Department would scramble the satellite signals right as we crossed the border, in order to prevent the Iraqis from using those same satellites to target missiles. The entire deployed command structure rose up in protest, insisting that these systems are the only way to navigate in a desert.

I had a GPS under the Christmas tree a month before I deployed, and it bailed me out of several highly embarrassing desert meanderings. I learned how to use it in less than an hour, it fit in my pocket, ran on AA batteries and cost $100. It was a cheery canary yellow and had an intuitive interface, built the way the human brain works.

The defense establishment, of course, couldn't go out and buy these excellent little gadgets; instead, they paid ten times the price for the huge, heavy, Precision Lightweight GPS Receiver (PLGR), which was the size and weight of a dictionary and everyone called *Plugger* and to a man hated. The PLGR system was nearly impenetrable in that engineers-rather-than-regular-people-must-have-designed-this way, and thus added to my frustration with our military-industrial complex.

———•••———

The Marines couldn't afford REI gadgets, so they were using these pieces of shit to navigate. Sid, Brian and I were determined that every man learn to use it. Being in the wrong place would get these guys killed.

Off the boys went on foot, across the desert floor on foot in teams of four, running six checkpoints for time. The three of us sat on a tall dune and watched them miles away. I felt like a chessmaster, moving pieces around on a huge board only I could fully see.

I pulled out a trusty paperback from my cargo pocket and read for a bit before taking a nap in the dirt, taking care first to move upwind of the bloated and rotting sheep lying nearby.

I awoke to watch the lads scampering along with the sky darkening behind them. The darkness wasn't rain. Instead a sandstorm came roaring down on us like the hand of an angry god.

———◆◆◆———

War drums were beating.

I sent Brian and Sid on a recon down to Camp Commando to retrieve gear we had left behind. In theory, I was supposed to be ready to go five days from now, and I didn't even have vehicles and radios yet. I figured the two of them would be more tactful than would I, and thus would get things done instead of yelling at people like I would. First rule of self-awareness: know your limitations.

———◆◆◆———

The I Royal Irish first objective once over the border was the GOSPs.

A GOSP is a gas-oil separation platform, the first step in the changing of crude oil from underground into something useful. The GOSPs were built by the British decades before, and so like everything the British did there was beautifully engineered, sensible and efficient. It was here, in these southern fields, that the Iraqi oil infrastructure began. The oil complexes in southern Iraq were nowhere near as extensive as those in the north stretching to Kurdistan, but they were a hell of a lot closer to the port complexes at Basrah and were thus crucial.

The White House had a list of objectives for American forces in the first hours of the war: protecting the GOSPs was right up there next to finding Saddam. The concern was that Saddam would blow them up, and if he did that the lone economic engine of someday-real-soon-we-promise Iraqi sovereignty would go with them. They had to be captured intact.

The brigade staff ordered up reconnaissance flights for us to see where we were going.

Each battalion's staff rode out to the open desert, following GPS to a point in the sand. We all stood in the rain and wind, laughing among ourselves, until we heard the low thwock-thwock of helicopter blades—as Michael Herr said, a sound that is *sharp and dull at the same time.*

———— •• ————

Militaries have naming schemes for aircraft that make sense only to them.

The Marines name their aircraft for evocative animals: those which do the same thing. The Harrier is a bird (and jet) that hovers and kills; the Hornet is a fast stinging striker; the Cobra is slender and venomous and strikes from hide; the Osprey is can fly in any direction; the Super Stallion can carry loads forever.

The U.S. Army keeps to Indian tribal names: Kiowa, Apache, Chinook, Blackhawk.

The U.S. Air Force uses animals, but with a twist. High-flying, pretty aircraft are Eagle or Falcon. Low-flying, dirty aircraft—favorites of the Marines—are Warthogs.

The British named their aircraft for agile, lithe creatures: Puma, Lynx and Gazelle.

———— •• ————

Two Puma helicopters roared in and landed nose-to-tail, and the officers piled on board. I had never been in a British helo, and in fact hadn't been airborne since we arrived in Kuwait. I was very happy to be off the ground again.

We roared north as a section, and then our dash-two aircraft broke off to the west to show the Paras their routes into Iraq and objectives beyond. We continued north and the Irish officers hung out of the doors or pressed against the windows, looking at our assembly areas, routes of march and the GOSPS themselves.

It was the most inhospitable place I had ever seen. Six bright-orange natural gas flares burned far in the distance, too bright to look at, shimmering and marking the six GOSPs where we would soon be standing. A huge thunderstorm was moving off to the east behind the GOSP structure and throwing sheets of rain before it, and the black sky made the flares look even more evil.

No humans moved anywhere. The Iraqis surely knew we were coming and had either fled or dug in by now. The pilots skirted right on top of the border, and we looked out on no-man's land of steel and sand and ugly and flame.

On the way home, the sun broke through and everyone seemed to cheer up as we turned back into Kuwait. Our Para brothers came back from their recon, and the pilots formed back up and dove for the deck, the agile, feline machines skimming along at fifty feet off the sand in loose formation at 150 miles an hour. I had a huge smile on my face.

Marcus looked at me, circled his finger around indicating everything around us and where we were headed, and grinned widely.

———•••———

Everyone needs a fan.

Sergeant Espinoza was mine.

He pulled me aside, looking me straight in the eye through expensive glasses that added to his air of maturity.

Sir, I don't know if it is my place to really say this... he began.

Whatever it is, I can take it, I told him.

I just want you to know that a lot of guys are starting to think about OCS because of you. You know, they look for officers to emulate, and...uh...well, Major Sewall isn't...

He stopped, unsure of how far he could push issues like this with another officer.

Well, sir, he isn't, maybe, the best example. You are the guy the Marines want to imprint on. They really like the fact that even though you are really intelligent and educated, you don't talk down to us like a lot of other officers do.

He said You are one of us.

———•••———

We were in a world without women.

———•••———

Yet I lie. We had two: a doctor and a writer.

Sarah Oliver was a British reporter, assigned to us by the London papers as on-the-scene chronicler of *British Lads In Action.*

She was lean and tough, charming, lovely, everyone's favorite sister. Her mane of thick red hair cascaded from beneath her helmet wherever she went. The fact that she had volunteered for this, to live out in the mud with us, impressed everyone.

———◆◆———

My entire time with British forces, I never saw one of their soldiers with the muscular, ripped physique of many American men, not one. In fact in civilian clothes only their huge quadriceps (built from endless hiking with heavy packs) gave any indication of their profession. With the exception of the bony, angular Mike Murdock, the Royal Irish officers were beefy and broad rather than muscular, and their pale skin accented their mild appearance.

They looked just like pictures of American men in World War II, before the advent of aerobics and heavy weight training and overeating.

However, the British were without question in superior field shape to any Americans I worked with, and their stamina and raw physical toughness were unparalleled. They could hike without complaint for days.

The stiff-upper-lip British reputation is also for real.

What was said of them during the American Civil War was true: British soldiers talk like ladies but fight like wildcats.

———◆◆———

17 MARCH 2003 ▶ FORT BLAIR MAYNE, NORTHERN KUWAIT

St. Patrick's Day.

With an Irish rifle battalion.

My watch alarm beeped me awake at 0530. I shoved bare feet into unlaced boots, and gallumped across the sand for ablutions. Quick shave and into the morning's uniform: utility trousers, boots, T-shirt and green fleece pullover.

At 0630, the officers gathered next to the mess tent to begin the day's festivities. A trash barrel was lined with plastic, and the Sergeant Major poured in fifth after fifth of rum, liberated from god knows where. The mess cooks worked over a huge steaming pot of tea, and when all officers had assembled poured it in with the rum to make *gunfire*, a traditional Irish drink. Each company commander took a large cooler of gunfire and his platoon commanders took stacks of paper cups.

Per the Saint Patrick's Day tradition, the troops stayed in bed late, and every one of them was served gunfire in a cup by an officer. They sat up in their sleeping bags, nursing their cups and chatting quietly, as the officers rolled tent by tent through the battalion.

Brian and I tagged along, ensuring that each Marine got a cup from one of us.

As the officers fanned out through the tents, the Royal Irish band formed up and began to play. Bagpipes, drums and fifes in the sand. The band marched through the center of every tent, the bagpipes startlingly loud in an enclosed space, and woke up any stragglers.

After breakfast came the chariot races. Each company had devised some sort of Doomsday machine, and each company commander rode his chariot and screamed at his boys to pull harder. Soldiers, stripped to the waist and painted in different colors, surged at their lines like draft horses. Staff members threw multicolored flares, so as the teams charged around the oval course around camp they disappeared in and out of a purple haze.

My Marines had scrounged up a telephone cable spool, and Sergeant Walsh, naturally, took charge of the Marine Corps entry into the race.

Sarah stood on the hood of a Rover, her long red hair blowing in the wind, snapping pictures and writing quickly, giggling at the absurdity of it all.

Colin Marks's boys soundly defeated all comers; we disputed the results, arguing that because Colin was so small and light his team had an unfair advantage.

Volleyball games sprang up, and soccer matches, and men lazily tossed softballs to one another. My boys had found a football somewhere, and a pickup game devolved from crashing about in the sand to a calm game of catch.

I sat next to the shower trailers, in the sun with Sid and his team, and chatted mildly, flipping through magazines and soaking in the day. The Irishmen started to burn red in the Kuwait sun; my Mexicans stripped down to shorts and flip-flops and just got a shade darker.

The day took on the air of a lazy picnic afternoon, and I couldn't help but think of it as the calm before the storm.

———•••———

At 1700, the battalion formed up, 700 strong, for the Saint Patrick's Day parade and pass in review.

The guest of honor was General Mike Jackson, commanding general of all British forces in theater. Like all Brits, he had a deep, fraternal affection for the Irish, and seemed to think of them as sort of cheerful, high-spirited mascots.

Marine generals tend to have a panache and polish and look the part, silver hair and broad shoulders and square jaws. General Jackson looked like a gaunt, aging wino who had found a uniform beneath a bush and put it on. The lads loved him, though, and he had a great reputation. Good enough for me.

The Marines and I watched the pass in review, standing atop vehicles parked to the side. A mind-bending sight: 700 soldiers in caubeens, bristling with snap and polish, marching beautifully across the desert floor. They swung their arms shoulder-high in the British way, and each officer, as his company approached the reviewing area, screamed out EYES, RIGHT. Hundreds of heads snapped 45 degrees to the right and each commander saluted the general with their Monty Python elbows-up, palm-forward salutes.

On Saint Patrick's Day, every member of the Royal Irish gets a live shamrock. Period. Doesn't matter where in the world they are; the tradition must be followed. Somehow, someone had shipped over crates of live shamrocks direct from the Auld Sod, and General Jackson distributed them among the lads.

A Gurkha bart followed, eaten outdoors at picnic tables, heaping bowls of meat and rice.

I was pleased to see Lieutenant Colonel Fred Padilla, the commander of 1st Battalion, 5th Marines, and his staff; they had promised to make it if they could.

Our first mission over the border would be to take over for the boys from 1/5, who would go over in front of us. The Marines call this a RIP/TOA: *relief in place and transfer of authority* for the battlefield. It was simple: a Marine comes out of a fighting hole, and a Royal Irish soldier goes in. Tim would take the battlefield from Fred.

It was at this seam between not only two battalions but two nations that ANGLICO would be operating. This is why we were there.

I found Tim Collins and brought the two staffs together; many of them had never actually talked to one another.

Colonel, what are you hearing from General Mattis or the RCT-5 guys? I asked Fred.

Well, we may not be able to stay here long he said. We are on a 24-hour string, but it is going to go to four hours pretty soon. I brought my comm folks with me to stay in touch with the rear, so if I run off, don't be mad at me.

No, sir, don't worry about that. Is there anything I can do from my end to help you?

No, Stan, I don't think so. He looked distracted and a bit far away. Your guys are fitting right in with my rifle companies. Great Marines.

Tim Collins walked up and made small talk. The three of us watched, bemused, as the Marine Sergeant Major and the Irish Regimental Sergeant Major fell deep into discussion; they had never met before. There was an instant bond which infantrymen around the world share, combined with their leadership billets.

Fred Padilla spoke up. Have you ever seen so much saltiness in one place?

I laughed. No, sir. Those two have more experience than most of the two battalions put together.

I thought about it for a second. Sure enough. Sixty years of infantry experience, at least, right in one place. Elders.

———•••———

After dinner the entertainment began. The entire battalion pulled plastic chairs into a huge semicircle to watch the festivities; the staff from 1/5 joined us for the show.

Robby Boyd had scrounged a guitar from somewhere, and he and his four-piece band played all the Irish folk tunes they knew. As they closed out their set, they played Country Roads and The Star Spangled Banner for the Marines, and we shouted our approval.

Skits followed in a talent show format. I knew the Irishmen were funny by nature; I had no idea how clever some of the lads would be.

The first was a takeoff on a British television show. This show leads the viewer room-by-room through a house of the rich and famous, pointing out objects and then culminating in a panel vote on whose house they think it is.

Robby's A Company soldiers did a takeoff on this show, with a host walking the audience through Robby's tent (And who might live in a tent like this?) He pointed out the cot (covers pulled tightly and evenly,) the clothes (everything folded just so,) and so on, poking fun at his tidy, neatnik reputation.

The host then drew up short in mock surprise and in deadpan British accent began going through the items on the shelf: Look at this! A GPS! And a spare GPS! And a spare, spare GPS! This person really likes to know where he is and where he's going!

The panel comprised:

The Sergeant Major, who leapt to his feet and shouted Who is Duty Company?;

Tim Collins, who kept hearing the host's references to *Bravo Two Zero* and shouting out, It's shite! That book is shite! It's a fairy tale! Get rid of it!; and

Tim's second-in-command, a very large major, who kept commenting on how hungry he was.

The assembled soldiers roared with laughter.

As the staff changed out props for the next skit, I noticed a commotion to my left.

Fred Padilla and his staff jumped up from their chairs and ran to their vehicles.

Sid and I exchanged glances.

———•••———

The next skit was, naturally enough, Tony Blair and George W. Bush discussing the war.

Bush, of course, was played as a rough-and-ready Texan, hitching up his belt, spreading his feet wide and distributing bellicose ideas. The soldier playing Bush had borrowed one of my Marines' Kevlar helmets, one size too big, which made the visuals even funnier.

Bush: So, Tony, who ya got who can fight with us?

Tony Blair was played as a crisp, proper British gent: quiet, effeminate, high-voiced, long-winded.

Well, George, right, smashing, so glad you asked. We in the United Kingdom so very much look forward to this chance to stand with our allies across the Pond...

He began going through the options of whom the British might send:

I Para: soldier runs out in full gear, starts doing pushups, and screams Airborne! Airborne! whenever he is asked his name.

Royal Marines: soldier runs from stage left with an immense pack towering over his head and an even bigger Union Jack flying from it, carrying an entire case of toilet paper. (On their initial deployment into theater, the Royals had complained all the way to Parliament about a lack of toilet paper. They were pilloried in the press when that got out, and of course the rest of the British forces in theater piled on.)

I Royal Irish: soldier playing the bagpipes enters stage right. His playing grows a bit hesitant, then he begins to wheeze and weave about, obviously drunk. He plays valiantly on until overcome by drink, at which point he collapses face-first to the sand in a crash of notes to screaming, roaring laughter.

The soldiers broke up and streamed back to their tents. Few had noticed the U.S. Marines' hurried exit. I knew there was only one reason they would have run off so quickly.

---

19 MARCH 2003 ▶ FORT BLAIR MAYNE, NORTHERN KUWAIT

Phil Caputo in *A Rumor of War* described the hours before his rifle battalion deployed from Okinawa to Vietnam. He painted a vivid picture of harried, frantic and tense preparations: Marines walking around in various stages of undress, weapons and ammunition everywhere, vehicles dodging crates of supplies.

Replace the humidity of Japan with the dry Arabian air, and the scene before me was a perfect match.

Almost 1100 men were inside the Royal Irish berm, 700 or so in the Royal Irish proper and another 400 or so attachments: engineers, communications teams, Gurkha admin officers, medical personnel, U.S. Marines. Every man was intently engaged in doing something. Weapons were cleaned, engines oiled and greased and fueled, ammunition loaded, unloaded, reloaded. Packs were unpacked and repacked; nothing worse than not being able to find something quickly and under pressure. Pale-skinned, red-haired soldiers laid ammunition belts of evil-looking rounds across the breeches of heavy machine guns.

Sergeant Wilson walked up next to me and stood for a moment. He held an undergraduate degree from UC Santa Barbara and had a wry, laid-back and educated attitude about everything.

He looked out at the men scurrying about across the sand and said It all seems surreal and walked away.

———•••———

WEDNESDAY, 19 MARCH 2003 ▶ FORT BLAIR MAYNE, NORTHERN KUWAIT

Collins called a meeting for 1500. Everyone trooped in early, even more tense and wired than they had been at an identical meeting seven hours before.

He went carefully around the table, asking specific questions and wanting to know, truly, if the lads were ready or not. Each company commander spoke up truthfully about maintenance and ammunition issues. Each insisted that his boys were ready.

Collins had seen combat at several levels, both on small teams and in large units like this, and as we got closer to time to cross the LOD he began to charge us up. We were awash in adrenaline as it was—the British in their reserved way, me showing it by talking to fast and laughing too quickly—and being led by this man amped us even more.

I fell right in line with the company commanders: Yes, sir, everything is fine, small issues but nothing we can't handle, lads are primed and leaning forward. We are ready when you are.

Collins leaned forward and spoke.

———•••———

It looks like D-Day has already happened. We can do ourselves a favor by getting the Iraqis to free their own country. We are looking for a truce, not capitulation, not surrender.

He looked directly at his rifle company commanders, his conduits to the men who would be pulling triggers.

Make a distinction between what you actually saw and what you heard about.

To the group he said Enjoy this. This is an adventure. This experience cannot be bought. Your grandchildren will ask you: what was it like? What did they tell you before you went?

Let's bring all these kids home. Their parents are really worried; we are their parents in locus.

Let us bring light to this country, which has had thirty years of darkness.

———•••———

Collins had scheduled a formation of the whole battalion for 1700, so we didn't have much time.

Collins held the tent flap open for me. Your lads ready, then, Stan? he asked in his singsong Belfast accent.

Yes, sir. The rest of my boys have already gone to the border. Time for us to get into the fight.

Right. See you at the Führer Rally.

He always referred to his speeches in this way, a small joke among the staff. These events were indeed a whiff of the Nazis: clear-eyed, pale-skinned, square-jawed young men, armed to the teeth, in a worshipful circle around their leader.

———•••———

I was that day a witness to history.

———•••———

19 MARCH 2003, 1700 ▶ FORT BLAIR MAYNE, NORTHERN KUWAIT

The Rally started promptly.

We formed up on three sides of a rectangle, with Collins standing alone on the fourth side. There was always a dash of the dramatic to him, and especially on this day. He wore a desert scarf as a kaffiyeh wrapped several times around his neck. His monstrous, expensive Suunto watch glinted from his left wrist. His kukri, presented to him as a commander of Gurkhas, hung from his left hip.

I stood directly to his right side, Richard next to me. I was the lone American in the front rank of the formation, and I stood out due to my different uniform. Nearly 1000 men stood straight and quiet on the sand, only eight of us American.

———•••———

Sarah stood across from me and a bit apart from the formation, notebook in hand.

———•••———

Collins leapt into his speech. What he said that day caught fire and made headlines around the world, but here is the thing: there was nothing unusual about it to us.

Collins made speeches like this all the time.

Tim Collins was a soldier through and through, but he was also a highly educated Irishman, with a touch of the poet that the Irish all seem to have. He wanted the boys to understand what they were about to get into, and wanted them to be mentally prepared as well as tactically focused.

As I stood and listened, I realized that Collins was one of the few men in the battalion who had killed a man or even heard a shot fired in anger. A lot of these lads were about to see their first dead body. Collins wanted simple rules followed: kill bad guys, but not civilians. *Uphold the honor of the regiment.* Protect the tribe.

Everything was about to change.

———•••———

Collins began.

———•••———

There are some who are alive at this moment who will not be alive shortly. Those who do not wish to go on that journey, we will not send. As for the others, I expect you to rock their world. Wipe them out if that is what they choose.

But if you are ferocious in battle remember to be magnanimous in victory.

Iraq is steeped in history. It is the site of the Garden of Eden, of the Great Flood and the birthplace of Abraham and the ancient city of Ur. Tread lightly there.

You will see things that no man could pay to see and you will have to go a long way to find a more decent, generous and upright people than the Iraqis. You will be embarrassed by their hospitality even though they have nothing. Don't treat them as refugees for they are in their own country. Their children will be poor, but in years to come they will know that the light of liberation in their lives was brought by you.

If there are casualties of war then remember that when they woke up and got dressed in the morning they did not plan to die this day. Allow them dignity in death.

Bury them properly and mark their graves.

It is my foremost intention to bring every single one of you out alive but there may be people among us who will not see the end of this campaign. We will put them in their sleeping bags and send them back. There will be no time for sorrow.

The enemy should be in no doubt that we are his nemesis and that we are bringing about his rightful destruction. There are many regional commanders who have stains on their souls and they are stoking the fires of hell for Saddam. He and his forces will be destroyed by this coalition for what they have done. As they die they will know their deeds have brought them to this place. Show them no pity.

It is a big step to take another human life. It is not to be done lightly. I know of men who have taken life needlessly in other conflicts; I can assure you they live with the mark of Cain upon them. If someone surrenders to you then remember they have that right in international law and ensure that one day they go home to their family.

The ones who wish to fight, well, we aim to please.

If you harm the regiment or its history by over-enthusiasm in killing or in cowardice, know it is your family who will suffer. You will be shunned unless your conduct is of the highest for your deeds will follow you down through history. We will bring shame on neither our uniform nor our nation.

It is not a question of if Saddam will use chemical weapons, it's a question of when. We know he has already devolved the decision to lower commanders, and that means he has already taken the decision himself. If we survive the first strike we will survive the attack.

As for ourselves, let's bring everyone home and leave Iraq a better place for us having been there.

Our business now is north.

———•••———

Sarah scribbled madly in her notebook.

———•••———

Collins continued, firm, direct, warm.

We will kill who needs to be killed. I want some of these Iraqis to be cowering in their holes and trying to be quiet when we approach. I want the last thing some of these guys hear to be their officer saying *Who the fuck did that?*

He turned and walked steadily away; the Sergeant Major took charge of the formation and dismissed everyone.

I, for lack of anything better to do, walked back toward the briefing tent. Collins stood in front.

Hey, sir, great speech, I said to him.

He smiled. Thanks, Stan. What no one knows is that there was one more person in the audience: me! I was listening to myself, too—I didn't know what was coming next.

You didn't rehearse that, sir?

No, mate, just let it flow. I don't practice those things.

I filed that away under Leadership Habits To Emulate, and went back to my tent.

———•••———

As we got geared up to move out, Sarah Oliver was realizing what had just happened.

One of the great speeches of modern times had just been delivered...and she was the only person who had written it down.

———•••———

20 MARCH 2003, 0345 ▸ FORT BLAIR MAYNE, NORTHERN KUWAIT

Ranger Lee Magowan, Collins's right-hand man, hustled into my tent, tripping over sprawled bodies and swearing quietly. He woke several grumbling people before finding me.

Uh, sir, right, call for you from Brigade.

Fuck.

I hopped into my boots, still in my black running shorts. I grabbed my fleece pullover and ran behind him across the camp, trying not to trip over anything in the dark.

The CP tent was hopping with activity. A dutiful young soldier recognized me and handed me the Ptarmigan phone. Why they named these phones after ptarmigans, with so many other birds from which to choose, always mystified me. Brian insisted on referring to these as the Penguin Phone, and I always, *always* giggled whenever I picked it up.

I expected the CO.

Sir, Major Coerr here.

It was my friend Neil LaSala, a chief warrant officer whom everyone called Gator, working on the brigade staff above me.

Hey, sir, Gator here. Brigade says to move your guys back up to 1/5. Right now.

Now? When are they leaving for the border?

Uh, don't know yet, sir. Word is that they are supposed to be moving out in two hours.

Two hours! Jesus Christ! I vented at poor Neil. I can't even get them there in two hours, let alone have them ready to move to Iraq! I knew this wasn't his fault; I had apologized in advance to everyone all the way back in California for my propensity to shoot the messenger.

Sir, we have also heard they are on six to eight hours' notice to move. I don't know what to tell you, but I guess you should send them up right now.

I blew out a huge breath.

OK, Neil, sorry. I will get them moving. I replied.

Yes, sir. Let us know what we can do from here. Gator out.

India Six out.

———•••———

Shit.

———•••———

I ran through the dark to start waking people.

I jogged tent by tent through the black, grabbing team leaders and getting them moving.

Marines have two seemingly contradictory traits: they are incredibly deep sleepers, a habit evolved so that the noises of men and machines 24 hours a day don't preclude getting any sleep at all.

They also pop wide awake instantly when something important happens. All my folks snapped upright and were dressed and moving within minutes.

It did indeed take them more than two hours to get moving.

Sid was running unusually slow getting his people going.

One of my RAF attachments informed me, five minutes prior to his team's departure, that his people didn't have any chemical suits.

Wilson's vehicle broke down. Again.

Walsh's VHF radio stopped working. Again.

We slapped fixes on everything, got Wilson's engine started, got them lined up.

Eleven vehicles idled in the sand as dawn broke over Blair Mayne.

———◆◆◆———

I walked from vehicle to vehicle in the flat predawn light, handing out cookies my mother had sent me.

I bid my Marines and my British soldiers farewell as they prepared to push north to join 1/5, Brian in command.

I was suddenly gripped by the realization that this was it: this was war. Some of these guys could be dead within the day. These were parents' sons and women's husbands and children's' fathers but they were my men. *Mine.*

The lads, grim and quiet, taut, strapped on weapons and radios and headsets and were off.

I turned from my teams and I choked up quietly alone as they drove away.

———•••———

0630

Three explosions, quick succession, to the northwest.

I poked my head out of my tent flap.

Men were running in every direction.

———•••———

0800

Tim Collins pulled us together for a quick pep talk; all the details were in place long before. He cycled quickly around the room to all commanders, all of whom said they and their boys are ready.

I said the same.

Collins leaned forward, arms on the plywood, massive watch clunking against the table.

He looked hard at us.

Good luck to you all he said, and rose and strode quickly from the room.

———•••———

I was in my Humvee at 0815.

Conde smiled and seemed relaxed, shaking his head at the beehive around him. We idled quietly inside the camp, a line of several hundred vehicles. I sent Scull on a mission to liberate a box of tea bags from the chow hall; he hustled there and back, afraid the convoy would leave without him.

And then, just like that, we started north.

———•••———

Vehicles snaked through the front gate of the Blair Mayne, rumbling in low gear across the sand. I felt a bit wistful at leaving the camp, and wondered if I would ever see that piece of land again. We moved out and away from the berms, joining an exodus of Rovers and trucks from the other battalions beetling across the desert, *Road Warrior* plumes of dust rising in parallel straight lines east and west.

16th UK Air Assault Brigade was on the move...all of it. The Royal Irish pulled into four long lines, between the two Para battalions, turned off engines, and immediately threw up camo nets.

———•••———

We were the largest single-day assault since OVERLORD.

In the distance to my right were other British battalions from other brigades; same to the left, stretching farther than I could see. An *entire British division* was assembled on the desert floor. Somewhere in front of us was the *entire First Marine Division and the entire First Marine Expeditionary Force.* Somewhere dozens of miles to my west was the *entire U.S. Army Third Infantry Division and the entire U.S. Army V Corps.* Behind us was the *entire 11th Marine Regiment,* field artillery, hundreds of guns, all of them pointed over our heads.

Scattered at small pads around us and on roads in front of us and at airfields far to our south was the *entire Third Marine Aircraft Wing* and squadron after squadron of British fighters and helicopters. The United States Air Force had *entire air wings* to our north, working out of Turkey, and heavy bombers spread across the Gulf States and Europe, ready to do whatever we needed.

At sea, turning circles in the Gulf, were *two entire U.S. Navy carrier air wings*, centered around two carrier battle groups, dozens of ships of war. Task Force *Tarawa* was out there, too, most of another Marine Aircraft Wing spread across two amphibious ready groups.

I was in the belly of a monstrous satanic doomsday animal, a slavering, voracious beast devouring fuel and ammunition and food and water, ready to chew through and cast aside in pieces anything in its path, insatiable, unstoppable.

———•••———

And then we stopped.

We sat.

———•••———

We knew this would be our lives for at least a day, maybe two. With nothing else to do, I wandered down the line of vehicles, stopping and chatting with the lads as I went. I found Marcus Readman sitting in a lawn chair beneath his net.

Hello, mate! he called out as I walked past. Come on in!

In meant ducking under the tent seam; I struggled into his little sanctuary. I accepted his offer of tea, and sat in the sand looking out over the rest of the British Army lined up to the south.

Good blokes, those, Marcus said, gesturing with his chin to the next line of trucks.

Who?

The Paras. Different than us, though. Their regiment is a bit snooty. He thrust out his lower jaw, affecting an upper-crust, just-in-from-the-riding-to-the-hounds British aristocrat accent. They talk like this, mate, don't you know. Good lads though: tough.

I thought about that. This regimental system was so foreign to me, but it made sense. Fighting not just for country, but for tribe, for the honor of the regiment for which your father and his father and his father had also fought.

I made it back to my Humvee. Scull had the BBC tuned up. One advantage to having all the comm gear in my vehicle was that I always had good access to the BBC World Service. Sure enough, as I walked up the oh-so-smooth announcer was intoning that explosions were heard just south of the border. The war was on.

———•••———

The Irish Regimental Sergeant Major wandered by and stood next to me, gazing out at the cold hard machinery of war.

He said Sir, just bring your boys home. This isn't important enough to have anyone hurt, and then he walked away.

———•••———

As we prepared to go into the fight I was not worried about being killed by Iraqis.

Here is what I *was* worried about:

Mines.

Booby traps.

Gas.

And getting shot by our own guys in the dark and confusion and rain and the fog of war.

———•••———

Combat leadership is at its core one thing and one thing only: the management of heavily-armed teenage boys.

———•••———

21 MARCH 2003 ▶ DA BRIGHTON
IRAQ-KUWAIT BORDER

We pulled into position at dusk and everyone dug.

Conde, Scull, Arreola and I swung shovels and axes into the sand, taking turns with the heavy pickax. A Lance Corporal, two Staff Sergeants and a Major: no rank when you get to this level. A shell coming in doesn't care who you are when shrapnel scythes through human bodies.

As I sweated and grunted, filthy and exhausted, my mind wandered to college classmates, no doubt comfortable ensconced in offices in Manhattan and Los Angeles and Washington, clucking their tongues at the depredations of George Bush and the Vulcans in the White House.

Well, they could come right out here and see it.

James Webb's character Hodges in *Fields of Fire* said it perfectly: fuck them.

Fuck anyone who hasn't been out here and done this.

———•••———

An explosion roared me awake in the dark...a *very large* explosion, much closer and bigger than the last.

Someone was shooting at us.

I went back to sleep.

———•••———

21 MARCH 2003, 0230 ▶ MAIN SUPPLY ROUTE DALLAS, IRAQ-KUWAIT BORDER

I awoke with a start.

My subconscious detected noise and movement and pulled me up. I shaved quickly in the Humvee mirror, shivering in the desert cold, stripped to the waist.

Conde started up the vehicle and we sat with the doors open and feet on the door frames. I had on a scarf, gloves, field jacket and watch cap.

The radios were alive with combat. Two hundred POWs; the Irish were going to take control of those prisoners so we were tuned into that steadily-climbing number.

A Cobra had shot and destroyed one of our own tanks.

———•••———

An officer with 1/5 was dead.

———•••———

Initial word, always wrong, was that he had stepped on a mine. It was later determined that he had been shot in the stomach, a horribly unlucky AK bullet that had hit him just below his flak jacket.

Second Lieutenant Therrel Childers, known as Shane, prior enlisted Marine and a well-liked infantry officer, was the first American killed on the ground.

When he was ambushed and murdered he had been unarmed, walking forward of his Marines to accept the surrender of an Iraqi unit.

———•••———

Jets were roaring overhead, from south to north, flights of four every few minutes all night long.

Cobras headed north also, division after division.

I listened to the radio, and worried about mines and booby traps and gas. I looked out at the surreal moonscape through my windscreen: black and white sand and scrub, orange fires, white sand, dark clouds behind. I made a quick cup of tea with my little British heat tab, just enough to get me going.

We were adrift, nomads now, young men in a dry month.

RUBICON

On your young shoulders rest the hopes of mankind.
—Major General James Mattis, Commanding
General, First Marine Division

Letter to his Marines before crossing the
line of departure, March 2003

Only four animals form groups of four or more males and foray out to kill other males.

Dolphins. Bonobos. Chimpanzees. Humans.

That list is also this one: the four animals with the largest brains.

———•••———

I grew up on a happy, leafy suburban street, the kind where every family had several kids all roughly the same age.

It even had the perfect suburban name: Oaklawn.

Free-roaming games of football and Frisbee and Mother May I and Red Rover and bicycle races and dodgeball games and bottle rocket fights raged up and down the street all day all summer every summer, and when dusk came we played hide and seek, because it was harder in the twilight and we felt like rebels as our mothers called for us to come in for dinner and we ignored them.

And then on special nights when it was full night and we felt brave after dinner we went back out and we played the only game that felt like it was for real and still even now is, the game that was no longer pretend:

Manhunt.

———•••———

21 MARCH 2003, 0500 ▶ DEMILITARIZED ZONE BETWEEN KUWAIT AND IRAQ

We headed for the breech in the berm along MSR Dallas. Collins led the formation.

The sun rose over my right shoulder, low and fat and pale at 0500. We creaked along behind Richard and in front of the Regimental Sergeant Major. The berm rose in front of us, the razorback of a vast horrible hog flopped between two countries which hated each other. I saw the cut our bulldozers had made, and renewed my respect for the poor engineers who had been up here by themselves for weeks, digging away as the Iraqis watched.

We suddenly stopped just short of the DMZ; I feared for a moment that something had happened to Collins's Rover.

No: Collins himself jumped from the left side door, ran a few steps forward to where the barbed wire started, turned, whipped out a camera, and snapped several photos of all of us lined up in the orange of dawn.

He hopped back in and off we went.

A jaunty sign at the side of the road informed us:

Warning: You Are Now Approaching The DMZ.

And just like that, there we were indeed, through the first set of berms. I hadn't realized that there was a no-shit DMZ here...I thought it was just a figure of speech. But there was a good 200 meters of open ground between two head-high berms, both topped with razor wire.

God only knew what kind of shit was buried in the ground right next to me: mines, booby traps, IEDs, artillery shells with proximity fuses.

And then we were through the second berms.

And then we were in Iraq.

———•••———

Phil Caputo was an officer in the Marines in Vietnam, and when someone asked him why he volunteered he said Having known nothing but security, comfort and peace, I hungered for danger, challenge and violence.

———•••———

It wasn't until we got clear of the second berm that I could actually hear and smell the fires we had seen for the last two days, from the GOSPs Saddam's boys had set ablaze. All these guys had to do was the engineering equivalent of throwing a match onto the wellheads, and they would burn for a thousand years.

That's just what they had done: our entire world was lit orange, partly from the rising sun but mostly from the bright-orange flames roaring away to the north. They felt equally hot. It was *exactly* like the movies, spiraling arcs of fire reaching 100 feet into the sky and throwing off nasty, thick, jet-black soot at the top. Nothing else burns like that.

———•••———

We pushed through the southern GOSPs, the Irish infantry companies peeling away from the convoy behind us and taking up their positions alongside the Marines of 1/5, the RIP/TOA in action.

Collins zoomed straight north, looking for Fred Padilla. I went with him.

We found Fred and his command staff at a road intersection, abeam a large compound which was in use as a temporary POW cage. Our vehicles pulled in next to theirs, and engines shut off.

Everyone took a deep breath in the sudden silence.

Fred hopped out of his command post, which was two monstrous amphibious tractors, Amtracs, parked back-to-back.

1/5 Sergeant Major Jones stood out of the circle of officers, one day's growth of beard and an amazingly filthy canteen cup making him look even more seasoned than he was.

Fred walked over to Tim and managed a tired smile.

I found out later from Brian that Fred had had to talk each company personally across the border in the thick fog and moonless night, to keep them from hitting or engaging each other. Combined with the flying steel and screaming impacts of the 11th Marines' regimental massing of fires onto preplanned targets in the GOSPs had meant a sleepless night for the 1/5 staff.

Fred shook hands with Tim. He was unshaven and looked exhausted.

How are you, Tim? Good to see you.

Good, mate, how are your lads?

Fred was calm and matter-of-fact. I had never been around officers during a war. I didn't know what to expect, but I knew this was how to do it. He was pitch-perfect for keeping his guys focused.

Well, we lost an officer last night. Shane Childers took a round in the stomach and bled out before we could get to him.

Jesus, Fred, I heard about that. How are his boys?

Fred looked at the ground. They aren't doing too well. The platoon sergeant took over. Shane was prior enlisted, and he and his platoon sergeant were very close. They are taking it hard.

They discussed the RIP for a moment, then Collins withdrew, to leave the Marines alone and let them pack up. We pulled over to the side of their CP and got our gear set up.

And just like that, 1/5 was on their way. I couldn't believe how quickly they broke down their comm gear and got on the road. That was the advantage of having your command in an armored vehicle...once you take down your antennas, everything else goes with you the way it is.

We walked over to the vehicles to mount back up. The Tim Collins Show was on fast-forward; I knew if I stuck near him, things were going to happen. As we strode along, Tim asked me Did you see our ex-Iraqi?

No, sir.

What the hell was he talking about?

Aye, right over there in the grass, he said over his shoulder as his vehicle started up.

Sure enough, twenty meters to our left lay a dead Iraqi soldier, face up. Hackworth was right: there was something unnerving about a man lying on his back on the battlefield. It means the guy is dead.

The young man had his hands folded across his chest, as if he had expired while looking at the clouds. I couldn't see how he had been killed. Round through the chest; he was otherwise, and except for being dead, untouched.

———•••———

Portuguese writer Jose Saramago says you normally don't see the dead mingling with the living apart from exceptional events such as war.

———•••———

Our dead Iraqi was far too young to be involved in something like this. All of us were. But I was older then than I am now.

———•••———

The padre walked by. I mentioned our dead Iraqi to him, and he told me he had already done seven burial services out in the desert, knowing that Muslims must be buried before nightfall on the day they die.

He had done those services all alone, a Christian man mourning Muslim boys.

The war was twelve hours old.

———•••———

As the morning sun rose, we pulled up to the site where Shane Childers had been killed, just next to the main north-south road through the GOSP complex.

I was angry and tense and sick standing at this site. I wondered if his parents had yet seen young officers in dress blues getting out of a government van in front of their house in Wyoming.

I wondered if the word was out among his high school buddies and old girlfriends and college roommate.

I wondered if his elementary school teacher would weep at her desk at this little boy who had become a man and gone adventuring and was coming home in a box.

The sand was dark with blood, in patches and splotches and ugly dried black splatters. The vehicle that had ambushed them sat halfway off the road, the sheet metal and windows riddled with bullet holes.

An Iraqi helmet covered in blood lay upside down in the sand, one bullet hole clean through front and back.

Shane Childers' boys had gotten revenge when their Lieutenant was killed. They had killed Shane so our teenagers killed them right back.

Those Iraqis were buried with their guilt, entombed under freshly-turned earth a few feet away.

Collins stood at with his hands on his hips, staring at that ground.

He walked to where three Iraqi fingers lay in the dirt, splattered with blood. He was as angry as I had ever seen him, trembling with rage over the death of this young man he had never met.

He stood over the fingers for a moment, and then lashed out at them with his foot, kicking them into a ditch and then kicking sand on top of them.

Fucking bastards, he seethed. Is this *fucking shite* country worth a young American's life? God *damn* it.

He reached down and picked up several full AK magazines, and flung them savagely into the ditch as well, and then kicked sand on top of them too.

He stormed back to his Rover in a dark fury and we drove on.

Collins set off to survey the battlefield.

Through the morning we checked on each rifle company, and more importantly showed the boys that the CO was there and keeping an eye on things. The Brits were digging in quickly; no one knew what was coming next.

On our journey north to go find Colin Marks' boys, Collins suddenly veered off the road and slammed to a stop. Conde skidded us to a stop behind him. Collins was already out of his door, stomping out into the desert.

I kept an eye on Collins and spoke loudly to Arreola: Staff Sergeant, go with him.

Aye, aye, sir. Already on the way. Arreola flung open his door and chased after him. Last thing I needed was to sit and watch our battalion commander get shot.

Come to think of it, if something happens I had better be there, too. I left Conde and Scull, hopped out and set off at a jog.

We caught up to Collins marching toward a D-30 site. The D-30 is a huge gun, and this one was pointed due south, right down the throat of where we had just come from. The Iraqis had wisely realized that the jig was up and had left the gun where it sat.

Rounds, fat and malevolent, were stacked neatly next to it. Uniform items were scattered in every direction; soldiers in this part of Iraq were primarily conscripts, with no interest in fighting—and even less in dying—for the regime. Each man kept his robes and sandals nearby, and in ten seconds could become just another innocent Bedouin wandering across the desert, minding his own business and wanting nothing to do with guns and war.

Arreola and I ran up behind Collins, and he whipped around, startled.

I grinned at him. Can't have the boss getting killed on the first day of the war, sir. He smiled and that and strode on.

We walked around the gun site, but gingerly; I was convinced that places like this were mined. A Bedouin (judging by his weathered skin and missing teeth, a real one) materialized, on foot and from the east, undoubtedly hoping that the soldiers had left behind food and water.

Collins shouted at him.

In Arabic.

———•••———

Collins ran off the Bedouin. Last thing he needed was an injured civilian to deal with.

The man glared at us, cursing the intruders on his land. And these nomads considered *all* of this their land...anywhere they could walk, they felt free to do so. He gave us a wide berth, staring at us all the time, a guard dog circling slowly.

He sauntered back into the wasteland.

Cheeky buggers, those Bedouins, Collins said with admiration. They don't give a damn about boundaries. Lines on a map don't mean a bloody thing to them. They will go across a border just to piss everyone off. They will steal you blind, and cheerfully.

————•••————

We stopped several times over the course of the day to go through Iraqi bunkers. These were the hovels where our POWs had lived and where their mates had died, waiting for us to come. Each was a large pit in the dirt, covered with a sheet of tin. They were surprisingly hard to spot, weathered and dirty and blending perfectly into the desert backdrop.

Each time we went down into one of these places, I had no trouble imagining how bad the lives of these men had been.

The bunkers were a horror: claustrophobic, airless, foul-smelling and choked with rotting food and vermin and dust. Dirty clothes hung from pitiful nails driven into wooden support beams. Food was sparse, and seemed to consist entirely of bags of rice and sugar and tomato paste and some spices. Each bunker had a family photo or two: smiling children, young wives.

Ammunition was kept beneath the bunks, as if the infidels would come all the way across the ocean, all the way through Kuwait, over the border, across the open desert, into this bunker and then not think to look under the bed.

Loaded rifles and loaded machine guns and linked ammunition and knives were scattered about, as if these units had left in a hurry. Which, come to think of it, they had.

———•••———

The weather was actually quite cool and pleasant, but inside these dirt pits it was unbearably hot. This was only March; I couldn't imagine living here during the Arabian summer. And I couldn't imagine looking out over the open desert to the south, knowing that hundreds of thousands of men, unstoppable, were coming to kill me.

How these guys fought at all was beyond me; I would have deserted long before. I hoped deep down that soldiers had only been assigned here for a few weeks at a time, that maybe units rotated through and then fell back to someplace more pleasant. It was too depressing to think of the alternative. I tried, and failed, to imagine keeping control of these soldiers in any way except at the end of a loaded rifle. I gained respect for the commanders who had kept these men together and actually convinced them to shoot at us when we came.

The rest of the Royal Irish command staff had been going through the bunkers as well. When we returned to the command post in mid-afternoon, an enormous pile of materiel had grown next to our position: rifles, crew-served weapons, knives, pistols, RPGs and their finned rounds, optics, magazines, grenades. Lethal impedimenta of the lethal trade.

———•••———

In the middle of the afternoon, the Regimental Sergeant Major pulled up with two Iraqi officers.

Both were Lieutenant Colonels; one had been battalion commander of the units whose bunkers we had just cleared, the other his number two man. I would have guessed each man was about 50, though they turned out to be my age, 35. Their faces wore a hard life poorly: sagging skin, permanent squints, sunburns, dirt, bags under their eyes. Men who lived in bunkers like those I had just seen would look like this.

The senior man had his mandatory Saddam-style black mustache, and a large belly bulged from his filthy green uniform. Collins called me over as senior American officer, and set everyone hopping to find bread, tea, coffee, sweets. We set up chairs around a folding table and made the men comfortable.

This was not going to be an interrogation from the movies.

Phil was a British officer from London but of Arab descent, fluent in Arabic. He sat with us and translated.

Americans are not used to dealing with Arabs. An American would sit down and say Tell me where the rest of your men are. An Arab would sit down for the same discussion and say For many years, my father and his father and his father walked this land, and all of us as a people joined in our love for Allah and his blessings....

Collins of course knew this. He knew everything.

In the Arab way, Collins began by chatting obliquely, asking about each man's village and their ancestors. They, in turn, made many statements about the land and the people and their wishes for a better Iraq. Our speech was stilted and formal, like reading from the Bible.

I spoke through Phil, looking directly at our new friends.

The American people want a better Iraq. We believe that this is the beginning of a new time for your people. We Americans join with our British friends in freeing you from Saddam so that this day may come.

Collins chimed in. I have brought my men, and my American comrades here, to help with this new country. We believe in the new Iraq, and we think that men like you should be able to be with your families and be free.

The discussion meandered like this for a while, with the commander growing increasingly agitated.

Phil said He says one of his men is hurt, out in the desert, and he is afraid that man is hiding from you.

Collins responded in BibleSpeak. Yes, let us go, right now, and find this soldier. There is no need for any more blood to be shed on this day.

Back into the desert we went, six of us, in Collins's Rover, 1000 pounds of soldiery cheek by jowl. Our Iraqi guided us. He knew this land intimately, and pointed the Rover this way and that across the open sand. He and I and Phil were smashed with Collins's radioman into the back, four of us in a space the size of the bed of a small pickup, and I feverishly hoped we were close.

We slammed to a halt.

The Iraqi commander leapt out, suddenly agile, like an overweight cat, and walked quickly and certainly to a bunker.

His bunker.

He dove into the entrance.

The five of us stepped back, drew weapons and clicked off safeties. God knew what he had down there. A rifle was least of our worries, but what if he had booby-trapped the goddamn thing and, knowing the jig was up, was going to take us all with him?

Mais non.

He emerged with a filthy polyester blanket, gaily colored. Yeah. Wounded soldier my foot. The old boy knew it was a time in the POW cages for him, and he wanted his blanket for the concrete floors.

———•••———

We were thoughtful pilgrims in an angry land.

———•••———

The afternoon drew cooler and the sun fell.

Collins was still on overdrive, and when he got a call of more POWs to the north, he was off like he had been shot out of a cannon. We went along.

We drove north at full speed into the gathering hellscape of this dusk, dodging puddles of crude oil, bright orange flames roaring all around us. Thick black smoke choked the air, an assault on the lungs and nose, a smell like a burning clutch or a steel mill;

there seemed to be no way out of it. Why Collins needed to be there to look at prisoners, I didn't know, but that was where the action would be.

We jogged on a side road due east, and pulled up next to a small gas compression station.

Ten British soldiers stood relaxed but wary, weapons pointing at the ground, facing what seemed to be the better part of one hundred prisoners sitting on a small hillside.

These men were absolutely whipped: the most pitiful, obedient, pathetic people I had ever seen. They sat silent, shivering in their single thin uniform shirts in the dropping evening chill.

A friend once told me about taking prisoners during Desert Storm and feeling sorry for them. I now understood.

These guys presented no danger to anyone, as far as I could tell. Hell, some of these guys could have been the *same* prisoners taken during Desert Storm. That was only twelve years before. These guys were much older than our young soldiers and Marines, and American forces in 1991 had been to here and beyond. These guys looked awfully tired of war.

Collins roared up and leapt from his seat. I trailed behind.

The Iraqis sat frozen, terrified, but their eyes followed his every move. Hell, Collins's *own* guys were afraid of him, and by the way he moved and spoke these POWs quickly understood that this was someone important. They followed me with interest as well, noting my American uniform, understanding intuitively that only officers carried pistols, and that whoever sat in the front passenger seat of a military vehicle was some sort of commander.

The POWs feared moving a muscle. The war was not even a day old, and these Brits hadn't had a chance to shoot anyone yet, and finally *right here* were some actual bad guys. They leaned forward almost imperceptibly, watching with anxious eyes as Collins spoke through Phil to their commander.

Their commander was another of Saddam's local boys, another man old before his time and beyond his years. He spoke English, it turned out. I stood to the side as Collins spoke and as the two commanders shook hands.

The Iraqi officer began in English: sir, these men are starving. None of them has eaten. More than thirty-six hours. Americans came, they did not shoot. Please, to give them food and to sleep, inside.

Collins smiled warmly. We will do that. We want to watch out for these men and then we want them to return to their families. Please tell them that they will be taken to shelter.

The Iraqi officer turned and addressed the men in Arabic.

———•••———

Before the first sentence was out of his mouth, the men erupted in cheers and leapt to their feet. They began to run toward the buses parked to the side of the clearing. What had been a quiet scene suddenly was chaos.

———•••———

Collins erupted. He screamed at them: *What the fuck are you doing?* Sit back down!

Quick as a snake, he unsnapped the holster on his sidearm, flipped off the safety, and cracked two shots into the air. Then two more.

The Iraqis froze. Several threw themselves face-down to the ground, terrified of being killed so close to the end of their war and within arm's reach of safety. A rush started, back to the hill where they had begun.

Get control of these men! Collins shouted at his British soldiers, who were frozen, wide-eyed, startled by the melee. They leapt into action, grabbing the Iraqis and turning them around to line up for the buses. Order restored, the prisoners filed onto the buses, quietly, orderly this time.

Collins stood with his hands on his hips, weapon now cooling back on his hip, glaring at the scene before him.

------◆◆◆------

Staff Sergeant Arreola was standing next to me. *Fuckin A, sir!* he whispered. That will teach those fuckers to get out of line again. Man, Colonel Collins takes no shit, does he?

No, he doesn't, I replied, but I wasn't so sure. These prisoners seemed completely harmless to me: unarmed, hungry, cold, beaten. Then again, they outnumbered us ten to one. Collins knew what he was doing.

He had been in combat before, and I hadn't. I would trust his judgment.

I hopped into the back of Collins's Rover, alongside our battalion commander prisoner of war. We headed into the dark, back to the compound where these POWs would live.

On the drive, I talked with this man, who spoke some English. He was tired, hungry, resigned but relieved of his burden of commanding men for a job doomed to failure. He had commanded the force assigned to guarding the oil infrastructure in the northern part of the GOSPs.

He told me that twenty of his men were volunteers, actual soldiers, the rest conscripts from the tiny villages around this part of the country. These are not real soldiers, he told me, not professionals ready to fight and die for Saddam.

These are security guards, I thought, with all the training we would give a mall cop in the United States. How would a mall cop do against the combined-arms machine of keyed-up British soldiers and U.S. Marines?

I asked him the question which had intrigued me for months. Did you know we were coming? Did the officers above you tell you to be ready for us?

No, my friend! he shouted over the crashing and grinding of the vehicle. No, they told us nothing! I did not speak to my superior officers for many days before the invasion began. They said the Americans were coming very soon, but then our Brigadier left. I think they perhaps ran, or gave up and are now with their families.

Many of my men ran as well. We had no warning.

But I knew you would come.

He looked sad, like he had failed in his tiny piece of the defense of his homeland. He himself was a real soldier, sent to the boondocks to command his rent-a-cops. I felt sorry for him and wondered where he would be a year from now.

Collins directed that the officers be given their own room, partially out of respect for their rank, partially to keep anything from getting organized among the prisoners.

Off to the cages went the commander with his number two man.

We pulled into the POW camp, and I bid him farewell as he was led away.

I never saw him again.

---

24 MARCH 2003 ▶ SOUTHERN IRAQ
I couldn't believe how beautiful it was.

The sun set slowly to our left, a dull orange ball sinking into the Hamar Canal. It was dead quiet, no manmade noise, the first time in weeks I hadn't heard some sort of machine operating or something exploding or burning. Shorebirds chirped and squawked cheerily, diving for fish in the dusk gloaming. Bats swooped and darted.

Signs of past wars: enormous piles of ugly, twisted metal half-sunk near the shoreline. The bridge on which I stood had been blown and rebuilt several times, judging by the tonnage of twisted burned steel in the water. Aside from the detritus of war, this was a gorgeous little piece of Mesopotamia.

The infantry officers on foot ahead of us stopped short of a gaping hole in the concrete. American planes had already bombed this bridge, but were only halfway through the job of dropping it entirely when someone realized this was the only way north further into Iraq for thirty miles in either direction.

That bomb had ripped out smaller chunks of the bridge as well; I could see between my boots forty feet down to the water where fish darted in the dusk.

Waiting for us back at the GOSP complex was a gift.

Collins walked up to me with a big grin and conspiratorial twinkle in his eye. Stan, I got you a present, he said.

OK, sir, what is it?

A Humvee! he announced, beaming.

While Richard and Brian and I were up at the Hamar Canal, Collins had been roaring around the GOSPs looking for trouble. On one of his escapades, he had found a brand-spanking new Humvee parked at the side of the road. It didn't run, for some reason (which was why it was parked, its occupants long-since departed with the rest of their unit) but Collins was thrilled to find a little gift for his Marines, and so threw a chain over the bumper and hauled it to Mike Murdock's command post, where we now stood.

And there it sat, the nicest Humvee I had ever seen.

It was even nice by stateside standards.

For Iraq, it was like it had just rolled off the assembly line.

It sparkled.

It gleamed.

It had four new tires.

Music swelled and the angels smiled.

———•••———

Ratfuck (Verb) (*Irregular*)

1. To take what you need from a collection of items and toss the rest.
2. To steal an item you need from those who in your estimation need it less.

Usage: *Major Coerr said to ratfuck the Humvee and distribute the parts through the teams.*

———•••———

Ratfucking is among the finest and oldest of Marine Corps traditions. Another is outright theft. The only rule: you never, *ever,* steal from other Marines.

Ratfucking: waiting for cover of darkness and then taking your favorite candy out of your kids' Halloween baskets while they sleep.

Theft: taking *all* of your kids' candy.

The first is widely accepted; the latter just not done.

This wasn't theft. This Hummer didn't belong to anyone. It was just a lucky find and the ratfuck was on.

I sent Arreola and Conde over with a tool box and they started disassembling it as I watched, surgical work, pulling it into component parts, cannibalizing pieces for other Humvees. I split the tires and engine parts throughout the teams, depending on need.

I had eyes only for one thing: the seats.

The new Humvees had thick, heavily-cushioned seats on springs. GM had finally responded to long complaints about the paper-thin butt padding on the old ones, which smooshed even flatter after large guys wearing flak jackets slammed around in them for a few thousand miles.

The pad on my seat in my ancient Humvee was down to the metal. The seats in my vehicle were so bad that we actually grew exhausted being bounced all over Mesopotamia on our off-road adventures.

So I pulled rank and gave Arreola strict instructions: the first item on the Ratfuck Agenda was to replace my old, flat seat with the cushy, fluffy bucket one from the new vehicle. This is called *priorities*.

I was a seven-year-old boy, and my father was putting me to sleep.

I slept in his workshop, drifting off each night with the smell of sawdust and 3-in-1 Oil.

He didn't have a bed for me. What he had was a World War II Marine Corps-issue jungle hammock, which of course to a boy is the coolest thing ever. I slept in that hammock for years and I can still smell the canvas.

I needed something to read this night, so he disappeared into the study and returned. He handed me a book I read cover to cover and which is now on my desk: the 1962 *Guidebook for Marines*.

———— •••• ————

We and the Iraqis we came to save were followers of incompatible gods.

———— •••• ————

The Bedouins came from literally nowhere and were now everywhere. They were walking in and around our positions, always moving slowly so we knew they were not a threat, smiling and waving to show how innocent and unarmed they were. Bullshit: every one of those bastards had a weapon, but of course we were not concerned about them. I would carry a rifle too, out in the badlands.

They were stealing everything they could find.

The Bedu realized that a new sheriff was in town, and that he didn't much care about theft. Collins made it clear to us: this is their country. If they want to loot and pillage and rob one another, we will not get in the middle of that. The only things they could not steal were weapons and ammunition.

I completely agreed with this outlook: if we start playing local cop, how will we ever leave?

I have always heard the phrase *stealing everything that isn't nailed down*, but had never seen such a thing in action.

The Bedouins even stole things that *were* nailed down.

Brian and I joined a small group watching in slack-jawed amazement as a small group of them rode up out of the wasteland in a small pickup truck. They pulled up next to an arc welder, an enormous machine roughly the size of an RV and which had to have weighed several tons. Tools materialized and they unbolted the goddamn thing from the concrete, and simply threw chains around it and dragged it out into the desert.

What they were going to do with it, I had no idea: it required huge amounts of power to run, and even if they got it running somehow, what were they going to weld? No matter. It was large and shiny and expensive, so they stole it.

And the Americans and British watched, bemused, with arms folded across our chests, and let the Iraqis pull apart their own country piece by piece.

——— •• ———

Collins was frozen, a bird dog, staring out onto MSR Dallas.

A large group of local men was walking right down the middle of the road.

Collins assumed they were Bedu, out for a stroll to show us who really ran the show in that part of the world.

One man held a box of food that was given to prisoners, a distinct and easily recognizable box even from this distance. Collins now stepped off the porch, carrying a rifle, and yelled at the man. He didn't seem truly angry, and assumed the Iraqi was simply a Bedouin who had stolen the food from down the road.

The man responded in Arabic, and Collins seemed to relax a bit. As the group made its way past us and began to walk out into the desert, one man at the back of the pack raised his hand in farewell.

His hand had a large black number written on it.

That meant he was a POW.

Collins flamed.

He raised his rifle and fired two shots into the air, and began to run towards the group. The Iraqis immediately went onto their stomachs on the pavement, lying flat, cringing and terrified. At the sound of rifle fire, soldiers and Marines ran from every direction, converging on the scene. Arreola and Scull whipped past me carrying rifles.

I stood back from the scene, my pistol still holstered. There were plenty of men there now, all with weapons pointing at the pathetic little group on the concrete. The words of an old Marine mentor who had led a long-range patrol company in Vietnam echoed: if you are fighting, you're not leading.

Collins was screaming at them in Arabic and in English, telling them to keep their heads down. Scull, closest to me, joined in, yelling down at the men with his weapon in his shoulder. The other soldiers, taking their cue from their commander, joined in the yelling, and the Iraqis didn't move.

The leader of the group was allowed to speak, and tried to explain what was happening. In the melee, it wasn't making any sense. Finally, the RSM, the man in charge of all the POWs, made it to the scene, and told Colonel Collins that these men *were* in fact POWs, but had been questioned and released, each with one box of food.

They were simply trying to get away from us and from war.

———•••———

I awoke at 0200, lying on my poncho liner on a filthy, decrepit bed I had scrounged.

Richard, who had been in the other bed in the room, was gathering his gear. In the manner of all military men since the dawn of time, he crashed about and swore quietly in the dark. His driver, whom everyone called Pez, came in to urge him along, and before I woke fully they had clanked and banged and crashed their way outside by flashlight.

I didn't see the need to get up to Hamar Bridge in the dark; what the hell would we accomplish that couldn't be done in the daylight? I went back to sleep.

———•••———

At 0400 Arreola came in, hunted and urgent and afraid I had overslept.

I was lacing my boots and my gear was already in the Humvee, and Arreola, satisfied, went back out. I bid a quiet farewell to the dark, close, filthy room Richard and I had called home for those short days; I wondered if I would ever see it again.

I once asked legendary *New York Times* columnist Johnny Apple how you got to the front lines in a combat zone. He responded You commute! You get a cab, and you keep throwing more money over the front seat each time the driver refuses to go any farther.

I was commuting to combat.

I had Conde instead of a cab driver, but it felt strange just heading off to work.

Especially this work, that of killing.

———————●•●———————

Each of us assumed his role.

Scull and Arreola were sitting in the back seats, doors open.

Arreola was, as usual, loaded for bear: flak on and Velcroed shut, helmet on tightly, gloves tightened down, weapon already out the window. I didn't have the heart to tell him the British Army controlled the sector of Iraq we would be driving through...he reminded me of a little kid dressed up to play cowboys and Indians with his buddies.

Scull was the opposite, also as usual. His flak jacket hung open, helmet on the floor at his feet, a cigarette already angling from his lip, the rest of them in the box in his top pocket where he could get at them quickly. His features were contorted in concentration as he fiddled with the radios, which sat astride the huge engine box in the middle of the Humvee, separating the two men on the left from the two on the right. The military Humvees are much beefier than the ones you see tooling through the suburbs.

I couldn't even reach Conde with my fingertips unless I lay prone across the middle of the vehicle.

Conde, as always, was alert and ready to go. The kid was in high school a year before and never seemed to need to eat, drink or pee. He was completely focused on anticipating my every need and being a step ahead of me. He also didn't need to shave, as far as I could tell.

Conde was strikingly handsome, dark eyes and perfectly smooth brown skin with a doe-eyed, innocent look, a Mexican movie star but with the impossible first name *Morgan*. Girls at his high school had no doubt swooned over him. He had made the mistake of showing all of us pictures of his older sisters, each of them drop-dead gorgeous, after which the other three of us decided we need to visit: soon.

He should have been the boyfriend of the heroine in a Mexican telenovela, not driving for me.

I schlepped my stuff over to my spiffy new freshly-ratfucked passenger seat and flopped in.

Conde smiled at me.

Ready to go, sir?

I was born ready I responded with a grin, and he put our Hummer in gear and drove us to war.

———•••———

We roared north in the growing light, the only vehicle on the roads. Off to each side we caught glimpses of movement: the

Irish infantrymen, in their fighting holes and looking out over the desert, one man up and one man down brewing up their morning tea. The moonscape whipped by my open window, orange and pink and sandy brown in the flat light of dawn. We came to the end of our road and took a hard right, and Conde floored it, driving right down the center of the road.

I daydreamed, looking out my window and wondering how things were going with the Paras up at the Bridge. I wondered how Jackson was doing. I listened to the lulling hiss of the radios. I lazily turned back to look out to the windshield.

I saw the puddle in the middle of the road at the same instant Arreola did.

He yelled Conde, watch out! while I braced my feet against the floorboards, too late to even yell.

Seeping in from the left side of the pavement was a huge slick of crude oil, leaking from the destroyed transmission lines the Iraqis had left behind as they fled before us. It was just dark enough that we couldn't see the black pool until we were right on top of it. We sailed through the pool at full speed, Conde standing on the brakes, my feet locked against the sandbags and my hands braced on the dashboard, Arreola and Scull screaming behind me.

Thus began two seconds during which I had much on my mind.

I had the mental image of us going sideways and a tire catching and the four of us, unseatbelted, cartwheeling gracefully skyward and away from the vehicle as it pitchpoled across the desert.

I had a sudden, extremely keen desire that I had pushed the issue of lack of seatbelts in our Humvees harder back in Kuwait.

After this thought, I wished I was driving.

After that, I wished Conde had my aviator eyesight.

Finally, I wished I had leaned harder on Conde not to drive so fast.

Conde reared back in his seat as the three of us screamed at him, but he didn't flinch and didn't overcorrect. We slid completely sideways at fifty miles an hour. Conde fought it, countersteered deftly, and we straightened out.

We flew out the other end of the slick, making a pretty roostertail of oil on the pavement for a hundred feet or so beyond the puddle.

Conde slammed on the brakes and we all got out. Our hearts slowed back to normal.

Scull spoke first: *Fuck.*

My Humvee was the center of all the logistics and communications for all our teams, so we carried extra of everything, as well as a double set of radios. There was so much gear inside the vehicle we even had it under our feet. Because we carried all the extra gear for everyone else, there was no room at all for our personal gear.

Master Scrounger Glenn Walsh had solved this problem when we were back in Blair Mayne. He had found, I dared not ask where, several steel ladders and a welding torch. He had cut the ladders to length and welded them to the front and sides of our vehicle, and this is where our packs were: strapped tight to the outside, hillbilly style.

Scull and Conde had their packs strapped to the front push bar of the vehicle, and those packs had taken the brunt of the oil. The right side of our once-brown Humvee was now black, coated in oil, and it dripped from the doors and the length of the chassis and even from the roof. Under the pressure from our tires the oil had shot right through the opening between my fabric door and the vehicle frame. My pack was relatively unscathed, but my right arm, which had been out the window, was soaked with oil, as was my flak jacket and right leg.

Scull had ducked behind me at the last moment and was thus clean, and he giggled at me.

Sorry, sir, he smiled.

Everything was in one piece, so we shrugged. Onward.

———•••———

We arrived at the Hamar Bridge, and I immediately set in my teams. Wilson and his boys went across the bridge; Davidson and his off lads to my east, at the bend in the canal. Weapons Company and their fast-moving WMICS dune buggies were already there, and Colin Marks was replacing the Paras with his lads.

I walked across the bridge with Bob Bruce, my counterpart with 3 Para commanding our sister ANGLICO teams, to get the full turnover.

I chatted with the wet and dirty Paras who had been occupying holes in Indian country all night. They looked happy to be leaving.

———•••———

I hopped back in the Humvee and we pulled in next to Richard, who was as usual ready go with his charts, matrices, frequencies, target lists and so forth. Artillery guys always think you can impose order on the battlefield through external means. Aviators think the opposite way: the battlefield will always be fluid, so you had better be ready to flex. Artillery guys are all about planning; aviators' motto is: he who plans early plans twice.

Artillery guys are necessarily trained to be precise, mathematical, and timely in everything they do. One round short or long, or early or late, could mean dead good guys, so they always focused on precision. Aviators are raised with a million things going on at once: two radios squawking in your ears, the world rushing by at hundreds of miles an hour, both hands and both feet at work, systems beeping and blinking and speaking to you. We are trained to be flexible and adaptable, to change in an instant.

Richard and I both knew what we were doing, though I was always telling him that his matrices would be worth shit when the bullets started to fly, and he always telling me that I needed to be back in the CP with Collins to control things in an orderly fashion from there.

We were both right. I ignored his advice, he ignored mine, and we got along great.

———•••———

We creaked to a halt, and the British guffawed at our filthy Humvee, which now smelled like a gas station. Richard walked around the front of his Rover to meet me.

Bloody hell, mate, what is all this? Uniform looks smart, eh? he asked, looking askance at my dripping sleeve and pant leg.

Yeah, like that? I said. Conde grinned sheepishly off to the side while Pez razzed him. Arreola dug up some rags and got Conde started on cleaning the vehicle from top to bottom.

———•••———

3 Para withdrew.

The Royal Irish had the watch.

———•••———

I had never been to a war before.

Once on the battlefield, I didn't know what to do.

Go over the bridge and try to stir something up? Not without a company, at least, with me.

Get some airplanes and have them go forward and look? Pretty uncool to get my boys shot down.

Stand right here and wait? Nothing else for it. So that's what I did.

Bob and I stood and chatted, looking across the canal in the bright, clear morning sun. I thought again about how beautiful it was here, and how Iraq could actually be a pretty nice place if they cleaned it up. Beautiful palm trees, farmland, rivers and canals, even a first-rate port.

In fact it reminded me of what my buddies had told me of Mogadishu. I daydreamed, thinking about what they had described: gorgeous white sand beaches sloping down to crystal-clear blue water, warm breeze coming in from the ocean. If only you could do away with the stench of the city and raw sewage in the streets, and of course the dead bodies scattered around, and then also of course the warlords, maybe Europeans would come there to vacation, and the country could...

—————••••—————

WHAM!

WHAMWHAMWHAM!

THE SHOW

God must have been angry when he made this place.
—Marine wife

Upon seeing Marine Corps Base Twentynine
Palms for the first time.

Hunter S. Thompson had a theory on life: *you pay the ticket, you take the ride.*

———•••———

Jesus! Fuck! What the hell was that?

I turned to Richard, and said Dude you need to move your boys back. Those rounds going out are awfully loud.

Richard looked tenser than usual, but looked up from his map and smiled at me.

Mate, that was incoming.

Incoming? They are shooting at us? Us, in particular? *Me?*

The radios squawked alive, querulous British voices trying to figure out what was going on, and pinning down whence the rounds had come, and Sir can we shoot back?

The British had a marvelous counter battery radar called the Cobra, which immediately picked up movement of an incoming round and calculated speed, trajectory and spin to spit out a ten-digit grid coordinate of where it had come from and even what system had launched it.

The Cobra pinned these guys down, and Richard gave the order to let the battery rip.

Richard's four 105mm guns roared in unison with shells headed back across the water to our unseen bad guys, their first of more than 1000 rounds they would put through those guns on this day.

Well, here we go.

Not looking up, Richard spat out coordinates to me.

Mate, bad guys Quebec Victor 4312 grid square: tanks, artillery, triple-A pieces. Can you get some planes for us?

Oh. Yeah!

Planes.

Radio.

War.

Time to clock in.

———•••———

When I was a young officer learning to fly the Cobra attack helicopter, I once had a hop with Stickman, so named because he was 6-4 and maybe 150 pounds.

Stickman was a very quiet, gentle guy, soft-spoken and thoughtful, reader of poetry and Marcus Aurelius.

I was asking him about strafing missions against individual targets and he said it's simple, you ram the twenty-millimeter cannon up the guy's ass and pull the trigger.

———•••———

So I got on the hook.

———•••———

Kairos

There is no way to tell how long that moment was, no way that
he who comes later will be able
To expand it as I did
It bent just as in 1905 he said it would, curving
In and around itself
One sharp crystal point emerged and that point was me

Me alone

Compress all of yourself and all that you are into one moment of
  intensity
Sharpen and bear on who it is that you might be
For now, now it is the time for that moment, else there may be
  no other
Coiling inward and preparing is a lifetime, all that you have been
  and have thought you would be
Is here, here, right here
The moment broadens as the sun up sharp through the
Refracted haze of dark and smoke
It is dusk and dark and then warmth and light and the light is not
  always warmth, not always
It is this day
Chronos as it always does is insistent in chopped seasoned
  increments, it is kairos of which I am here, the gathered
  instant, the perfect here now

The clarity of one million year old light

The haunting great magic moves and suffuses with the new light
The last, at last, to last
Release it all that coil, release with the greatest joy into the light
  Ultimate

Kairos at its work that single sharp point cracks and topples and

Again again soft in the light of the newest dawn

———•••———

All of us had UHF radios, which are great but only work line-of-sight, which meant that you had to have a straight line to the controlling agency. The curvature of the earth, or buildings or wires or trees, would interfere with the signal. To solve this problem, the Marine Corps had a Direct Air Support Center, or DASC, which did what their title implied and kept everyone organized.

The DASC guys, or *Daskateers* as everyone called them, usually worked out of big tents stuffed with computers, radar and communications gear, all of which required air conditioning and thus made these folks very popular in summer desert training.

For a war like this, where everyone was moving too fast to stop and set up like that, the powers that be put aloft a DASC (Airborne), or DASC(A), in the back of a huge cargo plane.

These were traffic cops of the sky, sending airplanes where they were needed, prioritizing all of us on the ground asking for planes, and generally keeping things under control in a very chaotic environment.

The DASC(A) for this war was called *SkyChief*, and he was circling 30,000 feet above me.

I keyed the mike.

SkyChief this is Manila India 6.

This is SkyChief, go, responded an efficient voice.

Uh...we are taking fire from grid QV 4312...you got anybody you can push to me?

Wait one...Yep, OK, stand by for Opah 15 this push.

Opah 15? Who the hell is that?

When all units got into theater, they had taken away everyone's call signs and given out new ones for each squadron and battalion. The thought was that otherwise you would have three or four units with the same names—Wolfpack, Vipers, Mavericks, and so on—and tasking would be too confusing.

But the other side of this decision: we now didn't even know what kind of airplanes were coming, let alone which squadron.

Turned out to be just the guys I needed.

———◆◆———

SEAL sniper Chris Kyle said In my experience Marines are gung ho no matter what.

They will all fight to the death.

Every one of them just wants to get out there and kill.

———◆◆———

To the northwest of me began the rhythmic thump of rotor blades. I could tell immediately that it was a two-bladed rotor system (here is how you know: if you can hear each blade, it is a two-bladed rotor head. If it sounds like a giant lawnmower, it has four blades or more.)

Cobras.

A deep, calm voice came up on my radio. His callsign was Grimace: an old friend.

With all the urgency of a guy deciding whether to have latte or espresso at Starbucks, he checked in with me.

Manila, this is Opah...I'm a flight of four Snakes. Whattya got?

I quickly outlined the fire we were taking and what and where the bad guys were.

Rounds were starting to fall more regularly now, and the Marines were starting to look at me with a little more urgency, willing me with their eyes to hurry up.

Yep, I can do that. Uh...I'm skoshi on fuel, but I can give you one run.

OK, Opah, I am right under checkpoint Softball, right at the south end of the bridge over the Hamar Canal.

Yeah, OK, I can find that. Be there in a sec.

The blades whomped louder and to my left front the boys materialized out of the clear blue sky. The Cobra airframe is 38 inches across, and when they are coming at you head on they are very difficult to see.

Four planes came into view, roared over the top of us, and circled slowly right above me at one hundred feet. Since I had been a Cobra pilot myself, I could tell a lot about these guys just by looking at them, and I was primarily interested in what weapons they were carrying. I craned my neck straight back to see.

Hellfire missiles. Laser-guided, pinpoint accurate, with a warhead that would go through forty inches of cold-rolled steel. They could kill any tank in the world.

What a coincidence! Just what I needed.

I passed the mission to them.

———◆◆◆———

The Marine Corps is a learning organization.

We had had so many men killed for so long that we finally created a new type of forward air control procedure, ranking missions according to the level of control required.

When I had first learned close air support, it was pretty simple: see the target, put some sort of a mark on it with artillery or mortars so the guys in the air could see what I wanted destroyed, call in the planes to shoot a missile at it or drop a bomb on top. That was pretty much it.

Now, with the advent of laser-guided weapons, bombs with GPS programmability, thermal sensors, and a much faster-moving battlefield, our guys realized the need to make things more flexible.

Type I control was the old way: see the target, and see the plane.

Under Type II control, you could see the plane or the target, but not both, so a degree of trust had to be there between pilot and the guy controlling him.

Type III control was the unknown: you couldn't see the target, couldn't see the plane as it closed with the bad guys, and so you were basically making a leap of faith that it would go well.

This was a Type III control.

I sent my brief over the radio, made clear to Grimace that he was *cleared hot*, which meant that he could kill whatever he found out there. I couldn't help from where I was. Then I waited.

———•••———

In the fall of 1994, I was working in the operations office for Third Battalion, Seventh Marines, deployed to Camp Hansen, Okinawa: the same small camp from which Phil Caputo had deployed to Vietnam 25 years earlier.

Our company clerk was a young Corporal named Mike Blakemore, an unusually bright and very effective young Marine who was rumored to have scored above 1400 on the SAT, and he came to me as one of his tribal elders and asked for a letter of recommendation as he applied to an officer program. I liked this kid and knew he would make a good officer, and wrote a detailed letter for him.

And then I forgot about it.

And nine years later here in the fight I had four Cobras working for me. Four Cobras meant eight pilots.

One of them was a young First Lieutenant named Mike Blakemore.

———•••———

The Cobras rocked their noses over and whickered off to the north in two flights of two, zipping over the water and disappearing out into the desert. The shells continued landing on us and I wondered what was happening out there.

A few more shells slammed in, then they tapered off, then stopped.

The radio came alive.

Manila India, we got four T-54s destroyed, pretty good secondaries as well. Uh...I took a lot of triple-A out there.

(Translation: *I destroyed four Soviet-era tanks. There were other explosions, not caused by my missiles, which means I hit ammunition or fuel stores. When I was leaving, the Iraqis shot surface-to-air guns at me, big fucking bullets made to take down helicopters, so please don't make me do that again.*)

There are a lot of guys north of you, but I gotta get some gas.

I'll be back.

———•••———

Many months later, I found out that he had been in a very dangerous situation.

In the process of destroying those four tanks, those Cobras had really put themselves on the line. Apparently the AAA had been coming up in sheets, and one gun was so well camouflaged that they flew right over it. The Iraqi opened up on the lead aircraft and missed; the second Cobra thereupon killed that piece and everyone standing near it.

———•••———

Eighteen months later, sitting in my office in San Diego, I wrote a three-page summary of what had happened.

Major Al Grinalds was awarded the Distinguished Flying Cross, second only to the Medal of Honor, for his actions that morning.

———•••———

Five years later I saw him and thanked him for saving my life.

———•••———

The tribe.

———•••———

I was still standing along the canal, enjoying my success in my first-ever taste of combat, when WHAMWHAM...rounds started coming in again.

Sergeant Wilson, my man across the bridge and the man farthest north of anyone in the British Army at that moment, called me on another radio.

Uh, sir...we are taking fire up here. What do you want me to do?

What kind of fire? I shot back. Shit. If bad guys were closing in on him, he was going to have a tough time getting back across the bridge under fire, and I sure as hell wasn't going to leave him hanging out there alone.

Artillery, sir, and I guess mortars.

OK, us too. Hang in there...I am working on it.

Yep, OK. Wilson out.

———•••———

The incoming fire intensified.

Machine guns, high and inaccurate but nonetheless attention-getting, snapped over our heads. I really hoped these guys were as bad at adjusting fire as reputed. I went back to work.

The counterbattery radar spit out the grid to us: same one to which I had just sent Al.

Fuck! Again?

The rounds started coming in faster, and a recon plane that SkyChief sent out there told me that the bad guys were massing. Tanks, AAA pieces, artillery and mortars, all getting together. They were out in the open, at least, and I knew I had them right where I wanted them, if I could just get some airplanes.

———•••———

I had Iraqis moving in front of me....*lots* of Iraqis moving in front of me. I needed planes, lots of planes. Richard's lads were burning out their barrels shooting artillery at these guys: I needed to do my part.

I pushed and prompted and begged and threatened my new buddies at SkyChief.

I got nothing.

The plus of consolidating air control in one agency was that things were organized and everyone could talk.

The minus was that he had to prioritize strike aircraft, and I knew the Marines were stepping into it on the road to my west, moving into Nasiriyah. They had more guys in danger, so they got the planes.

I spent more than ninety minutes trying to get something—anything—to help me. No one came.

The SkyChief boys, to their credit, were pushing just as hard as I was. They knew I was with a British unit, and I think they felt sorry for me. There was no doubt in anyone's mind that the Marines—not the British Army—was the focus of all the efforts in the southern part of the country.

When Al and the boys had shown up they were actually on their way back from the north when they heard my call for help.

They weren't even assigned to me. They just came over to help a brother.

———•••———

Mihaly Csikszentmihalyi described *flow*.

Flow requires two things: you must be engaged at the edge of your abilities.

And the task at hand must be exactly right for those abilities: not too easy, and not too difficult.

When you are in flow you are in a state of complete absorption, superseding in your mind all other things, to include physical needs and the passage of time.

———— •• ————

With the radio in my hand, I summoned fire and death from the sky and with my words people who awoke that morning would never again.

We fought all afternoon, mission after mission, SkyChief finally opening her kimono and giving me what I wanted, American and British aircraft stacked over me loaded with missiles and bombs waiting their turn to kill.

Do not believe those who tell you that war is about helping people and doing right by those who cannot help themselves and bringing to the benighted our special truth. War is about killing, killing and destruction and death and ending anyone in your way. In this way you help people yes but you do it by killing.

I did it easy and intense and focused, running missions from memory, doing math in my head under pressure, the three-dimensional trigonometry of jets moving at 600 miles an hour and bombs falling from thousands of feet in the sky while artillery rounds arced in below them. Richard was as dialed in as I was and we snapped numbers to one another, killing, killing faster and better and keeping our brothers alive and ending, ending those who would not capitulate. I did it fast and efficient and it made sense and it worked and everything I had been training and studying for since 1985 came together and I gathered into one point of energy and light and I was a king, a king of the battlefield, the king of all I surveyed.

No. Not a king. I was a new god.

———◆◆———

Conde took a photograph of me during Grimace's first mission.

He was standing three feet in front of me, pointing a camera right at me, and I didn't even see him.

Arreola that afternoon forced me to eat. I hadn't done so since the night before.

Combat anorexia.

Flow.

———◆◆———

Wilson held on. So did I. Our combat families were intact.

Darkness and quiet fell over the battlefield. I put myself on watch and put the boys down in their sleeping bags.

Three radios hissed at me in the gloaming, a smattering of male voices cracking through and issuing terse, rapid-fire acronyms.

It was dead silent along the Hamar Canal. Shorebirds emerged from wherever they had hidden during the shelling and squawked and wheeled and spun cheerily over the water again. Ducks quacked and snuffled quietly in the reeds below me. I thought about the last 24 hours: the shithole CP with Richard and into combat, the elements: dead bodies, blood, fire, oil, water.

The radio traffic picked up. Somebody was really getting into a fight: it was the guys trying to get into, and through, Nasiriyah.

First Marines' aviators and fire support coordinators were calling for everything they could get, and SkyChief was pushing everyone in theater to them. Every airplane in the lower half of Iraq was in support, circling in stacks, waiting for their turn in the fight.

The voices on the radio grew more panicked and more intense, and I could hear shooting in the background. I sat and worried about my friends in First Marines and listened to someone else's war.

———•••———

The shooting slackened, stopped, and then started up again in the night. Sporadic, inaccurate, alarming, unseen.

———•••———

I had spent a full day in killing and I wondered if it was the best day of my life.

———•••———

Morning broke early and cold. Rounds came in.

SkyChief was on 278.525, the little green numbers burned into my brain.

I begged him for airplanes from my oasis.

SkyChief asked me Are you taking fire?

Well, no, not right this second. But I was a second ago and am going to be pretty soon.

You are not taking fire?

No, goddamn it. Not taking fire.

OK, stand by.

Five minutes went by.

Ten.

I pestered them again.

SkyChief, how are we doing on those aircraft?

The guy 30,000 feet above me said, are you taking fire? *It would reallllly be better if you were taking fire.*

Ah.

Yep! Now that you mention it...What a coincidence! I *am* taking fire.

Great! he said. Stand by for push.

I fought again, all day.

Missions 25-7 and 2509 were Kermit 61, two A-10 Warthogs from my Air Force: good men, different tribe.

These guys were carrying Maverick missiles, Mk-82 bombs and plenty of rounds in their huge 30mm cannons beneath their squat noses. We killed five artillery pieces at QU 424987, and then destroyed two mortar sections at 407992.

Both of these systems were starting to get the range on me...until we silenced them. Forever.

Mission 25-13 was at 380048- artillery again. Two Marine F/A-18 Hornets checked in with me: my favorite guys, long-duration and lots of lift, which means lots of bombs.

I couldn't see what I was shooting at; I needed someone to get north of me and get some eyes on the target, and then run other attack airplanes.

These guys could do that. The Hornets dropped a JDAM for me, six Mk-83 1000-pound bombs, and two Rockeye. Huge explosions. Lead aircraft told me he saw flashes, which meant secondary explosions and steel-on-steel contact.

I was getting tired, still in flow but half a step slow. I screwed up basic mathematics not once, but twice, trying to add numbers in my head. Fatigue and trying to work too fast combined to make mistakes. I had to force myself to slow down, add things slowly and methodically, and finally got it right.

———•••———

People searching the battlefields where the huge clashes of the Civil War took place find small trinkets, even now: dog tags, cups, spoons. Sometimes they find knives or even whole weapons.

Sometimes they find something truly unique: two bullets which hit each other midair and joined, missiles struck over sacred ground fused in heat and violence, buried and cold waiting for light.

———•••———

Afternoon.

The weather closed in, fast, a slamming door.

Desert weather is not a gradual change from one state to another: it is like stepping from a warm room into a maelstrom. We went from a pleasant, bright-blue morning to howling wind, rain, and a driving sandstorm.

Sid called me.

Hey, Stan, boy, I need some airplanes out here!

I smiled and answered OK, Sid, whattya got?

Sid tended to sound very excited on the radios. This was an amusing trait of his, particularly because he had seen more combat than the rest of us put together, not to mention three decades as a cop and SWAT member and commander of hundreds of cops in the Los Angeles ghettos. He had somehow never lost his gee-whiz farm-boy Andy Griffith outlook on life, and it came through in his voice.

My little combat family could all hear the radio when someone called. When Sid came up on the net all four of us grinned.

Wow! Holy smokes, it is stinkin' horrible weather down here! Man, I can't see a thing! This sand is blowing all over the place! I need a plane to guide us!

Uh, Sid, if you can't see well enough to drive, then I guarantee a plane isn't going to see well enough to fly. Let me try.

And I did. I tried for over an hour to get someone—anyone—pushed down to him, but all aircraft in the southern half of the country were grounded. The weather was deteriorating sharply. By the end of the day, visibility was so bad that Sid was out in front of his Humvee while Sergeant Sullivan drove at two miles per hour, following him like a stalking horse.

———•••———

My Army brothers were far to my west, off road, V Corps pushing hard to Baghdad, sweeping in an immense arc to the left of the Marines' route of march. The Marines bogged down in Nasiriyah, but Mattis expected this and pushed through quickly. Not a marathon. A sprint.

———•••———

That night, the rain sheeted down on us all, soaking equally the saved and the damned.

———•••———

I gave myself the watch again, and read letters and fought to stay awake. The Humvee roof leaked, the cheap rubber parting and fraying and letting the rain pour in. I wrapped myself like a burrito in my rubberized air mattress, trying to keep the rain off.

The entire Hummer was fogged up, Mom's station wagon on prom night. I worried about our radios; if the rain leaked onto them we had a serious problem. I also worried about the Iraqis, but I knew they were far less capable than we were at night.

The entire Third Marine Air Wing was grounded. We infantrymen were on our own.

———•••———

Was it to be now? We were deus ex machina, but to now there had been a whole lot more machine than god.

———•••———

On June 7, 1988 I was standing in a formation of 250 young men, NROTC and Naval Academy midshipmen soon to enter our senior years, at Marine Corps Officer Candidates School in Quantico, Virginia.

We had been there one day and were already asleep on our feet from exhaustion.

The student company commander took the report of the student platoon commanders who said everyone is here and he executed an about face to address First Sergeant Hernandez, the terrifying high priest to our band of novitiates who was standing on a landing looming above us, and he announced *Company First Sergeant, two hundred and fifty Marines present!* and the priest screamed in reply Marines! *MARINES?* I don't see any Marines! All I see is a bunch of fat college boys!

———•••———

Jack Laurence of CBS News, a very talented TV reporter and author of the magnificent memoir *The Cat From Hue,* was out in the jungle in Vietnam with a Marine rifle company.

Somehow a Marine from another unit had been separated from his brothers, and this company had found him alone in the jungle.

Laurence rolled tape and approached the company commander.

This man was wearing filthy utilities, exhausted, unshaven, thirty pounds underweight, heavy with responsibility for two hundred men in the most dangerous place in the world. A cigarette hung from the corner of his mouth. He could not have been twenty-five years old. A hard, intense man with eyes of a veteran, a young man too old for this.

Laurence led in with reference to the man they just discovered and asked will you take care of this man?

The Captain stares at Laurence as if he is insane.

Captain: He's a Marine.

Laurence: What?

Captain: He's a Marine. I'll take care of him.

———•••———

Peleliu

Satan is here
Vulpine
Shredding coral, viperous dark, an evil sun
Barbed wire razors explosives bullets flame and death
Desiccated heat and blood on the rocks
Boys are crueler than men in this place, privates harder than
    veterans
All have resigned from the human race

The boys carve off ears from corpses
They are only angry about stepping through rotting human
    bodies because of the smell it leaves
On their boots
They are more casually violent than the darkest smiling drill
instructor dream
Each man has bloody gold teeth in his breast pocket
Chilling nonchalant evil

These are the same boys who did both dishes duty and drying
duty so their mothers could

Sit after supper
Who fixed tractors in the rain and bought lemonade from little
kids down the road and
Learned to throw a curve next to the barn
Who ran to help the family on the next farm over

Bring in their crop
While the heavy storm built
Billowing upwards on a black horizon

———•••———

26 MARCH 2003 ▶ HAMAR CANAL, SOUTHERN IRAQ
I was sound asleep on the ground and two artillery rounds whined
overhead and slammed in right next to us.

Scull bolted upright, still in his sleeping bag, a prairie dog poking
his head up.

We were getting used to it. Scull sat for a moment and then went
back to sleep.

———•••———

We grumbled awake, each man in his morning routine, little old
ladies now, comfortable in each other, not speaking, each making
a cup of tea, eating...

Then seven rounds came in, one after the other.

Same guys from yesterday, still shooting at us.

Mother*fuckers.*

Okay. That's it. I am getting tired of this.

I got SkyChief up and clocked in to work. I did my morning commute: three steps to the side of my Hummer.

Two Harriers showed up carrying GBU, and I ran them onto grid QV 2932. We killed two GHN-45s, massive Soviet guns the Iraqis had probably bought twenty years ago.

Davidson was still off to my east, at the curve in the canal. Walsh was south, behind me working cordon and sweep missions in the GOSPs.

Sid was off on a mission with another unit, having been stolen briefly from the Irish.

Poor old Wilson and his team were still hunkered down across the bridge, alone and brave, looking east to see what was moving.

---

27 MARCH 2003 ▶ HAMAR CANAL TO RAMAYLAH

We awoke to a cold, dark, rainy morning. Heavy fog hung over the Hamar Canal, and dawn was different from night only in degrees of gray.

It felt nothing like the Arabian desert...more like the weather our brothers at Chateau Thierry or Korea went through. I snorted awake upright in my seat. Rounds exploded, but just far enough away to be someone else's war.

I heard a squall of rusty metal and looked over at Richard and his boys. Richard was just opening his door, and stepped out into six inches of viscous, orange mud. Hell, this is the bloody Somme! he exclaimed, and slurped around to the back of his wagon, swearing quietly at his now-filthy boots.

We drove back up onto the MSR to meet up with the lads from 3 Para. It seemed like a lifetime ago that we had taken over from them, and now here they were, refreshed and rested and ready to take the reins.

I huddled with Bob Bruce and his number two man, gave them the scoop on what I had done, and then met up with Richard as he finished briefing the 3 Para fire support guys. While I waited, I put on a pair of thick wool socks I had rescued from Blair Mayne as we prepared to pull out last week and a hundred years ago. I had intended to use them to clean things, thinking there would be no need for such heavy winter socks, but my boots and socks were soaked and my feet were rapidly going numb.

Richard led us out, his driver keeping the pedal on the floor as all British drivers did (Oh, aye, sir, gotta keep a moving target, lots of rounds falling about, eh? No sense waiting for one to fall on us!) Which made sense, I guess...where else should you speed but in a place where artillery is falling?

Except for this: the very nature of artillery is that you don't know where it is going to land. *Maybe we were driving right to where it is going to land.* The British attitude didn't make it easy on our big heavy Hummer trying to keep up with the lighter, more nimble Rovers.

We zoomed south, away from incoming artillery and back to the Irish, our brothers, our tribe.

We took a brief detour through the wrong village, had a brief delay to pull Richard's Rover out of the mud, but finally found the Irish CP in the village of Ramaylah.

———•••———

Collins had moved the CP into a schoolhouse compound, and I agreed with the location he had chosen. These compounds were all over Iraq. I could never figure out why the Iraqis had felt it necessary to put ten foot-high walls around all their elementary schools, but they were absolutely perfect for housing rifle companies. Lots of room in the schools themselves, great places to put guards, towers for our snipers, walls thick enough to keep out direct-fire ordnance, latrines, lots of individual rooms to split everyone up.

We rolled through the gate and into the courtyard, our muddy vehicles leaving tracks on the concrete. We backed side-by-side against a loading dock and my comm boys jumped out and threw up antennas and joked and chatted with their British mates.

———•••———

I walked across the compound, taking my oil-soaked, muddy, soaking wet pack off the Hummer on the way.

I found Marcus Readman sitting on a bed, lovingly cleaning an AK-47 he had scrounged up somewhere. Mike Murdock sat on a chair with a missing leg. They both were filthy and tired but happy.

Hello, mate! Marcus cried. So you got into a bit of a spat, we heard.

Yeah, we did, I told him.

I was not nonchalant or modest. I was in shock.

Though they wouldn't admit it, the British rifle company commanders didn't quite know what to make of the ANGLICO teams.

Deep down, they didn't think they needed us, and they didn't truly understand or appreciate combined arms. We had just proven them wrong.

Marcus looked at me with a new respect.

He had a look on his face that I would come to recognize.

Envy.

I HATE IRAQ NAZIS

I suggest the Apache has deteriorated, judging by a few of the specimens I've seen on my way out here.

If you saw them, sir, they weren't Apache.
—Henry Fonda and John Wayne, *Fort Apache*

I went to find Collins.

Just outside the wall of the compound was the headquarters, now defunct, for the local Ba'ath Party thugs and enforcers. This, too, was typical...the equivalent of a Gambino capo setting up shop right next to an elementary school in Brooklyn, or a Nazi commander establishing a headquarters in a Polish village. Assholes. The boys in Collins's CP party tore down the Ba'ath Party sign first.

Collins was making a point: this would be his office, outside the walls, with the people we were there to help. New sheriff in town.

He made himself right at home in the former Party leader's office, and when he started exploring his new digs found a set of brass knuckles and handcuffs in the upper drawer of this guy's desk.

The Ba'ath Party had had the imprimatur of Saddam Hussein, and everyone knew that these guys were untouchable. Any Ba'ath commander, especially one in charge of a city, was appointed and vetted by either a very senior officer or by Saddam himself, and like the Nazis this is how the regime had kept power: jackboots in every village, no matter how small, to remind every Iraqi who was in charge. Thirty years of rape, torture, murder, extortion and disappearances weren't enough, I guess; this jerk had to beat people up personally, as well.

One of the village leaders came for a sitdown with Collins. When he realized the meeting was to be held in that room, he started to shake and refused to walk in.

In the United States, white people have brown people—yard guys, nannies, cooks, trashmen—clean up their neighborhoods for them.

In wartime Iraq, brown people had white people—soldiers and Marines, British and American—cleaning up their neighborhoods for them.

We were the immigrants, outsiders. They stared at us as we passed.

———•••———

I walked into Collins's office and he was bustling about, setting things up. He had a broad smile on his face when he saw me; he had heard of the fight we were in and was pleased that the Irish, or at least their attachments, had finally drawn blood. He seemed a bit wistful that there hadn't been an infantry engagement, but he would take what he could get. He was tense, anxious to get into a fight, a caged tiger.

———•••———

I walked back outside and sat on a picnic bench beneath an eave still dripping with steady drizzle. I was in a daze.

Sarah came out from a door across from me. Her long red hair, eye-catching to any man even in normal times, snapped my head up. She was carrying a wet shirt which she had just washed and was preparing to hang to dry. I must have looked drained, because she walked over to me with a smile on her face.

Hello, Stan. Haven't seen you for a bit? she said in her lovely clipped London accent.

Yeah, we've been out and about. Brian, Richard and I just got back from a scrap up at the bridge north of here.

Her eyes flashed—a fight!—but then dulled again. American Marines weren't her beat. She wanted, almost as badly as did Collins, for the Irish to get into a good fight and give her something to write about. In my mind's eye, I saw an e-mail from her *Mail on Sunday* editors: *Sarah, bloody great story, keep it up, proud of you, but we aren't interested in the Yanks. Give us something to print about our lads!*

I told her about what we had done. She listened carefully and asked Reporter Questions, but also seemed genuinely concerned about all of us and the fire we had been under. I knew she wouldn't write it down, but it was nice to talk to a civilian every once in a while. And a woman. And a friend.

———•••———

I took a walk through the schoolhouse. It was cute, everything half-sized like an elementary school anywhere. Little desks sat side by side, lined up neatly before a blackboard, two kids to a desk. There were kid drawings on the walls, and the file cabinets were full of graded tests with comments in Arabic but, of course, in the ubiquitous red ink that teachers use everywhere. Red ink. Even here.

A younger, leaner, thickly-mustachioed Saddam glared down from every classroom, every hallway, every room.

No child could move with seeing the Benevolent Leader watching his every step, and I was just realizing how truly Stalinist, how Nazi, this country had been. These paintings, combined with the new CP next door, slapped me in the face with just how repressive the regime had been. Good riddance.

———•••———

We were the ultimate kid fantasy: not only do soldiers from another land come in and out of your neighborhood hourly, providing no end of excitement, but they occupy and shut down your school, thereby handing you and your little mates the ultimate snow day.

No school today! Or tomorrow. Or, maybe, ever again.

———•••———

Collins was not one for lots of rules, but the ones he had he was serious about.

One of them was this: *you will never hand anything to an Iraqi.*

I completely agreed. Such an action makes people supplicants in their own land, subordinated to the conquerors.

———•••———

The three sines qua non of the Third World, right outside the compound: smiling brown children, chickens running loose, and soccer balls. Tijuana, Port au Prince, Kinshasa, Bombay, Rio, Ramaylah...they are all the same.

Little kids were everywhere. Impish faces with huge bright eyes looked in on us through the gate and watched our every move as we left the compound, whether on foot or in a truck. They seemed content to just watch us going by.

Since Collins's CP was next to, but not inside, the compound wall, everyone had to run the Munchkin Gauntlet each time he needed to go between the buildings. These kids were not the grasping, whining, poverty-stricken urchins of Central America or Africa, but rather were just bored, cheerful little kids enlivened by foreign soldiers living in their midst.

———••———

Collins was doing exactly the right things. He had a knack, an intuitive feel for the situation, and he seemed to know the right moves to make.

The Special Air Service is not a place for men of uncertain courage. Our own Delta Force was founded by Army legend Charlie Beckwith, who survived a tour with SAS and returned determined to create an identical American unit. SAS is the toughest military organization in the world.

As an alumnus of this fearsome warrior tribe Tim Collins understood at the molecular level the nuances and subtleties of violence, and he was the finest small unit leader I had ever seen. He was not a follow-me-lads, once-more-dear-friends-into-the-breach kind of guy, but a thinker and a fighter. I knew he would keep us alive, and would keep alive the innocent Iraqis who were victims in all of this.

He was completely unhindered by self-doubt or hesitation of any kind, and this bold, decisive, never-look-back leadership resonated with the Arabs, who respect men of power and strength. What surprised me was the continuum of force he used, ranging from quiet, smiling negotiation over tea and cookies with village leaders to forceful, coiled aggression. Both were appropriate, both were effective.

The boys in the Irish were all scholars, and had a wistfulness for their place in history, steeped as each was in the study of British empire, of colonialism and the Raj and the days when the sun never set on those in British uniform. I had expected that this would translate into a desire for occupation here, and I fully thought these guys would be prepared to stay here for a year or two, at the least.

Not so. Collins and his officers wanted to get things stabilized and get out, and to that end this village, and Iraq itself, had to stand on its own.

———•••———

The boys found a fire hydrant under pressure.

We rooted through the refinery buildings and found a crescent wrench the size of your arm and wrenched the goddamn thing open, and it gushed an unending roar of clean fresh water, and we ran to our packs for bars of soap and stripped naked and hopped under the tsunami finally finally finally clean, and then we danced in it barefoot on the pavement like little kids in Harlem, and got out of the spray to let other guys have a turn and by the time we got our shorts back on in the desert oven hot and made it back to our packs we were dry and we put our filthy clothes back on.

———•••———

I held two degrees in political science. I had never seen it in action.

———•••———

This was a true three-block war.

One day I was blowing things up and killing tanks and killing people and sleeping in the mud. This day, I was clean and rested and walking village streets, smiling and speaking my few words of Arabic to the locals. From destroying artillery pieces to establishing a police force to putting economics to work...same battalion, same province, same men, same day.

The first thing we had worried about was killing bad guys in uniform. The second thing we worried about was security: no security means no peace, which means no country, and Collins made goddamn sure everyone knew there was a new sheriff in town.

He had very direct meetings with the local leaders, at which he put forth his philosophy: We are here for all of you. I want a free Iraq as much as you do, but you must run your own country. I want *your* boys on the streets, *your* men in uniform keeping the peace, backed up with mine. If there is any real trouble, I will take over, and if I find any rebellion among old loyalists beginning I will ensure those troublemakers wind up dead. If we have to fight, we will.

We will have peaceful streets here: your children will go to school, your wives will go to market, you will have jobs and quiet. You will have peace.

———◆◆———

The next thing we worried about was the local economy.

We could not simply dump money onto the locals. Microeconomics tells us British pounds sterling would go through the millenia-old system like a bolus and disappear, leaving the Iraqis as welfare recipients, robbing them of pride, and most significant devaluing the dinar and wiping out the villagers' savings. It would be like force-feeding rich food to a starving man.

Irish second-in-command Andrew Cullen requested and received an infusion of cash from the British government, thousands of pounds sterling, which the Irish then changed into Iraqi dinar. This cash was used to put Iraqis to work, immediately, Collins carrying through on his promise, local boys as a security force for the village itself and the GOSPs to the south. Iraqis were given back their uniforms and, more significantly, their weapons and ammunition, and they were put onto the streets as police.

Those dinar then worked back into the local economy, allowing for reopening of the markets and normal microtrade among the people. The very first transaction was a haircut for Tim Collins himself, from the village barber.

It was pitch-perfect, and indeed the entire time we were there we had not one bombing, booby trap or injury to Iraqis, Marines or Irish soldiers. Not one.

———•••———

This village seemed untouched by the war, but it was not.

A man came into the compound under guard and asked for the senior officer. He was badly shaken, worried, trembling, and came to find the Westerners. We would have the answers.

His daughter, he said through Phil, had been caught in a crossfire of some kind, and had been badly burned. She had been taken away by the Americans and he hadn't heard a thing since. He had no way to find her, no one to ask for help, so he came to us.

Collins summoned me and I got on the radios immediately, passing the information up to Brigade through my brother Terry.

I hoped for the best, but I knew how poorly information moved in theater, and I didn't have much faith that we would find her. We never did.

———•••———

We went to check on the lads.

My combat family pulled up to a huge complex, a massive training camp of some kind, replete with gigantic crossed swords over the gate, which Colin Marks' boys had taken over.

Corporal Duperroy was standing watch at the gate, which immediately made me furious. Standing watch and checking vehicles: not an ANGLICO mission.

I hopped out of my vehicle and summoned Duperroy and Macis: the two of mine on Davidson's team. Both dragged over to me, beaten and unhappy.

I looked hard into their eyes.

Tell me what's going on, I demanded.

They looked at each other, the silent message *Tell him what we talked about.*

Duperroy, senior man, spoke.

Sir, we need to get off this team. We are...uh...a little concerned about Lieutenant Davidson.

Yeah? How so? I wanted to hear it from them, but I already knew where this was going. I felt my chest tightening with anger.

Well, he continued, Lance Corporal Macis and I are thinking maybe there is something wrong with him. He has been killing dogs around here...I guess that's OK, and other people are doing it, but he is really into it. He has been wearing us out with watches and duties, all kinds of extra bullshit we aren't supposed to be doing. That's why everyone is so tired and burned out.

He paused.

Sir, there's something else. We were OK with the dog thing, but yesterday there was an Iraqi leaving the compound, on foot. He was just trying to walk out to the street...and Davidson shot at him. He shot down at his feet, maybe two feet away. He thought it was funny. Me and Macis are getting worried that something is going to happen, something bad. We don't want to be here when it does. He is scaring us.

My heart pounded with anger. I should have seen this coming.

All of Davidson's right-mate, no-worries bullshit convinced me that he would be steady and aggressive. He was aggressive all right, but in the way that a small-town cop, now carrying a gun, is aggressive against the guys who picked on him in high school. Davidson was a small guy, and I had an image of him being brutalized in the notorious British school system. Now he was big man, with the power of God over the locals.

He probably *could* kill a civilian. But not on my watch.

It was suddenly clear to me. This is why his guys wanted to get away from him. This is why Nosha was so happy as a member of Walsh's team. This is why Slap and Chili always looked a bit longingly at me whenever I came to say hello. They all wanted to get away from Davidson, having seen through his act long ago. I had the picture now.

I looked from Duperroy to Macis, right in their faces. This stops right now. You guys are off this team. I am bringing you back with the rest of us. I don't own Davidson, but I am going to let people above me know what's going on.

Duperroy smiled. OK, sir, we were hoping to come back. We just... we don't want to be here if something really bad happens.

I walked away and sat in my Hummer, fuming. God *damn* it. I can't believe I let things go this far. I should have been more aggressive about fixing this earlier.

No way around it: My fault.

My. Fucking. Fault.

———◆◆———

My teams spread themselves over the battlefield.

Brian and his team stayed with me.

Sid, along with Robby Boyd's company, remained south of us, working as an aerial react team.

Sergeant Wilson, able to sleep at last after two very tense days alone with his team in Indian country north of the canal, moved back in with Mike Murdock and was traveling throughout the GOSPs.

Davidson, chastised, arrogant, convinced he was right all along, moved back to Colin and D Company, and they split the GOSP mission with Mike.

Marcus was summoned down to Basrah, in an effort to give some more firepower to the Commandos preparing to take that city, and Walsh took Cruz and Lopez—and Macis, now back on his team—along for what they hoped would be a big fight.

I didn't have comm with any of them, but trusted my small-unit leaders to do the right thing without guidance from me.

———— •••• ————

I think private gun ownership is stupid, and so it was of no small amusement to my boys that I now carried three weapons on my body: Beretta in a cop-issue drop holster; Gurkha kukri on my left hip (put there, per Marcus's direction, only *after* we crossed the border); and an RPK assault rifle I picked out of the CP stash.

I had wanted to carry an Iraqi weapon for a simple reason: Soviet weapons worked better when they were dirty. They were not as accurate as were American rifles, but then again the M-16 didn't work unless it was *perfectly clean*. We were hoist on our own petard: the M-16 was so tightly machined, with internal tolerances so perfect, that it didn't work with sand or dirt or water... in short, all the things we were covered with all day, every day.

I clearly remembered a David Hackworth story about pulling an AK out of a pit in Vietnam in which it had been buried, racking back the slide, and firing off an entire magazine. *That* is an infantry weapon, so magnificent that C.J. Chivers wrote an entire book about it. So I carried one. On top of this, the Marine Corps' obsession with weapons accountability meant very deep, court-martial-type trouble for anyone who lost his rifle, so I hadn't taken an M-16 from California. If I lost this Soviet weapon, so what? I would pick up another one.

———•••———

Every military unit has a Gear Queer.

Everyone in the Marines is a gear queer to an extent, and the crappy equipment with which the Marine Corps saddles people almost requires that you go out and spend money on comfort items for the field. Buying a better GoreTex sleeping bag or a better helmet liner or a more-comfortable drop holster, all critical for the most basic comfort in the worst conditions, did not put you into Queer status. That was the norm.

There can only be one Gear Queer. This is the guy who always goes out and buys the coolest and latest whiz-bang gadget from REI or Blackhawk to stand out from his peers.

The ANGLICO Gear Queer was Sergeant Bunch.

As Brian and I stood with Sid drinking coffee in the desert one morning, Bunch appeared out of nowhere. He was a big, handsome, square-jawed kid, all broad shoulders and ripped muscle and eight-pack abdominals, which he took pains to show off by walking around without his shirt as often as possible. He looked like a movie star, always outfitted in the latest and coolest gadgetry and Blackhawk catalog Delta Force- SEAL-Ranger-SOG holster, belt, sling, hat, sunglasses, knee pads.

He indeed had designs on being an actor, and implied to everyone that he was in fact earning his living in action movies. His several, very brief, appearances on screen in movies like *Blackhawk Down* were impressive, until we quizzed him very hard (and publicly) about just how many lines he had spoken on screen.

The answer (none) had earned Bunch an unfortunate sobriquet: Extra.

Extra strode up to us, expensive sunglasses balanced coolly on his nose, expensive speed-lace boots enabling him to sneak up quietly on an unsuspecting foe, super-duper tactical rifle sling holding his M-16 ready for the gunfight soon to erupt. He was wearing tactical kneepads, a la Mogadishu, just in case a huge urban battle broke out here in the Mesopotamian desert.

He didn't belong to me, and we had no idea where he had come from. He sheepishly filled us in.

1 Para was still far in the rear, having rolled the dice and come up empty. The rumor was that one unit was going to jump into Qalat Sikar Airfield and take it, and 1 Para was designated to be that unit.

Big deal for a British airborne unit, but even bigger deal for the U.S. Marine attachments, who would have been the first Marines with a combat jump since World War II.

It was a big *risk*, though: enormously cool if it happened, but if it didn't, they were left behind. And as it happened they were in fact left behind while their sister unit, 3 Para, and we Irish pushed into the war.

They had been sitting for a week in safety, doing nothing.

Poor Extra. This was his first foray into the war.

———◆◆———

We were summoned back to Brigade for a meeting.

Sitting at the entrance to the compound was something I hadn't expected.

Two tanks.

I couldn't believe it. American MIAI Abrams Main Battle Tanks, 60-ton behemoths sitting right at the entrance to 16th UK Air Assault Brigade CP, as if to ward off a pending Iraqi attack.

Every time I was up close to one of these machines, the similes roared through my brain: *like a dinosaur, like an elephant, a beached whale, a house on tracks, a mastodon unearthed from the tundra*. They were simply enormous, and their main guns packed an enormous punch. Big machine, big gun, so of course all Marines loved them.

I had forgotten that Terry was a school-trained tanker. He and his Marines had been bombing along in their Humvee several days prior, and had seen these tanks off in the distance. Not an unusual sight on the battlefield, but what was unusual was the Marines were standing on top of them, waving their shirts in desperate hope of flagging someone down.

One tank had run out of fuel, and the unit left another tank behind to protect that one and then just left. That had been days prior, and no one had come back or contacted these poor guys since. Running out of water, food and batteries, they resorted to flagging someone down to rescue them. Terry and his boys had happily done so, and now Terry had Rommel fantasies of commanding his own tiny tank unit.

———•••———

Conde drove us in and parked us on the far side of a moat.

A moat. *A fucking moat.*

I had no idea why the Iraqis would have built such a thing, but I supposed it was an irrigation canal which had collapsed through disuse. We balanced our way across on a rickety wooden bridge and found the ANGLICO area. Our boys had just thrown up their hooches in the shadow of the main building and were living out of their vehicles. The whole setup reminded me of the embassy scenes from the marvelous movie *The Killing Fields*: squat central building from the Early Stalin era, small ones clustered around it, palm trees in every direction, invaders living in the dirt, locals and refugees outside the walls.

I went inside and entered the hornet's nest.

Every time I was around any staff unit of any size, even one with as good-quality lads as the British, I remembered why I had sworn to never serve on a staff. The same men who were speaking tensely and urgently into radio handsets and telephones in Kuwait were doing the same thing here, sitting on the same wooden-seated folding chairs, talking to the same commanders on the same frequencies and telling them to do things with their units they didn't want to do.

I pretended to try to find my ANGLICO commanders, then fled. I couldn't get out fast enough.

---•◆•---

31 MARCH 2003 ▶ AR-RAMAYLAH, IRAQ

Collins was starting to ease off. He was from the same school as those under whom I grew up in the Marine Corps...you can always get softer on people, but you can never get tougher.

He had been rough on the Ba'ath Party assholes he found, and for good reason.

He was not a violent man by nature, and was in fact quite witty and cheerful, but he *understood violence*. If Iraq was to be stable, the Ba'ath Party, now dethroned, had to be afraid of us. There was no way around it. Collins was starting to feel that the village was under control, and could run itself. The Irish were like a full-grown tiger in a very small cage, thrashing around in frustration with nowhere to go. We needed to get these guys back out into the field where they could run.

Killing stopped. Nation-building continued.

Collins was quite proud that the village school would reopen this day. It turned out that the headmaster was among the worst Ba'ath Party brutalizers and offenders of law and order; Collins sacked him and started anew. I told Collins that now that school was back in session, he had gone from the hero of all these little kids to their mortal enemy.

He made clear that the school would have a nice, crisp Iraqi flag— *not* British, *not* American—flying in front before reopening, and completely barred the press from the event. And this was to be an *original* Iraqi flag, not the bastardized version Saddam had invented. In his view, this was for Iraqis only.

This was their country, their people, their flag, their tribe.

———◆◆◆———

Brian and I were headed out of the compound the next morning and met an SUV coming in the gate. The SUV was new, clean, functional and sparkling. Unusual for Iraq.

The vehicle had stopped and the occupants were getting out to show their IDs to the guards. The double-gate was being guarded on a rotation of the rifle companies, and today it was the Gurkhas in charge. The dark-skinned Nepali held the ID cards like tarot cards and could not read them and had no idea what to do.

If the vehicle was unusual, so were the men standing next to it: big, fat, and American. I pulled alongside and hopped out.

One guy saw our vehicle with USMC painted on the side, and broke into a huge grin. His huge belly hung over a big belt buckle. His red face was already starting to burn. Pure Texas.

He walked over to shake hands. All raht! Man, I's hopin' I'd see some Americans soon. Can ya tell these fellas who we are? They won't let us in, and boy, ah don't want to stay out here a second longer than ah have to.

He looked at me, Brian and Arreola, each carrying two weapons. Looks like you fellas are safe out here, though.

I laughed and agreed, and started asking questions. These were the first American civilians I had spoken to in months. Sure enough, they were engineers from Texas, oil refinery guys, and we actually knew a lot of the same people in Houston. I got a kick out of seeing these good 'ol Texas boys in the middle of this shithole, and I smoothed things over with the mistrustful Gurkhas on the gate.

————••••————

Now that things were under control, the civilians arrived, driving up from Kuwait. Right behind the capitalists were the anticapitalists: UNHCR, and then the Red Cross, within the hour. Oil men and do-gooders. We were hitting for the cycle.

That made sense to me, as this was a humanitarian crisis on top of a military event, but all in all I would rather spend time with my new buddies from Texas. I was leery of the humanitarian people, as they tended to want to give orders to the military. The humanitarian people viewed U.S. soldiers and Marines as their own protection force, which pissed me off though I knew they had a job to do. But so did I.

————••••————

And then we got pulled away.

The British Third Army Air Corps, 3 AAC, was a quick-moving helicopter unit, agile and aggressive but without their own indirect fire support or much close air support beyond what they brought with them. They were the sorts of guys who could track down bad guys but then not do much about it; ANGLICO was the opposite, able to kill a whole lot of people but not go out and find them. We were yin to their yang.

They had been slavering over us since we arrived in theater, casting covetous eyes on our radios and veteran fire support experts, and took their case to the commanding general. They had made inroads by working in with Robby Boyd and Sid, and now they won, grabbing all of India from our brothers in the Royal Irish.

So off to the AAC it was.

The Irish bade us a wistful goodbye as they worked in Ramaylah. I missed them already.

The now-all-Marine teams and I drove down the road, refugees, from the Irish to our new home.

The lads at 3 AAC had happily occupied an abandoned airfield near Ramaylah. It was perfect for them, with paved runways and fuel pits and lots of space for men and toys. I liked the way the AAC worked *in principle*: lots of movement and quick action and screening and reconnaissance, and as an attack helicopter pilot myself I was always been a fan of tree-limbs-in-the-skids helicopter flying.

But these guys seemed hugely disorganized and couldn't quite figure out where they fit in the big scheme of things. The individual pilots, like helicopter guys everywhere, were intense and smart and aggressive, but I was not overly impressed with the leaders. They seemed to be making it up as they went.

The pilots and senior officers gathered in a run-down, filthy building at the center of the airfield. Sandbags lined the halls and rimmed the offices, one deep to keep out the water if another monsoon storm hit.

Our first brief was very brief and down-and-dirty: helicopters will fly screening and reconnaissance missions, and if we see anything, we scoop up you lads and get fire and air going. Righto? Jolly good!

Nothing wrong so far. This was precisely the sort of thing ANGLICO was supposed to do, and the faster we moved, the better I felt.

We joined up in the middle of a huge convoy staging inside the gate. One platoon of riflemen from 3 Para went with us, to be used as muscle if we dug up some bad guys. 81mm mortars went along, as did a British Forward Observation Officer team, with the decidedly unwarlike nom de guerre of FOO. The FOO lads were a stripped-down version of us but thought the same way we did, and I liked them. So far.

———•••———

As we sat baking in the sun, some of the ANGLICO Brigade staff guys showed up with mail for us. Mail had, as usual, been sitting somewhere for weeks on end, then was released in a flood.

Sorting through the tsunami was like Christmas morning: endless packages with endless goodies. My Duke Blue Devils had lost to Kansas in the Sweet Sixteen. For a second, I was sitting in my filthy hot vehicle but back in Cameron Indoor Stadium, right next to the court, surrounded by fellow 19-year-olds who had made 1540 on their SATs and now were screaming at the top of their lungs, their faces painted blue. A different then and a different me.

———•••———

We zoomed north.

Next to the road ran a fuel pipeline that the engineers had laid, running jet fuel from Kuwait all the way to Baghdad. Along that pipeline, I saw the guys who I determined officially had the Worst Job in The War.

Four guys, living completely alone, were monitoring and maintaining a pump which kept that fuel moving north.

These poor guys had the worst of all worlds.

Their job was ungodly boring.

They were twenty feet from a heavily-traveled thoroughfare, ensuring ear-splitting noise as tanks, tracks, Humvees, Rovers, flatbed trucks, troop trucks, 18-wheel fuel trucks, self-propelled artillery pieces, motorcycles, dune buggies, and on and on roared past in an endless grinding stream, ensuring they were covered every thirty seconds with a fresh coat of dirt.

They were all of four strong, so they could be rolled up at any time if an Iraqi unit made it across Route Tampa. Only two guys could sleep at a time while the others stood watch.

But these were teenagers and when we drove past I looked back at their brown world and saw for one second a Frisbee framed against the baking sky over their generators and pump and pipeline and world, and then they slid into my past.

––––•••––––

I thought I knew the meaning of *The Middle of Nowhere*... until I got to LSA Viper.

The Marine Corps—the creative, thoughtful, imaginative institution that named officer's basic training school The Basic School and called a hilly running loop The Hill Trail—called all these little base camps Life Support Areas. That always sounded to me like a geodesic dome on the moon, but the letters LSA in blue ink on my map meant good things: hot chow, tents, computers (*with Internet*), and, most important, Marine infantry.

As we approached Viper, all the Paras were called away, back to Ramaylah. They were absolutely critical a few hours before, but someone had decided they were in the wrong place, so now those poor lads had to retrace the path we had just taken, this time at night. Surely, someone at the top must have known what he was doing, but who that person might be and what his plan was remained unclear to us.

Viper was the good guys' fort out on floor of the wasteland in *The Road Warrior,* a heavily-armed fortress oasis in the middle of nothing. Marine Corps and American flags snapped brightly, the only splashes of color against a sere backdrop of sand and brown. Tents squatted against the sandstorms and wind in drill instructor-straight lines, as the military mind imposed its own order on the surroundings. The gate guards wouldn't let us in, as if we were terrorists who had stolen more than twenty vehicles, painted them with American and British markings, and then oh by the way grown white skin and blond hair and found American accents to add to the deception.

Conde and Arreola were happy, though: the gate guards for some reason were all young Hispanic females. Yeah, boy! said Conde as we rolled at last into the camp. He had good hunting prospects, at least for the next day or so. Add that to the LSA pluses.

---

27 MARCH 2003 ▶ MIDDLE OF NOWHERE, IRAQ
3d AAC established a forward arming and refueling point and a laager area far out into the desert away from the cities. They

were still hoping to use Sid's team for an OP mission, in Indian country near Viper.

The (justified) fear among American and British planners was that with the speed of the division's movement north, entire Iraqi units were left in the field, simply bypassed and unaccounted-for. The Iraqi 51st Mechanized guys we had had it out with a few days before were such a unit, and the British wanted eyes and ears out on likely routes they and others like them may take to try to get up to Baghdad.

Brian and I went out there to say hello.

Sid and his boys were parked in a row of vehicles, all hunkered down among sand dunes in the driving rain.

Sid's boys were cheerful and productive, as they always were: this is the mark of a good small-unit leader. Hunter had lost some of his wide-eyed innocence, but still wore two knives slung on his skinny hips, like a little kid dressed up in dad's clothes.

Sid and Robby had been planning a company-size insert and patrol, with Sid's team to be inserted even farther out in no-man's land, but things were on hold while the weather lashed the entire coalition force with rain. I was able to score some great maps, from a 3 AAC intelligence officer who took pity on me, and had a great time back ever-so briefly among helicopter pilots.

There was here, as with the Irish, a great sense of urgency, but also of frustration as the British fell ever-further behind the Marines roaring towards Baghdad. There were grumblings about the wimpiness of Tony Blair and his unwillingness to let his lads take the fight to the bad guys. They—that would be *we*—wanted off the leash.

———•••———

29 MARCH 2003 ▶ AR-RAMAYLAH CENTRAL GAS FACILITY

My Marines came to me and told me that they had gone through the buildings of the refinery, checking for anything dangerous or interesting, and that as they did this Sergeant Sullivan carried a length of steel pipe and methodically destroyed anything he could, smashing windows and computers and wooden door frames in explosions of pointless violence. I shrugged at this and ignored them and worried about something else.

———•••———

Santos stood in the doorway of the company command post, glareblind in the noonday sun after spending the morning indoors.

He wore shorts and a flak jacket and boots on bare feet.

He squinted at us dreamily. He seemed genuinely pleased that we had come to say hello.

Hey, sir, what's going on? he said. We are doing some pretty cool stuff down here. Come on inside and I can tell you about the Eagle flights. Really cool...I wish we did a lot more of that kind of stuff. How come the Marines don't do that? Really fun.

He stopped for a moment as a thought slid into his brain. He was moving at half speed. I wondered if he had just woken from a nap.

Hey, sir, you want to take a good shit? We have a great shitter built in the back. We found a toilet seat and cleaned it up and everything. There is a big old hole so there aren't too many flies. C'mon. Come take a look.

Without waiting for a response he turned and wandered away, around the corner of the building.

———•••———

Brian and I exchanged a glance and went to have a look. Santos stood proudly next to his handwork, a kid waiting to show his project to Dad.

It was indeed lovely. It was truly Iraq's Best Shitter.

———•••———

Sid's Humvee had a broken parking brake.

Whenever he stopped on an incline, he had to chock his wheels. He used Iraqi helmets he had scrounged.

The Iraqi villagers saw each time he did this and assumed he had executed prisoners for their helmets to hold his vehicle in place and they were afraid of him.

———•••———

For the most part, Main Supply Route Tampa was the same as a highway in the United States: painted lanes, guardrails, nice new pavement.

One quirk to the road, though, was that the Bedouins and shepherds grew tired of having to cross at the bridges (which were also huge, modern and beautifully built) and so had cut into the railings and walls next to the freeway.

I shuddered to think about what would happen to a camel herd moseying (if there was ever an animal to which the verb mosey applied, the camel was it) across an eight-lane superhighway.

These cuts in the railing were also access points for villagers, many of whom had little cars and trucks, and they assumed that they could pop through these entrances, turn right onto the tarmac, and just drive along the freeway until they felt like exiting again. This was the equivalent of exiting a little two-lane farm road and making a 90-degree right turn directly onto an interstate highway. You don't realize how important a long on-ramp is until you try to get onto a highway without one.

The Iraqi system meant that you could be roaring along at 80 miles per hour and have a car suddenly stop in front of you, preparing to exit; or the obverse: pull onto the highway (even more exciting) in front of you, resulting in a closing rate of 79 miles per hour.

This was on top of the Arab drivers, who drove far too slow or far too fast, often on the wrong side of the highway, ignored all signs indicating a rule of any sort, and in general did whatever they wanted.

A few days of this were going to be the end of Conde.

——— •••• ———

We knew where we wanted to be, but had no idea how to get to it.

We could actually *see* the dirt road heading north away from the highway, but there was no exit to it anywhere in either direction. The British FOO team in their Rover in front of us finally gave up and all of us shut down, pulled out binoculars, and got out.

Right on the highway.

There is something unnerving about standing still in the middle of a highway. The brain just can't accept that such a familiar setting was being used in such a strange way; the lines in the middle of the road were supposed to be whipping past the window at 80 mph, not still under your boot.

The desolation here was breathtaking. Far to the south we could barely make out Viper, a dark memory against the sand. No human, no camel, no bird, no vehicle, nothing moved for miles in any direction. We were the last men on earth.

———••———

Strangest of all: there was a tiny shack, right in the middle of the overpass.

It was made of wood and badly damaged, a little one-room shotgun shack straight out of *Hee Haw*, sitting, absurd, on the concrete arching over the highway

What the *fuck*?

All I could imagine was that it had been some sort of lookout post for the Iraqis, since bombed or shot to pieces.

I wondered how *that* job had been assigned: *Hey, Ahmed! Mohammed! C'mere*, you two. Listen. You two are going to sit right here, out in the open, raised over the highway where you can be seen for miles. When the entire First Marine Division comes up the road, right underneath you, use this radio right here and tell us. OK?

———•••———

This place was bad: dark and wrong and forlorn and evil.

Philosophers believe that the soul continues even in inanimate objects. Ever wonder why they have to disclose to you if someone has died in the house you want to buy? That's why. The buildings at Dachau are just buildings, but they are not, haunted, ghosts adrift, *djinns* floating, immense horror and satanic evil.

Maybe I felt adrift from the Irish and from the rest of the Marine Corps, marooned with the AAC, in a sea of Brits I didn't really know.

I felt the lost Shia souls Saddam's henchmen had murdered and raped and thrown into open graves.

I felt the tension and apprehension and anger of the entire First Marine Division, which had just gone up this very road on their date with destiny in Baghdad.

I knew how exposed we were going to be when this mission came together, and the fact that if we got caught out in the open we were in serious trouble. The huge, unblinking searchlight of Marine Air had shone brightly, warm and brief and loving, on me and now had moved on, north, past Nasiriyah on the run to Baghdad where the Dirt People needed them far more than I did.

In the middle of 500,000 men I felt alone.

———•••———

Standing in the desert next to the road was a man in a wetsuit.

Now, *that's* unusual. Not exactly wetsuity-sort of land around here.

I actually laughed out loud, and I made Conde stop to find out what this guy's story was. Turned out he was part of a British military diver EOD team, checking the bridge we were about to cross. The obvious question: was the bridge rigged to explode? It was. Did you guys defuse the goddamn thing? We did. So we can go across? Yep, mate, no worries.

It was one of the great mysteries of the war why Saddam and his generals didn't give the order to start blowing bridges as they retreated.

All of southern Iraq is bisected by water—rivers, canals, irrigation ditches—running east to west, while the roads ran north-south. If they had blown the bridges, it would have slowed us down, if not stopped us cold. General Mattis was all about speed and tempo. If the Iraqis had frozen us in place, even for a day or two while we got bridging equipment up, they would have not only slowed our advance, but bunched us up against the water as guys poured north and backed up against units stopped in front of them. This would have left us exposed and our positions out in the open, highly vulnerable.

I said a silent blessing, again, to whoever at CentCom had given us the go order eighteen hours early, preventing just such an event. Maybe someone above us did know what he was doing, after all.

We said farewell to our dripping-wet new friend, and headed up onto the bridge.

———•••———

We turned west, up to the crossing, and stopped short.

I suddenly realized how narrow this crossing really was. It had sure looked a lot bigger from a distance. Railroad tracks ran engineer-straight across the ties suspended over the water, then faded right and out of sight behind two hills on the other side.

I was pondering how we were going to do this when around the hills on the far side came a camel. Not unusual: seeing a camel out here was like seeing a deer in the States. I just hoped the stupid thing wouldn't come out onto the bridge; that would be quite a Mexican standoff if we were halfway across.

Then another camel came around the corner, then another, then ten more, then a hundred, then thousands. Popping up from the furry, long-nosed brown sea appeared an Iraqi in a red kaffiyeh: the driver of the herd.

We weren't going anywhere for a while. There was nothing else for it. We and the British turned off our vehicles and got out.

The camels ambled across the bridge and came over us, a grunting, foul, reeking tsunami of bad breath and crooked yellow teeth and ugly, guttural rumblings. Camels are huge but skittish and stupid, and they hate humans. They streamed across the bridge and down both sides of our little convoy, closing ranks again behind us like a stream around rocks. It smelled like a junior high locker room: reeking, wet, filthy animals that slept in dirt and their own shit. They glared at us from the sides of their eyes, and bared their teeth and rumbled deep in their chests.

The driver surfed along the middle of the wave, shouting at his stupid charges. He glared at us too. He was a handsome, high-cheekboned Bedu, dark skin and dark eyes beneath the kaffiyeh. His saddle was seasoned and worn and looked comfortable. A little boy, about ten years old, rode his own smaller camel on his own smaller saddle, and shouted lustily in his small voice in Arabic, an imitation of his father. *Take Your Son to Work Day.*

The humans split around us and turned to glare again when they were behind our vehicles. I could read their expressions: we have been here for 5000 years, and this is our land. Go away, back to your land, wherever that is. Leave us in peace.

The last camel shambled (*moseyed*) away and the tracks were now clear. The Rover went first, and he rolled carefully ahead in front of us on its much-narrower wheelbase, straddling the tracks, one wheel inside them and one outside.

I told Conde to hold still, and I got out. I walked forward, carefully hopscotching from tie to tie. I turned around, looking at the bridge and at our vehicle, judging how much room for error we had, trying not to think about what would happen if one wheel went off the side. Not enough room.

From here our Humvee looked like a sumo wrestler squatting on a dining room table. The bridge was about a foot wider than the vehicle. I looked at the water between my feet, four stories down and maybe five feet deep. No railing, nothing to keep us from going over the side. Too dangerous.

The Rover, safely across, churned away and around the corner and disappeared, knowing little and caring less about the stupid Americans and their fat, heavy truck.

If we didn't get over this bridge, we had a five- or six-hour drive to find another way into our position from the west: back across our dirt roads, back to Tampa, north to find another hole in the highway guardrail, and this time setting off cross-country in the west, in Bad Guy Territory, completely alone. *If you saw them, sir, they weren't Apache...*

I looked over my shoulder at the Rover, which had reappeared when they realized we were no longer behind them. They were waiting for us.

I looked back at my little combat family, waiting, impassive, in the Hummer for my decision.

They looked at me.

OK, Mister Officer, what now?

We had to get across.

A Humvee is about the length of the average SUV in an American driveway, but it is more like a Mack truck in width. I knew Conde couldn't see his right front wheel, so he would have to guide off of the one in front of him.

I hopscotched slowly back, trying not to look down at an awful lot of Iraqi air straight down. I swung to my seat, got in.

Conde looked at me.

I puffed out my cheeks, looked straight ahead, and gave him the word.

Go ahead, but *slow*. Keep your wheel just barely outside the track, maybe even touching it, and whatever you do, don't make any sudden turns. You have less than a tire width on each side.

OK, sir! He said cheerfully, and put our little truck in gear.

I closed my eyes for a moment as we lurched forward.

Marines and soldiers had already died when their vehicles (usually tanks and personnel carriers) rolled off the roads into the canals, trapping them inside, upside down, underwater. I said a little atheist prayer and hoped that Conde had had enough sleep the night before.

We started across.

Conde was deft and gentle and rolled us ever-so-slowly along. The left side of the vehicle bumped slowly up and down as the left front tire gripped, climbed and then slipped off the steel of the track, over and over. The rubber of the huge tires squeaked as they did this, and each time Conde gently rolled us back down onto the ties.

I suddenly wondered what would happen if a train came around the hills in front of us. We had absolutely nowhere to go but forward; there was no way we could do this in reverse.

As Conde inched along, the Brits actually got out to watch us, their arms crossed on their chests, wondering if things were about to get much more exciting.

We made steady progress, squeak-thumping due west, and I began to relax. Our British mates slowly drew closer, and then we were across. Conde steered us down off the tracks with aplomb. We all began to breathe again.

The next day we were pulled back, back to the Irish.

They were indeed gearing up to move north, but I felt a twinge of guilt as I weighed my responsibility to the AAC. I had committed to them, and fundamentally they were into my thing: speed, action and air-ground coordination. I explained all this to Tim Collins. He was unmoved. He wanted us back.

This lasted one evening.

Richard came into the room I shared with Brian and Arreola at 0200, walking straight to my rack in the far corner.

Mate, that was Brigade, he said. They said to get your ANGLICOs back up with the AAC. They need you up there.

God damn it, Richard! I vented (again) at the (innocent) messenger (again). We just came from there, for fuck's sake! How urgent can it be?

Don't know, mate. Not my idea. Better get moving.

Fuck that, I retorted. I am not going out there alone at night. They can fucking wait.

Richard glared at me and walked out.

My bravado impressed not one soul. The next morning, sure enough, we were back on the road.

We made it in one long haul this time, same goddamn route, same bridge, all the way out to the same goddamned fucking railroad crossing Bridge of Death over the Gorge of Eternal Peril, squeak-bumping across a bit faster and with more confidence this time. We pulled right back into the same goddamn spot we were in the day before, right next to the same goddamn British team who had watched the four of us almost die the day prior. Exhausted and cranky from all the cross-country driving and exasperated at people above me at Brigade who could not get their shit together, I threw open my door and stomped alone up the hill to take a look around.

As far as I could see across the water to the west, camels were coming. *Always with the fucking camels.* The herders were driving them from or to something, but this water was the cleanest around, and camels by the hundreds were lined and drinking in their awkward, splay-footed style. Finished and refreshed, they climbed in an unending brown stream, an hour long, an hour of camels, sixty minutes of ugly, onto the bridge behind me and they trudged east.

Three of them, for some reason, separated from their mates and descended into our camp to check us out. They were chased away by rambunctious, bored soldiers.

I jumped and slid my way back down the hill to our little camp.

———•••———

The British FOO team was packing up to move.

———•••———

We had been there less than two hours.

I walked over to the commander. *You've got to be fucking kidding.*

He stared at me, British, imperious, superior, snippy.

No. AAC needs us back at the airfield. Don't know what's up next, but we are part of it.

But they *just fucking told us* they needed us here! *I just fucking came from there!* Just now! Now they want us back?

Don't know about your lads, but we're going. See you later.

I couldn't believe it. I just couldn't believe it. Four moves in two days? *Jesus H Fucking Christ.*

That was the final straw. I stomped over to the Hummer and threw myself down into the seat, doing a slow burn while I clenched my jaw and glared straight ahead.

We swallowed hard and drove back with the FOO teams, seeking unity in numbers. I then told Conde to split off to the Irish camp in Ramaylah, back with my Irish, my mates, my tribe, men who wanted us, while the FOO continued to the airfield.

I got back to Tim, back with my people.

I then called the AAC and told them: *fuck you.* I quit.

You get your shit together, you can call us. You want us, you get a general on the hook to tell Collins why.

I had *had it.* We were finished working with them. I never saw any of them again.

———◆◆———

Good rumors have four characteristics: they always come right from the mouth of someone who *knows*; they are always just

reasonable enough to be believable; they always reference someone who is not there at the moment you hear it; and they are
always wrong.

Back with the Irish, the rumors flew. We are going home! 3d
ANGLICO has seats on airplanes 19 July! Meneses heard it straight
from the CO! The UK is pulling out all her forces 19 May! So
specific a day? Oh, yes, sir, heard it in the chow hall! The Irish are
going to start anti-guerrilla ops in either Baghdad or Basrah...any
day now, sir! No shit. Heard it from my buddy at Brigade.

---

8 APRIL 2003 ▶ AR-RAMAYLAH, IRAQ

The word had come down numerous times unchanging from the
British command: *No British unit will move north of the Euphrates.*

This was typical of the Tony Blair Third Way centrist pussy
we-want-to-stand-with-our-American-brothers-but-don't-want-
anyone-to-actually-get-killed stance on the world.

Tim Collins, cheerful, dynamic and aggressive as ever, ignored the
rule and mounted everyone up to push as far as he could for as
long as he could until someone figured it out and told him to stop.
Forgiveness is easier to obtain than permission. He reminded me
of a toddler with a smile on his face, pushing a cup slowly towards
the edge of the table, looking directly at the adults to see when
they would stop him.

Conde now knew what to do when Collins started to get antsy.

The four of us loaded up our gear and sat outside on the refinery
loading docks in the pleasant night air, waiting for something to
happen. Conde was a bird dog, following the British Sergeant

Major, Collins's driver, for over an hour, and when the Sergeant Major got into his Rover, Conde got into the Humvee, pulled it directly behind, put it in neutral, left the engine running, and just watched the door.

Sure enough, Collins burst through the door, strode swiftly across the loading dock, and headed for the left-side door of his Rover. He hopped in without a sideways glance.

Conde put the Hummer in gear as the three of us piled in, and he stayed right on the Rover's bumper as we left the camp. Not only would Collins leave us behind (bad enough) but we had no idea where we were going (worse by far.) There was never a brief, never a meeting or map study of any kind to indicate what was coming next. *This was a man of action.* Collins just hopped in and went. If we didn't stay with him, we would be lost, at night, alone in the middle of a war zone.

We roared out of the compound just before sunset, a long line of vehicles, their drivers similarly astute, snaking through dead-quiet streets.

We pulled off the road into a huge assembly area, battalion assets filling in behind us.

At 0130 we started out again, a much-larger force this time, and headed north, due north, across open countryside.

South of the village of Aradha, Iraqi guides joined us, and after a brief, mysterious tete-a-tete, Collins led us onward.

PARIS, 1944

And you will swear as you enter Vegas
That you're not a gambling man.
—Steely Dan, *Do It Again*

8 APRIL 2003 ▶ MIDDLE OF NIGHT
ABU SAKHR, IRAQ

Before our engines even cut off, we were swarmed by the townsfolk.

This happened everywhere, but the farther north we went the more urgency the people seemed to have. Swarming, pushing, pointing, smiling, shouting in Arabic, asking questions (how long are you staying *this time?* was a theme), singing with joy, they followed through on the White House's insistence that we would be greeted with open arms in Iraq. If only they had only strewn flower petals at our feet.

As it was, we *were* heroes, to these people at least. I had the sense that Saddam hadn't really cared too much about the villages and hovels far to the south, except as they affected his control of the oil fields. The larger the city, the more north you went, the more brutally he had repressed the people, and that relief among those people now was palpable. All we had done was drive up and park, but we felt like the Allies marching on Paris.

Fathers, shy but insistent, pushed through the crowd. I met little children: Ali, Hasem, Hassad, Mustafa. I guessed their ages as about three...most, I discovered through sign language, were five or six or older. My son had just turned three and these children were smaller than that: malnutrition. Fathers were given the task of bringing the children to meet us, and they beamed widely as we knelt down to talk face-to-face to their little ones. Children were the most prized—and, perhaps, only—possessions of these simple people.

All Iraqi children knew the standard three or four phrases in English: *George Bush! George Bush!* was their favorite, and they also knew *what's your name?* and *thank you.* They figured out swiftly that we were intrigued with their currency (with Saddam's face on it, it would soon be like Nazi currency and rare) and would run after our vehicles, holding up their 250 dinar notes and shouting *Mistah! Mistah! Dollar?*

The children were absolutely adorable, beautiful little sprites with brown faces and straight, gleaming white teeth. These gorgeous little pixie girls were clear and fresh and huggable, not yet beaten down by drudgery and poor hygiene. I could not reconcile these little girls with the grown women: fat, stooped, angry, toothless crones covered in black, beaten down by a lifetime of suffering.

The people were hugely friendly. Arabs as a group are a friendly people, and the Iraqis even more so than their neighbors. I felt sure these people would have taken us in and stuffed us full of food had Collins allowed it. Like those in Latin cultures, they wanted to stand inches from you when they spoke, inside the comfort zone of an American but natural and friendly to them.

———•••———

The cheerful people and the beautiful children belied the condition of their country. Nothing, anywhere, was beautiful or delicate or well-designed. It was all poorly-built, broken, filthy, crumbling, broken and slipshod, every single item in every direction and at any distance. Not one thing worked.

The exception was the machinery of Saddam's oil wealth: the refineries—built by the British—and the highway system, immaculate and well-designed and built by the British.

The water was horrifying. They shit in it, peed in it, washed clothes in it...and bathed in it, drank from it, and washed their babies in it. Before it even got to their villages, it was dumped with truly frightening chemicals from manufacturing and weapons production upstream. Anyone who whines about the cost of the EPA in this country should spend ten minutes in an Iraqi village.

No one had a job, *not one person.* It wasn't just that jobs were abandoned because of the invasion, though that would be a natural guess. It was that no one anywhere we went moved with any purpose except the farmers. No one in a city was walking briskly to or from a job, carrying papers, opening or closing a shop, selling things, going to or from anywhere important or interesting. They mostly stood beside the road and watched us.

The people were poor, but this was not the grinding, abject poverty of Calcutta or Bangkok or Port au Prince. This was a simple lack of wherewithal, not the filthy, sinister, clutching poor of larger cities. They had horrible teeth (understandable), were all skinny (same) and for some reason seemed to have an unusually high incidence of some sort of mental retardation (not.)

Many, many Iraqis with whom we came in contact seemed to have Downs Syndrome. I couldn't understand it: a genetic disease can't be caused by environment, can it? Or must these poor people be tortured by all of life?

——————•••——————

We weren't quite sure what to do with all these people, and we were tense and ready for someone to start shooting, but finally realized that the joy was genuine. To the south, the white flags and waving were to keep from getting shot. North of here, we were soon to find, the smiles and handshakes were glares and crossed arms.

Here, it felt spontaneous.

A Führer rally formed.

Collins climbed onto the hood of a Rover; Phil stood next to him with a megaphone. He put his hands on his hips. The showman.

There will be no more guns. No more guns!

A moment passed as Phil translated this, and his Arabic had a tinny quality as it bounced from the megaphone through the large town square. A huge roar went up from the gathered. *No more guns! Good! Boosh! George Boosh!*

Collins continued. Look at your streets. Look at your village. There must be no more guns. You now live in a free Iraq.

Phil stayed a step behind, speaking rapid-fire Arabic, and when his sentence ended, a bigger roar rose. The people screamed, cheered, hugged. They held up their arms, thumbs up. This was our payoff for all the suffering we had endured for the preceding months: the looks on the faces of these beaten people in a beaten land.

———◆◆◆———

After 45 minutes in Abu Sakhr, we pushed on to the much-larger city of Medinah.

The radios came alive as we drove through the scattered palm trees south of the city. The country was growing more beautiful the farther north we pushed, desolate open desert giving way to farmland through the magic of forced irrigation. The Tigris River ran parallel to our direction of travel on the right; farms spread along the road on our left. Huge palm trees stood framed in front of the rising morning sun.

Mesopotamia, Sumer: biblical land.

We traveled above the floodplain, the road elevated over the surrounding farms, and by this vantage point we could see down into the yards and homes of the peasant Iraqis. They were doing what farmers anywhere did: picking crops, fixing machinery, shooing cows wandering through the yard. Children frolicked and shouted at each other, giggling as they avoided the reprimands of their mothers who stood, head to toe in black even in their homes, and called to the little ones from their huts.

We were a large force and we were causing a commotion as we ground northward. Our massive knobby tires and huge engines made a giant noise in the morning silence, and through the filthy windshield I could see children streaming from their homes ahead, running on perpendicular paths from their huts set back from the road, desperate to get to the road and see the army going by.

The faster, bigger kids made it first, and stood almost on the tarmac, waving and cheering and jumping excitedly on bare feet. The mothers stared at us from behind the walls surrounding their homes, daring us with hard black eyes to harm their children. Not one adult lifted a hand.

The men, hard, lean and leathery, stood next to the road and on the edges of their fields, carrying the hard, heavy implements of the subsistence farmer. They mostly glared, though some waved tentatively. They were friendlier than their wives, but still had the hunted, looking-over-their-shoulders tension of the generation Saddam had conscripted, tortured, threatened, murdered.

————— •• —————

We entered Medinah as conquering heroes.

We began to slow, the crowds growing so large that they actually blocked the street. This was the first and last time I experienced what the men who liberated Paris must have felt, people pressing in from all sides, screaming and cheering. These were Shia, families on whose necks Saddam had kept a boot since 1965, and they were still afraid of him. We were the first Western army to arrive here, and the country had held its breath as we pushed out of Kuwait and over Saddam's forces.

But here was the difference: Allied boys in France had killed an invading, occupying army. *We* had killed these people's sons and brothers and countrymen, Iraqi boys, many innocent, dragooned into service. These men had been defending *their own* country.

I thought these people would be furious, viewing us as the invaders. Not so. We were liberators, bigger men who had arrived with bigger guns to throw off the Ba'athist regime and give these people back their land. Their threat was from within. We were the good guys.

The deeper we pushed into town, the larger the crowds grew. The closer the people came to us, physically, the less afraid they seemed, as if these white men with big guns and sunglasses and brown boots could ward off the evil which had held them. They were finally giving themselves over to their emotions, releasing the anguish and tensions of thirty years.

————— •• —————

This was why we had come.

We rolled off the main street through town down back roads and alleys to the east, maneuvering our way to the riverfront.

Townsfolk lined the streets in all directions, waving and cheering. Liberation Day.

———— •• ————

Just before we reached the center of town, the convoy ground to a halt. We simply could move no farther, the crowd now filling the street and pushing each other, ten deep from the sidewalk and into the street. It was like trying to drive through Times Square on New Year's Eve. People were now up and onto the vehicles, banging happily on our hood and giving thumbs-up with both hands, climbing onto the hoods of the Hummers and Rovers, screaming, crying.

Conde gave up with a grin and shut off the engine. We *all* had stupid grins on our faces.

Except Arreola. Fuck, sir, this is bad. This is bad. We can't stop like this.

Staff Sergeant, I hear you. I said. What do you propose we do? Run over somebody?

Well, no, sir, but one of these people could have a bomb.

That's true. But we came here to kick Saddam's ass, not shoot civilians. Collins is out here with us, and they have machine guns on the tops of vehicles in front of us and behind.

Conde giggled and looked over at me. I think I've got a new friend, sir. An Iraqi was hanging halfway in his window, holding Conde's hand and pumping it madly. Conde recoiled across the hump in the middle of the Hummer, toward me, and now smiled nervously, unsure what to do.

Well, get out and say hello, I told him, and I did the same. This was why we were here.

I creaked my door open, pushing the flimsy canvas outward, pushing back the crowd to clear a little space to extract myself. I made a big show of taking off my flak jacket and helmet, and leaving my rifle on the floorboards. I was completely vulnerable, notwithstanding the British machinegunners, further back in the convoy, who scowled behind sunglasses from atop their gun mounts and never took their fingers off their triggers. The crowd grew even louder, sure that I was someone important because I was sitting in the front but not driving, pleased that I wasn't there to hurt anyone.

Excited Arabic chatter bounced off the walls of the close brown buildings, echoing up and down the urban canyon in which we were now parked. As Americans do everywhere in the world, I communicated with sign language. The Iraqis were, for some reason, intrigued with my photos of Jackson taped to the windshield of the Humvee. They were fascinated with his blond hair and white skin, my towheaded little boy in the pictures.

Men approached and very deliberately went through the hand signals: pointing at their own chests, then at their children, then me, then Jackson. This is my son...that is yours? They held up fingers to show the age of their children (invariably wide-eyed and silent at these huge mysterious strangers), then raising eyebrows to me...how old is yours? I remembered this was *Arabic* numerals, perfect for going along with the Arabic language, and held up three fingers. Men whose children were also three years old were particularly delighted with this and laughed out loud.

———•••———

A man came out of the crowd and focused on my face and pushed his way to me.

I was being pressed in on all sides by hugely friendly Iraqis, all trying to hug me, hand me things, ask me to hold their child, shouting in Arabic.

The man shoved them out of the way and made his way to me, focused with intent and purpose. I got a chill looking at him, realizing that if he meant me harm, I was completely hemmed in.

But he just wanted to talk.

He kept saying, over and over, All is peaceful here. There needs to be no shooting. These people do not mean to hurt you. They only want to talk.

I said slowly and loudly where did you learn your English and he said without an accent I went to the University of Michigan.

———•••———

Walsh and his boys had dismounted and were on foot, patrolling and poking around the city. Walsh was a street cop, trained in the barrios and ghettos of Los Angeles. He could smell out things I, raised soft in the comfortable suburbs, just could not. He also had the instinct all street cops have: get out and see what is going on. Get out of your car and talk and listen and smell and think.

My radio squawked.

Sir, Sergeant Walsh.

Yeah, Glenn-Bob, go ahead.

Uh, Cruzer and I found something you may want to see, he said flatly.

OK, let me get set up and I'll be over there.

Sir, I think maybe you should come over here right now. I think this is something Colonel Collins is going to be interested in.

Hmm. Okay. We are a block or two from you now. Give a shout when you see us coming.

We extricated ourselves from our groupies and pushed forward. We rounded the last corner, turning back to the north, and I saw the Euphrates in front of me. Walsh and Cruz were right on the sidewalk, urgent looks on their faces.

I hadn't seen them in a couple of days, and was shocked at how much weight they had lost even in that short time. We had been moving twenty hours a day and it showed on them. Cruz was usually the size of an NFL linebacker, and was suffering more than the smaller (that is to say: normal-sized) guys from the diminished food supply in the field. Walsh's uniform hung on him, and his head looked like it was too big for his body. He wore the radio headset for his team and no helmet, and he had grown truly the most egregious combat mustache in world history, a thick caterpillar under his nose that he cultivated sideways and trimmed out to meet his sideburns, next to his ears. He looked like a Civil War general.

Both broke into big smiles as I told Conde to let me out.

———•••———

I hopped to the sidewalk, flak and helmet back on, pistol on my right thigh, rifle in my left hand.

Sir, you aren't going to believe this, Walsh said.

They led me another half-block towards the river. Like all Iraqis, the citizens of Medinah built huge walls around their homes, twice as high as my head, creating the feeling of a maze on the back streets and giving each family a compound. I moved from the sidewalk to the middle of the street, forcing myself to walk in the open, remembering from *Black Hawk Down* that Delta Force operators told the Rangers to keep away from the Mogadishu walls: that is where bullets tend to travel. You are actually safer in the middle of the street in an urban fight, though it is *very* hard to break the habit of hugging against something.

I had a tingling on the back of my neck, like someone was watching me or something was about to happen.

Walsh and Cruz strode off the street and turned to a large compound's gate. With an air of triumph, Walsh swung back the door and stepped inside. I followed him.

We were in a large yard, thirty meters by thirty meters, the recess area for a school. The school itself, shabby and tired and dirty, squatted at one end of the compound, overlooking the river on one side and this yard on the other.

The yard was completely covered, six feet deep, with weapons and ammunition.

Machine guns, AK series weapons, RPKs, rifles, pistols, knives, telescopic sights, and weapon parts lay in stacks against the walls. Thousands upon thousands of rounds were stacked or lined up neatly by type: mortar rounds here, artillery rounds in the corner, tens of thousands of rounds of linked machine gun ammunition, RPG grenades next to their launchers.

I had never seen anything like it. This must have been the resupply point for the Iraqi Army and Ba'ath and Fedayeen for this entire province. They could have held off a battalion with all this ordnance, had they picked it up and shot it at us.

Walsh had a gleam in his eye. See what I mean, sir?

I was stunned. Yeah, Sergeant Walsh, excellent work. I gotta tell Collins about this.

Walsh and Cruz accompanied me across the street to our headquarters building, leaving behind British soldiers to guard the ammo dump and make sure nothing walked away. We went through the huge gate, already under guard by the Irish duty company, and walked across the compound. The convoy was breaking down, soldiers stripping off sweaty flak vests and setting down weapons and comm gear, drivers checking under their hoods in the safety behind the wall.

I found Collins busily taking charge of outfitting our new home. He motioned me outside as I tried to tell him what Walsh had found, but I was babbling and stuttering and just could not get it across.

So I showed him.

I took him across the street, our little entourage growing, as it always did, with grinning soldiers just following Collins wherever he went, sure something interesting would happen.

We went back through the gate, and he gave a long, low whistle.

Bloody ammo dump, eh? he said, and walked gingerly around the rounds stacked in all directions. He paused occasionally to pick up something dark and dirty and evil. Each time he did this all of us cringed and turned away, ready for the thing to go off in his hand. This stuff had been out in the elements for god knew how long.

He poked around a bit. Shrugged. Walked back to our outpost.

I trailed him back to the compound and out to a low wall against which the vehicles were parked, and he plopped down. His driver handed him a cup of tea, and he exhaled, exhausted.

He took a sip from his cup and stared into space. Right, Stan, good work by your lads. I don't think the Iraqis will be back for it, do you?

He was right, of course. There really was no reason for me to be worked up about this. No sir, just don't want to have a nasty explosion, or have one of your boys pick something up.

There is shite strewn everywhere, he said, and all you can do is make sure the lads have the sense not to mess with things. That school is a tremendous facility for us. I will get the boys to stack that stuff away and keep an eye on it.

Stan, he said, This is what war zones are like.

———•••———

The next morning we had visitors. An older man wearing a red kaffiyeh was allowed through the Medinah compound gates, under guard, bringing with him a tiny little boy who carried a large crate on a string. In the way of those who live hardscrabble lives, this man could have been 25 or 50...there was no way to know. He appeared harmless and the British were nonplussed.

It became clear that he was simply a local merchant who had brought tea to the Ba'ath officers every day at this time. He had figured, not unreasonably, that just because the building was under new management was no reason to stop his capitalism. He was completely unafraid and walked, head high, into the lion's den.

Walsh and I joined Collins and several Royal Irish soldiers around our new friends. The boy served tea to us in the Arab way. We had no idea what to do so this little tyke held a class for us.

The tea was boiling, burning hot and very good and very sweet. The little boy poured it into a cup on a saucer, then lifted the cup, dribbled a bit of tea onto the saucer itself, and drank from the saucer.

The big tough western warriors, three times his size in our flak jackets and boots, surrounded this little boy who came up to our waists and watched carefully and imitated him. The tea, nearly boiling when served, cooled rapidly on the saucer and was perfect to drink at that moment. Ah. Maybe we don't know everything, after all.

———•••———

8 APRIL 2003 ▶ AFTERNOON
MEDINAH, IRAQ

We all trooped inside to check out our new home.

There was no mistaking the raw anger and vengeance with which the townsfolk had destroyed this building.

This had been the headquarters for the local gendarmerie, and this structure therefore stood for everything the locals hated about Saddam and the Ba'ath thugs he foisted upon these people. It was filthy and destroyed, like every single thing we had seen in Iraq.

I knew what had happened.

The Americans had gone over the border, routing all in their path... the Hitlerite call had come from Baghdad for all to stand and fight to the death...local forces had gone out and had been destroyed, or had abandoned their mates and fled...the Ba'ath honchos had realized the jig was up and took off as well...and then, like a sea of ants, the people of Medinah had flowed over the walls and through the gates and systematically taken this building to pieces.

They had stolen or broken every single thing in the structure.

They had ripped phone cords out of the walls and wiring from the sockets and metal doorframes from the wood.

They had taken every photo of their fearless leader from the walls and broken the glass and torn the picture in half.

They had thrown those photos of Saddam on the floor.

They had then systematically shit on every one of those photos.

They had then shit in every square foot of every room, pissed on the walls, pissed on the floor, and broken every window on all four sides of the building.

Not one single thing was in its original state.

There was not one clean square inch anywhere.

There was not one spot you could put a boot down and touch bare floor.

There was not one place you could stand and draw a deep breath without sucking in stench and shit and filth and rot and dust and dirt and shit and urine and anger and revenge and fear.

Brian and I put our teams on the roof.

With nothing else to do, I joined all the boys sitting on a wall: another day, another homeless encampment. There were ten or twelve of us, grown men, all just staring into space, refugees, stateless, hobos, our worldly possessions in dirty piles around us. Coffee and tea brewed on little cookstoves, and a few guys nibbled on cookies from their ration packs. We all just sat, absorbing our new surroundings.

I hadn't had one full minute to relax when Richard marched out of the building. He passed me on the way to his wagon.

Right, mate, let's go. Are you ready? he said to me. As always, he was squared away and ready, carrying maps and frequency lists and about five steps ahead of me. Everything about him was discipline and order and he cooked off energy just standing there.

I must have looked startled. Ready for what? I truly didn't know what he was talking about.

He looked at me like I was an idiot. We are headed north. Commander's reconnaissance, airfield takedown at Qalat Sikar. Did Tim not tell you?

No, Collins didn't fucking tell me. No one told me anything. I jumped up and, as usual, chased along behind the rest of the staff, who all, as usual, seemed to know more than I did.

I was so far behind the curve that I couldn't even take Marines with me. I had barely time to grab my map and gear before the staff poured out of the CP, piling into the back of vehicles. I shanghaied a space with Richard, smashed into the back of Andrew's Rover, and we were off.

We drove north, honking and weaving our way through the ever-present swarm of cheerful urchins in the road. We veered off the paved road and began to follow dirt roads, concave tracks worn into the tops of the levees. We were in the land of the Marsh Arabs, and these levees were the sophisticated, brilliant system these people had used over thousands of years to maximize the sparse water available into irrigation canals.

The roads were quite good but punctuated by spine-compressing ruts and ditches running perpendicular to our route of travel, and several times our vehicle simply launched into space and then slammed down, clawing for purchase on ground that had been mostly washed away. Survival for the Marine Cobra pilot and ANGLICO officer and gentleman smashed in the back meant holding your butt off of the seat, supporting yourself with feet wedged against the vehicle frame and hanging like a monkey on the roll bar overhead. It was a highly undignified way to travel.

We slid off the elevated roads and down onto the desert floor, tacking north and west toward Qalat Sikar. I understood the need for a leaders' reconnaissance, but one OP would have no trouble seeing this herd of vehicles coming toward him, engines roaring and gears crashing, throwing dust thirty feet into the air. I simply didn't understand what we were doing or why we were doing it, but as usual the British brigade staff was throwing things together at the last minute. If we were really doing an airfield takedown, they were going to need a hell of a lot of air, and that meant me.

We slowed and our little samba line contracted. We took one final hard turn to the right, driving along the base of a huge berm running east-west, providing a perfect place to hide our vehicles and us.

The company commanders clustered around Collins, hands on hips, alert and engaged. He outlined quickly what he had in mind: This will be our LOD, we will move two companies up and keep one back, manpack all radios and carry only weapons and ammo. Right, let's have a look.

Just like in the movies, we crawled up the sandy slope, hands and knees, to look at the airfield. Everyone stopped a foot short of the top, pulling out maps and binoculars. One at a time, officers very slowly raised their heads until their eyes were just over the top, slowly raising their binos to get a view of the target.

I lay next to Mike Murdock. He slid down the hill a foot or two and then raised to his knees, still below the crest of our little berm, and slowly straightened to see for himself. Ay...right...yep, I see it...hmmmm... he mumbled quietly in his thick accent, then slowly coiled back down and handed his glasses to me.

Yeah, good target there. This will be quite an event, eh? he said with a grin.

I took the glasses and wormed my way to the top. I hiked myself to my elbows and had a look.

———•••———

You have got to be fucking kidding.

———•••———

The airfield, the objective of the attack, was a cluster of trees almost four kilometers away.

Two and a half miles.

Between where we lay and the cluster was nothing: no high ground, no cover, no concealment, no vegetation. *Nothing.* There were some very small dips and cuts in the ground where flash floods had cut serpentine streambeds, providing what infantry officers call microterrain. Maybe twelve inches of dirt suitable for hiding a man or two from direct fire. But that was it.

Fucking Brigade. Fucking goddamn staff officer idiots.

This was perhaps the stupidest idea I had heard in my Marine Corps career. They were going to put several hundred men out on this open ground, have them run, in searing heat in flak jackets, and attack what we could only assume was a reinforced position. In broad daylight. There was no plan for air support, no artillery coverage, nothing. I had a very sharp image of myself, radio on my back, sprinting alongside Collins across the sand. It was Pickett's charge. If any Iraqis were left, they would wipe us out wholesale.

And besides, I couldn't see anything. Everyone else was whispering and saying sage, knowing infantry things, but I saw not one sign of any bad guys. There was a little cluster of trees. That was it. No vehicles, no antennas, no people. Nothing.

I slid back down the berm, badly shaken. I just couldn't understand any way in which this could work, unless the Iraqis were gone. And in that case, why do it in the first place? We all slithered back to the bottom of our berm and gathered.

Richard smiled at me. Bet you are wishing you had taken an M-16, eh? That AK is going to be worth shite at these distances. And there won't be any more ammo, either.

He was right, but I wasn't in the mood.

This is fucking stupid, I snapped. Do you think this is a good idea?

He was unflappable as ever. No, mate, but guess we will make it work, eh?

No, Richard, we won't, I snarled. I can't believe Brigade wants us to do this. You never, *never* send men downrange when you can send steel instead.

Yeah, well, we are doing it, so get ready.

I walked back to the vehicle, tense and angry. I talked to myself: OK, tough guy, now what?

I was at a decision point. I *had to* assume that there were whole battalions of Iraqis dug in out there, somewhere, ready for us and surrounded by mines and machine guns and artillery pre-planned targets. This was a bad, dangerous idea, and it was going to get people killed. It was my duty to tell my commander what I thought.

Brigade wants to do this? I thought. Fine. I want wall-to-wall air for half a day before the first man steps out from behind cover.

My mind flipped and rolled, creating and discarding scenarios in which I could talk Collins out of this. At the least, I could convince him to do it at night, and to give me the day to line up aircraft overhead, loaded with bombs and missiles.

I sat in the back of Andrew's vehicle, fuming and unhappy. Officers swung into the vehicles and engines coughed to life.

Andrew sat in the left seat and we backed and filled and backed and filled and turned around on our little dirt road. His radio crackled, something unintelligible, and he snatched it up. He turned to us.

Never mind, lads, he said in his beautiful, clipped London accent. Attack is off.

---

9 APRIL 2003 ▶ MEDINAH HOUSE, IRAQ

Iraqis began to cluster on the levee in front of the compound.

This levee was a twenty-foot berm, obviously put there to keep out the Euphrates if it flooded, and even as I watched the British engineers had their huge bulldozers out, pushing more dirt on top of it to give us some protection. Armies love dirt: they live in it, hide behind it, sculpt it to their needs, bury themselves in it. The Irish needed a bigger barrier between them and the townspeople, so they built one, just like that.

A lone British soldier was standing at the edge of the berm, shouting at the Iraqis to move so the engineers could work. Bugger off! Fuck off, all of you! he shouted at the uncomprehending Arabs, flinging his left arm in a backhanded arc, his right hand on the barrel of his rifle, finger on the trigger.

He was alone out there, and there were probably 300 Iraqis trying to get past him. The Iraqis couldn't understand a word of his commands but could not mistake the tone. They backed away like buzzards hopping warily away from a kill when a bigger creature arrives, but staying just far enough away to avoid being yelled at (or, perhaps, shot) while still watching what was going on. They hadn't had this much excitement in years.

———•••———

Lionel Trilling said that the poet writes out of some mutilation he has suffered. He writes out of the darkness of spirit or not at all.

———•••———

Shark

It is in the travel that we reach our full flower
Movement itself
Drawing us out of their world and back to the one
With which we are familiar, the one in which
The internal combustion engine makes us

Dominant, not just of that place and
This time but of all places and all times
We are
Driven, driving, our machines make us whole
So it is in that momentum that we are actualized masters
Without it we are right back down on foot
With the goddamn savages

Slow, slower, stopped
We could stay here but we sure as hell aren't going to *live* here,
Who could live here? Why would you?
Can't get to where we need to be
Not just slow, but slower than they, relative slow
Less used to the land
Unaccustomed to the space and the light
The time from one point to the next
So we are not just not dominant

We are inferior, weighed down with gear
Impedimenta of all of us who have been through
Renaissance and Enlightenment
Those who came out of the Dark Ages and
Became whole, if we don't have our machines
We have slid back in time and we may as well
Just fight with hands and clubs
Even then we would probably lose because we
Don't live in sand, we are concrete people with hard souls
The people tell us many of their number have never been even
        out of this village
        or over those mountains
Sidelit in sunset, shadows sharp parallel
Ridgeline and treeline barriers
While I on the other hand could speak into this radio right

Goddamn now and we would be
Standing in O'Hare
Tomorrow afternoon
In the same clothes we stand up in
We are not supplying the shooters
We are supplying the targets

———•••———

We had Sarah, and a second woman.

Our battalion roster had one doctor and one woman. They were the same person.

She was a tiny young British Army medical officer, the battalion surgeon. They just could not find uniforms to fit someone that small, so she made do swimming in her clothes.

The only bush hat they could find for her was several sizes too big and in it she looked like an English woman tending her garden and we all called her Daisy.

———•••———

9 APRIL 2003 ▶ MEDINAH HOUSE, IRAQ
There was a commotion at the gate.

Soldiers sprinted through the compound, calling for Daisy, while several others flung open the gate and wrestled with a large bundle. The bundle turned out to be an Iraqi, badly hurt.

Daisy raced from the building and out into the courtyard, her medics right behind her. She commanded the man be carried into her makeshift surgery, a small outbuilding hard against the berm and the river.

The Iraqi moaned in agony, writhing slowly. A huge bright stain of blood seeped through his robes and pooled on the litter.

He was a Ba'ath Party member, gut-shot three times by locals up the road in Qurnah. Collins and I had worried about this, revenge killings by the oppressed populace once they realized we were here to stay. Thirty years of suffering. Payback was on.

The soldiers laid him on a wooden table and Daisy bent over him, upside down above his head as doctors do. She was working with limited equipment and in filthy surroundings, and she was simply not equipped for surgery. More important, she was not trained for it.

Daisy, like most of the young battalion surgeons in the British Army, had really just begun her training. The British Army has a different theory than ours on how to train their doctors. They use a system whereby aspiring young medical students attend an extra year of undergraduate school and then go into a residency-type program, rather than the grueling four-year med school our doctors attend before an equally grueling four-year minimum residency.

The U.S. Army and Navy send doctors to fleet units before their residencies, but after medical school; our doctors are actual MDs but have not yet chosen a specialty.

Every doctor I had worked with in the Marines had been a varsity guy: a real MD, most of them college athletes, studs who chose to live in the mud with the Marines rather than work in the safe and antiseptic environs of a hospital. They were the sorts of guys who could triage and work on multiple traumatic injuries at once: experienced combat surgeons.

Daisy was not such a doctor: *she was a second-year med student.* She had told us that she had done a short rotation in a city hospital in London and had actually only *seen* a few gunshots in her brief training. She had never actually worked on a gunshot victim.

This was not what our wounded Iraqi needed.

Brian and I watched in horror as we realized the extent of her medical care for this man: speaking soothing words and holding his hand.

Richard, equally appalled, ran to his radios to call for a medevac.

The wounded man, now unnervingly silent, was taken into the city, through the gauntlet of little kids and across the bridge to a landing zone across the river.

The British scrambled a Lynx helicopter at Richard's behest, and it landed fifteen minutes later in the clearing. We watched from our rooftop as the man was loaded aboard and secured.

The helicopter trembled and broke free of the ground and the pilot rocked the nose over, gaining speed out of ground effect and then banking hard and fast back to the south, where the coalition hospital at Shaibah could handle a case of this severity.

Daisy returned to the compound looking shaken and angry and ashamed, and she walked quickly into the building and did not look up.

———•••———

Daisy

The man's eyes were wild with pain and terrified and the snow
    white of his dishdasha was
Stained bright red, arterial blood
He had come to us because we were big and scary and armed
    and white
So we must be the men in charge
The people who would know what to do

Our doctor ran from where she was sitting in the shade as we
    laid him on a table in the
Filthy dispensary / operating room / living quarters
Where she did her work
He lay flat and still as the stain spread

She was a new doctor, sweet girl adrift in a sea
Of filthy violent men
She had the same gear as the rest of the lads, and the desert hat
    they gave her was the smallest they could find though
    still far too big, so rather than like a soldier
She looked an English lady working in her garden
We all called her Daisy

Daisy was at his head, upside down to him, speaking soft female
    words in a language he did not understand

Rather than using the tools of modern medicine to combat the
    tools of modern war
She simply spoke to him
Helpless, she had never seen a gunshot before
We had come to him with violence and now he came to us
In the most vulnerable moment of his life

Daisy spoke to him, a low soothing British accent

Of all the people in the battalion not one could help him
We could kill but we could not heal

---

10 APRIL 2003 ▶ MEDINAH HOUSE, IRAQ
Walsh had an inch and took a mile.

He sidled up to me and Brian and we sat on the low wall in front of the CP, drowsy, bored.

Hey, sir, got a question for you, he said, a mischievous grin on his face and twinkle in his eye.

I set my paperback down and looked warily at him. Something was up.

Okay, Sergeant Walsh. What?

Uh, Carlos and I were walking around out by the river. There are a bunch of little kids, and some teenagers I guess, jumping off the bridge and swimming around. They want us to join them. What do you think?

I smiled up at him. Figured it would be something like this.

Well, Sergeant Walsh, you're a big boy. Do you think this is a good idea? Do you have any idea how polluted that river is? Not only do the Iraqis shit in it and wash clothes in it, but there are chemical plants up north that dump all their hazardous waste into it. It is one of the filthiest rivers in the world.

Just at that moment, as if I had cued it up myself, an Iraqi walked down to the river's edge thirty feet away, hiked up his man-dress, squatted, and shit into the water.

I pointed, triumphant, to this perfect illustration of why this was a terrible idea.

Walsh was undeterred.

Yes sir, I know. But only once in your life do you get to swim in the Euphrates River. Just thought I would ask. He looked crest-fallen, like a little kid forced to practice the piano while his friends played outside.

Goddamn it.

I softened.

All right. But here is what you will do. You and Carlos, *only*, will go up there and do that.

First, I want to see an Iraqi your size jump off, in case there is something unpleasant underwater.

Second, you will jump off *one time*, swim to the shore, and then right back in here.

Third, for fuck's sake don't let Collins see you...he will kill us both.

All right, sir! No worries! he said, brightening, released from piano practice.

Last thing, I said. When you come back in here, you guys are both going to take a Cipro, right in front of me. You fucking knuckleheads, I finished.

Cipro would protect them from the basic filth of the river. Anything else truly nasty wouldn't manifest for weeks, if at all.

 Yes, sir! he said, now cheered up, piano practice forgotten. He ran off to find Lopez.

Sure enough, he and Lopez emerged moments later, wearing only green shirts and shorts and boots, carrying towels and rifles. Several Marines, armed, went with them, to watch and protect them. Collins would have –should have—relieved me on the spot had he seen how I was allowing these guys to go over the wall.

They checked out with me and went through the gate and over the berm, out to the river.

Little kids swarmed them immediately, dozens of them, thrilled that some of the Americans were going to come play with them. Lopez and Walsh joked and talked with the little ones, their faces bright and engaged. Well, this was why we came here. Hearts and minds. Fuck Tony Blair's rules.

They walked in front of the berm down to the bridge, then climbed the short, steep hill next to it up onto the pavement. The crowd around them grew, kids hopping and dancing alongside my Marines, running in the funny sideways way little kids do.

A few munchkins bolted from the crowd, legs pumping, running furiously back down off of the bridge to roust their friends to come see the show. A larger number, rousted, flowed back up onto the bridge.

Brian shook his head slowly next to me as we stood and watched. I can't believe it, he said. This is really not a good idea.

He was right, of course, but what the hell.

Walsh and Lopez strode to the apex of the bridge.

Walsh was first. Of course.

He walked to the railing and handed his rifle to Carlos.

Walsh stood on the cement support for the bridge guardrail, fifty feet up, and with a flourish took off his skivvy shirt. He waved it in circles over his head like a stripper.

The kids, hundreds of them, cheered and howled and shrieked with excitement.

Walsh now stepped over the railing, his toes on the edge of the cement, five stories above the Euphrates. Like all of ours, the sunburn on his arms stopped abruptly at mid-bicep, with pasty white flesh above. His ribs stuck out from his frame and he still had on his boots and his shorts and nothing else.

More kids flowed up the bridge from Medinah itself, running for all they were worth so as not to miss whatever was about to happen.

The screaming and laughing hit a fever pitch.

Sergeant Glenn Walsh, United States Marines, Los Angeles Sheriff's Deputy, showman, gathered himself, bent his knees, and with a yell leapt into the Euphrates.

As he fell, I closed my eyes.

I conjured up a sunken, rusting tank or truck or something horrible five feet underwater, all sharp edges and twisted, tetanus-causing spikes of steel. I thought of compound fractures and tetanus and spinal cord injuries and about how I was going to explain this. I had a mental image of myself in my formal uniform, sitting rigidly in a chair in front of a panel of stern, balding senior officers, all of whom would ask me why I had thought this was a good idea and *specifically approved it.*

Walsh's slammed in, a cannon of water.

His head popped up in the river, leading to another eruption of cheers from above.

He waved to his new fan club, and stroked to shore.

More kids, in a frenzy of exuberance, ran downhill away from the center and began leaping from farther down the bridge, closer to the water. This was more excitement than they had had in years.

Lopez, always quieter than Walsh, nonetheless had a huge grin on his face as he stepped over the railing, took off his shirt to more great cheers, and leapt without ado into the filthy polluted foul dank dark water below.

The two Marines gathered on shore, retrieving their rifles from Lance Corporal Macis, congratulating each other.

They waded over to me in triumph. I just grinned at them as they each took their Cipro antibiotic as I had commanded.

They sloshed back into the compound, huge smiles on their faces, heroes for a day.

———•••———

The Brigadier let us off the leash.

In mid-afternoon, the British government changed its policy. Strange to be right there at the very tip of the spear when an entire nation shifts course and affects your life directly.

16th UK Air Assault Brigade called in early afternoon and passed the word to Collins: *you are authorized to proceed north of the Euphrates.* The Euphrates was serving as the boundary line between the British forces and Task Force Tarawa, the East Coast Marines who came in off the ships south of Kuwait, and this boundary was suddenly dropped. We were free to run.

Pamplona.

From a complete stasis we went to full sprint. Collins didn't need to be told twice; he had been straining at the leash to cross the Euphrates since January, and now they had unclipped him.

I ran through Medinah House, rousting first Arreola and then the two of us grabbing all the ANGLICO Marines we could find. We threw together four teams and I gave them a five-minute warning order to be ready to go.

At this point in the game, the drivers had all been around Collins enough to know what to do, and they pulled up behind Conde as tightly as they could, engines idling, Marines standing next to their doors. Conde didn't even get out of his seat and simply watched the bumper of the CO's Rover.

As usual, Collins burst from the building at a trot, stomped directly to his vehicle, and roared away without a look back or a brief of any kind. We were ready for him this time and ANGLICO roared out through the gate hot on his tail.

His Sergeant Major drove, weaving through the tight streets of Medinah, swerving around little kids who materialized to wave and cheer and proclaim Good! Boosh! Good! Boosh! and hope for a glimpse of their new heroes: Walsh and Lopez.

We stayed right on his bumper. If he hopped on the brakes, we were going to have a Keystone cops five-vehicle fender-bender. The British Rover's huge long-range low-frequency antenna, twenty feet high, clanged off of the wires strung haphazardly in the Third World way across all the streets and alleys, and I desperately hoped that antenna was grounded somehow.

Then a last quick right turn, and we were on Walsh's bridge over the Euphrates. The children and teenagers who were clustered on the bridge to look at us in our CP now swarmed onto the road to see us up close. Collins screamed at them Fuck off! All of you fuck off! and shooed them out of the way. The bright brown faces, undeterred, beamed at us as we went by, and as we cleared the thick of the crowd we accelerated. I hoped the kids around here would get used to us soon, or there was going to be an accident.

We hit the open road north of the Euphrates and the Rover opened up. The Brits for some reason felt it mandatory to drive at the absolute top speed everywhere they went, and fortunately Conde had it floored already and refused to get dropped. The Medinah 500 proceeded north.

———— •••• ————

We were heading far north of any reinforcements, running out from under the protective umbrella of artillery, and I realized that I had better do my job and get some fire support ready. Richard wouldn't be able to help: his guns were out of range. It was up to me if any bad guys got any bad ideas.

I needed a JTAR: a Joint Tactical Air Request, a formal request keeping attack jets ready, circling above me in case I ran into something. I got on the hook to Brigade, trying to at least pretend I was going through proper channels, and then immediately remembered why I usually went around them.

I got Terry on the hook. Thank god. Terry was a good man: a gentle, caring officer, a friend.

Hey, Terry! Thank god. Stan here. Dude, I need to do up a JTAR for convoy escort.

Terry responded from far to the south, nearly out of range. Hey Stan, his voice crackled faintly. What are you doing and where are you?

I explained where I was and where I was headed, and how fast we were moving.

Wait one, he said, and then went silent. Conde kept the Humvee floored. Farms whipped by.

Stan, bad news, buddy. Can't do that JTAR.

Why not? I said, my anger rising.

Well, you aren't going to like this. New rules. You can't even be *assigned* an aircraft, let alone get one to shoot for you, unless you have been shot at.

Goddamn it, Terry, I think it is a little late to start the process after we take fire, don't you? I yelled, shooting the innocent (and on my side) messenger, as usual.

Yeah, Stan, I hear you, buddy, but that's the rule. I know it sucks. I can't really do much about it from here. It came from Higher.

Higher.

The wrench in every good plan. Higher meant higher headquarters, the unspoken message being: don't blame me (I'm on your side) but we both have our hands tied by someone above us.

It really *wasn't* his fault, of course, and I wisely unkeyed the mike before I released profane intense invective in an angry stream at the windshield. I reared back and hurled the handset at the dashboard.

Weren't these the same fucking idiots who two days ago wanted us to take down Qalat Sikar? Are we here to fight a war, or what?

If we can't shoot people, then why the hell are we here?

I calmed down, called back, and apologized to Terry for yelling at him. As if his life wasn't bad enough, working eighteen-hour days in that beehive, he didn't need abuse from me.

I threw the handset back onto the radio set and fumed. Conde, nonplussed, used to my violent profanity and physical abuse of the radio, drove on in silence.

Arreola yelled over the roar of the wind from the back seat. What the fuck, sir? We can't get a plane...what are we supposed to do if we take fire?

Can't tell ya, Staff Sergeant, I yelled over my shoulder. I guess we get shot, then call, then wait an hour for the helo to get here. Of course, we will be dead and the bad guys will be in Iran by then.

That's bullshit, Scull observed, and we roared north as the shadows began to settle over Mesopotamia.

We were at that moment the farthest north of any unit of the British Army.

We roared into the center of the village of Tawal, slowing to a crawl as the people, jubilant, surrounded us in a great seething sea of joy.

They pounded on the hoods, cheering, screaming, waving, shouting Good! Boosh! Boosh! Number one! Good! Good! We poked our way through the small village center and accelerated out the other side. The battalion spread out and picked up speed.

Word about us had spread, somehow, and by the time we got to Qurnah a huge crowd had formed, waiting for us. I couldn't believe they had telephones, so how the hell did they pass the word? Cell phones, maybe? But they did, somehow, in the way poor people all over the world seem to know when something is about to happen.

Collins led us into the center of Qurnah and parked on a giant stone court in front of a massive, imposing stone building. No, not a building...my mind immediately came up with the word *edifice*, and that's what it was. A perfect example of the Early Saddam style, it looked for all the world like the Museum of Modern Art in New York. God knows what it had been, but it was most certainly part of the government. No one else had that kind of money to build something this big, or the desire to put so much effort into something so unnecessary.

I checked my GPS out of habit: grid 318335. I would need that number if anything happened.

The Irish left vehicles parked in every direction, clustering around the town square and not quite sure what was coming next. I looked to my right, across the street, and saw why Collins had stopped here.

A statue of Saddam. I smiled and shook my head.

I knew what was coming next.

————◆◆◆————

The city people were beginning to cluster and were growing by the minute into a real crowd. Collins hopped out of his seat and waded out into the sea of Iraqis. After several moments of accepting the congratulations and thanks of the locals clustered around him, he marched across the square.

They didn't know who this man was, but he was obviously in charge. They followed him in a great flood, the admiring ring around him growing quickly to a throng of over a thousand: Tim Collins, Pied Piper of Qurnah.

He strode into the street and across, and headed for the huge metal statue of Saddam. Somehow, there was electricity here, not only the emotional kind but the actual kind, and the streetlights came on as dusk rolled in.

The mustachioed, lean Benevolent Leader, fifteen feet tall, stood on a cement pedestal about four feet high, one arm raised to the sky. The villagers, swelling into the thousands, went into paroxysms of joy and celebration, dancing, ululating, raising their arms, cheering.

Collins summoned a soldier onboard a small British vehicle called an ATMP, an off-road vehicle that looked like a combat golf cart, six huge knobby wheels and a bed in back for transporting supplies back and forth. One driver sat on it and controlled it with handlebars like a motorcycle. Several British lads ran forward at Collins's behest and threw ropes over Saddam, fastening them to the buggy. With a flourish, Collins gave the order to pull the statue down.

The villagers shrieked with excitement. British soldiers and U.S. Marines with huge grins ringed the square. Little children ran back and forth in the twilight.

The soldier at the controls gunned the engine and roared ahead... flew forward...and nothing happened. His buggy jumped onto its front wheels, slammed back to the ground, and stopped dead. The kid backed up a few feet, gunned the throttle and released the clutch...shot forward...slammed down...stopped dead again. The crowd murmured, confused, and quieted.

Collins leapt into action and summoned a Rover. The Brits quickly switched vehicles and hooked up the much-heavier truck to poor old Saddam.

The crowd noise swelled again as the driver revved his engine. He popped the clutch and roared down the sidewalk.

With a huge crack, the statue began to lean, lean, lean...and then with a squalling ripping metal sound creaked over, facedown on the pavement.

The Iraqis went into a frenzy. They streamed over and around the fence circling the square. Men climbed on the statue and removed their shoes, beating them against the last vestige of their departed dictator. Even showing the bottom of your foot to an Arab shows disrespect, and beating something with a shoe was considered the ultimate insult. Some were laughing, some were crying, all were screaming, caught in a huge surf of emotion and pent-up aggression. They had been oppressed for so long, and this was all the revenge they would get.

If only Dick Cheney could see this.

Collins smiled broadly and posed for pictures with the now-prone Saddam. Always the showman. It was now completely dark, and time for us to move.

The infantrymen, now stepping lighter and smiling more broadly with the boost in spirits, piled back into their trucks and Rovers and Pinzgauer vehicles. I expected to continue north, but in the mysterious and silly way that staff officers decide things we were... sent back to Medinah.

The combat snake turned itself about and we slithered through the square and wound our way back the way we had come. In the gloaming we followed the crude oil pipeline next to the highway and it whickered past, south. Villagers in small furtive groups out in the hinterlands pounded on that pipeline with hammers and chisels, knowing one inch away was the fuel that ran their world. We westerners ignored them and flew fast the wrong way, past farms now dark and quiet and uninterested, buttoned against the night.

———•••———

The next day, the sun set quickly, dropping from the sky and leaving its heat behind. We all chatted quietly in little groups, when Collins got the word to move back out, north again, back to Qurnah.

As usual, he got the call over the radio and sprang into action, gathering up his key staff and rushing outside. I was now a seasoned veteran of these moves, and I was one step ahead of him, sending Arreola to grab team leaders and get them ready. ANGLICO was lined up and ready to go, engines idling, when Collins charged out of the CP, threw his bergen into the command Rover, and roared off. We raced through the dark, zooming through the town square where Saddam fell the night before, and pushed past it and on to the center of Qurnah.

We pulled up at the site the Royal Irish staff had chosen as most likely to hold all of us: a riverfront hotel. The Hotel Qurnah had a huge wraparound deck in the rear, bordered to the north by the Tigris and to the east by the Euphrates. It was a beautiful spot. But this was not to be a pleasant evening.

We stood around for a few minutes, waiting for someone to tell us what to do. Sid, a novice in the Keep Up With Collins game, was wide-eyed. Geez, he said in his Tom Sawyer way, still in shock. Do things always happen that fast with the command group? We were still swallowing our chow when you guys pulled out. I assured him that it was always like this, and we just had to hold on tight to the tail of the tiger.

————— •••• —————

We stood on a city street hard against the Tigris. Across from the hotel stood, of course, the Ba'ath Party headquarters building. It was, again and of course, abandoned.

Arreola stood in the middle of the street, hands on his hips. He was fixated on the Iraqi flag flying above the building. He stared at it for a minute, and then stated flatly That's coming down.

He led a liberation party into the building, and moments later his head popped up on the roof, silhouetted against the rapidly-darkening sky. He untangled the lines and the flag dropped swiftly.

Collins was in a rage. I had no idea why he was so upset, but on occasion he snapped and this was one of those times. He was a dynamic, aggressive leader, and men like that snap every week or so. This is the way Collins was, simply his roaring Irish temper.

No matter the cause, tonight he was in a cold fury. He stood in front of the hotel, vehicles in a small circle around him, about twenty meters from where I stood. He sharply summoned one of our young officers, Graham Shannon, he who was the *fat little toad* the Sergeants Major had babysat when he was a baby and his father a member of I Royal Irish.

I sensed what was about to happen. I ran to the ersatz Ba'ath building and yelled up to Arreola to bring his little team down to the street: right now. Even from four stories up and in the gathering dark, Arreola could read my expression and ran back downstairs.

Arreola and I walked up to the little conclave of officers gathered in front of the hotel. Sid and Brian wisely stayed out of range.

Collins was in a complete rage.

Where the fuck is C Company? he screamed.

Poor Graham hemmed and hawed, both trying to cover for the absent Colin Marks (how do you lose an entire rifle company?) and legitimately unsure where the supporting company was. He remained respectful and almost stood at attention, taking the brunt of Collins's fury on behalf of the rest of us.

Why the fuck is C Company not where they are supposed to be? Collins roared.

He turned and unloaded on me.

Why do I have all the bloody ANGLICOs here but no infantry? He for some reason always used ANGLICO as a noun—especially when he was mad at us.

Collins was mad at officers who hadn't brought enough people, and at those who had brought too many. There was no winning with him on this night.

I stood my ground.

Sir, I knew you were moving out, and wasn't sure what we needed. I brought 'em all to be ready for anything.

We don't need all these fucking people! he screamed. We don't need every bloody ANGLICO in the fucking country here with us! He wasn't even looking at me, simply venting his free-floating rage at the closest target.

Yes, sir, I responded, my stomach tense and churning. I'll send them back right now.

I whispered for Arreola to go find Brian. Brian had anticipated this and came around the corner of the Humvee, fully aware of what was going on.

I leaned over to him. Take your team and Sid's team and go back to Medinah. I don't know what's going on but you guys don't need to be here to get yelled at. Take the map out of my Hummer. Be quiet about it.

Brian nodded quickly and hustled off, and my teams were on the road in minutes.

———•••———

My combat family stayed with Collins. Where he was, there too would the action be.

We set up for the night. We flopped down on the sidewalk across from the hotel, sleeping next to our Humvee, homeless people, winos, refugees, lying on the sidewalk with all our belongings in little piles next to us.

This turned out to be a terrible decision, as the spot where we threw ourselves down turned out to have the highest mosquito-human ratio in the Arabian Gulf, perhaps the world, and possibly in the history of the world.

We all faced the same dilemma confronted with these pests: cover up in your sleeping bag and pour sweat all night, or throw off the bag, let the breeze take sweat away from you, and endure the bites. These mosquitos lived and bred in the filthiest water imaginable, and I tried not to think of the disease they carried.

I chose to sweat.

I lay in my bivy sack, soaked, shoulder digging into the concrete, next to the right front tire of my little rolling home. It was an unknowable time, the strange twilight that could have been ten at night or four in the morning. I didn't dare look at my watch, for fear of finding out how little sleep I had had. A streetlight beat down on us, making our efforts at sleep even more feeble. There was no way it put off any heat, but it still made me feel even hotter.

My mind did lazy flips, running over issues and problems as the resting mind does.

We were in southeastern Iraq. The Euphrates River Valley.

Mesopotamia.

Sumer.

Adam.

Eve.

The Tigris ran in front of us, the Euphrates branched off to the south, and the Shaat-al-Arab intersected those two rivers. Three rivers. I was at that confluence.

My eyes snapped open, the tire rubber a foot in front of my nose snapping into focus.

Holy shit. I was in the Garden of Eden.

---

11 APRIL 2003, 0700 ▶ THE GARDEN OF EDEN

After my few snatches of sleep, I woke on the pavement, sore and hot and soaked and cranky. I didn't even make it to my feet before brewing my first cup of tea, sitting in my sad soaking wet filthy little bed, a refugee, sipping the hot, sweet liquid before the sun got too hot for me to do so. My bivy sack now had several months' worth of dirt and sweat and oil and grease on it, and was growing rapidly more unsavory. Come to think of it, so was I.

Choosing to sweat had been a Hobson's Choice. During the night, I had somehow put one hand out of my little breathing hole in my sleep. Mosquitoes coated that hand all night, and when I woke were a thick black seething fuzz. It was now swollen twice normal size, like I was wearing a thick glove made of skin. I couldn't feel it that morning and the nerves died that day. In the cold even now I cannot feel it.

The Garden of Eden is a fucking shithole.

Every little kid grows up with one idea of the Garden of Eden: paradise. Birds chirping, butterflies sketching this way and that, trees lush with fruit gleaming in the sunshine, flowers. I sat up on the pavement, grubby and sweaty and unshaven and underweight and angry and tired and sipped my tea and looked out over The Garden of Paradise.

Trash was strewn in every direction. Mosquitoes gave up on my hand and now hung heavy in the air, even at this time of morning.

Every building in every direction was slapdashed together, crumbling and broken and poorly designed and shoddily built, sketched with bullet holes, with the usual exception of the sturdy Ba'ath Party HQ on which Arreola had led last night's foray.

The entire place reeked with the typical Third World stench of cooking fires and pollution and open trash pits and human shit and dead rotting animals.

A thin fog hung over the Euphrates, the only attractive thing in view. That fog would burn off, taking the only brief artistic dash with it.

I stood up and pulled on my filthy trousers and boots. I had taken my rigger's belt all the way down, and I now cranked the Koch fitting with a full arm pull around my narrow hips. I had lost an astonishing amount of weight, to include, Sid always reminded me, my entire ass, which he insisted I had left behind somewhere in Kuwait. I could fasten my pant buttons and belt where it had been in January and without touching either I could pull my pants to my ankles.

Nothing else to do, I walked over to the hotel.

Ah. This was more like it, much more Sunday School than our hobo camp across the street. The view looking north from the wraparound deck was much nicer: smallholdings and vineyards and animals and palm trees. Waterfowl turned and swooped in the morning light, looking for the fish which ran thick in these waters. Doves fluttered quietly by, and swifts zoomed and darted and squeaked. Fish sploshed quietly in the river, feeding on the mosquitoes which coated everything; the birds fed on the fish.

Iraqis bent over their soil on the other side. The farmers' boats, dugout canoes, were moored next to their little farms, and I realized that they lived not on a peninsula, but on an island.

I looked straight down, at the bottom of the bulwark holding up the patio, and of course saw dead bloated rotting animals and piles of trash and filth. I stepped back one step and looked out again, blocking my own view from the ugly reality below, it was lovely again, and I thought about Jesus Christ.

———•••———

An interpreter.

Ali had been raised in Kuwait. I assumed he had gone up to the coalition and then been sent to 16th UK and then down to us. I had met him several days prior, and his dark skin and Arab features led me to expect the pidgin English of the Arab.

I asked him, enunciating slowly and carefully, where he was from. I expected some Arabic word for some exotic city, and he had replied Seattle.

Oh.

He turned out to be a Kuwaiti who had emigrated for school. I had the distinct impression that daddy was a wealthy businessman of some type and our new friend Ali was a dilettante.

But this dilettante had had the Iraqis kick down the door of his home in Kuwait five different times during their invasion and repression of that little state in 1990 and 1991. Ali had been taken five times and released four; the last time, he was rescued by U.S. forces. He remembered the individual soldier on whom as a boy he had imprinted during that significant emotional event—*He was very black. Very big. Very muscular. You could only see his eyes at night*—and he had sworn his love to the United States at that moment. When his country became the staging ground for *this* event, he had returned to help in whatever way he could. He was serving with us without pay, except for the only pay that mattered.

———•••———

On the television series *True Detective*, Matthew McConaughey said *The world needs bad men because we keep other bad men from the door.*

———•••———

Ali appeared now on the deck next to me and we watched an approaching boat. Collins, back to his normal cheerful self now in the light of day, waited with us.

Two men leapt from the boat in the shallow water and pulled it onto the trash-strewn beach below our little parapet. They walked quickly on a little footpath I couldn't even see, climbing the rocks quickly to our level.

They approached us, barefoot and shy, eyes downcast, subservient. Their clothes were filthy, as you would expect of those of subsistence farmers, and they were lean and brown. Their eyes were sharp, though, taking everything in. I mused that the GPS in my pocket was probably worth more than everything they owned.

Ali greeted them in soft but firm Arabic. One man, apparently the spokesman, spoke quickly, deferential and afraid. He was terrified of authority of any kind, natural for a man who had lived under Saddam.

Ali turned to Collins, speaking in bursts in the halting way that interpreters do.

This man was in the army. He has boots which were given to him by the regime. He swears that he uses them only to work in his fields. He wants to know if you will allow him to keep them.

Collins's eyes were soft and his manner gentle and warm. Yes, yes, of course, tell him that he may keep anything he has. We are not here for him.

Ali forwarded this and the man smiled. He spoke again.

His father, uncles, brothers, and nephews all also fought for the regime. They are spread throughout the country. They wish to return home. Can they come back?

Collins reassured the man that they could. The men both smiled, relieved.

He wants to be a policeman. Can he do that?

Collins said that many policemen would be needed. Of course he could serve his country in this way. The men beamed. They began to relax.

Ali spoke back and forth, Arabic to them, English to us. They told us you would bomb the country flat. They said you would kill all of us.

Collins smiled at that, and spoke directly to the men. Iraq is now free. You may do anything you wish. Saddam is not coming back.

I thought the men would hug him, but instead beamed shyly again and took their leave. I watched them paddle slowly back across the Euphrates, hoping they would live through all of this. It was for people like this that we had come.

———— •• ————

Brian and I laid claim to one of the hotel rooms: it was dank and filthy and managed to be stuffy despite windows to three rivers. It was wet and foul and broken and old and tired and decrepit and *does anything in this shit country fucking work?* like everything else in the Third World, and the windows had been fastened shut and then covered with some sort of film for god knows what reason.

We had beds, though, the first we had seen in months. We got our heads down for an hour in the heat of the afternoon. Brian followed his usual bedtime pattern: a quick read through one of his huntin' fishin' shootin' magazines, spreading of the magazine across his chest, and then drifting off to sleep flat on his back, arms at his side. My own personal corpse. I slept heavily and well.

We woke in late afternoon, and wandered into the ballroom for our first and last planning meeting for our move: north, always north, now to the city of Amarah.

As various officers presented their ideas and plans for moving the lads up, my mind wandered, bored and restless. I snuck a peek out through the sheer curtains blowing before the huge plate glass windows looking out over the Tigris. I wondered if, in this very room, Saddam's officers had planned a military event headed in the other direction. This is just the sort of place the Ba'ath thugs would have commandeered for their officers.

Late afternoon, the meeting over, we meandered out onto the patio, which really did have a gorgeous and commanding view of the water. The sun was setting and the birds and fish competed for the mosquitoes which were coming up as everything cooled off. I went back to the room and dug out a bottle of Jameson's Irish Whiskey I had secreted in my pack, and brought it and my canteen cup back outside.

———•••———

The very word whiskey is from Gaelic, meaning *water of life*, and this is indeed how the I Royal Irish officers viewed it. I splashed the water of life around to the company commanders, who had magically appeared when the whiskey came out as a cat does when the can opener starts, and I was taking my first sip when we heard the high-pitched whine of a Rover engine.

The CO's vehicle was backing onto the veranda. We all turned to watch. No one could figure out why the CO needed his wagon out here, but with Collins something interesting was always afoot.

Collins hopped out and walked around the rear of his Rover, smiling at us. A canteen cup appeared in his hand, too, as if by magic, and I splashed whiskey in for him as well. He stood back to command the show.

Ranger Lee Magowan, our young man about town, fixer, doer, seer and prognosticator and expediter of all things Collins, walked around the other side of the vehicle and opened the rear hatch.

He disappeared inside.

There was a brief scuffle and a crashing and slamming within and then Magowan reemerged. He was leading a sheep by the collar.

The sheep decided he did not want to meet us and he stood inside the vehicle, front feet braced, looking out at us, and bleated loudly and indignantly.

Collins laughed and said, Aye, he knows what is about to happen to him, eh?

I looked at the huge steel drum, cut in half, from which leapt flames from the huge and now roaring-hot fire the Sergeant Major had stoked hours before. I suddenly realized that our new four-legged friend was the banquet.

On cue, Collins withdrew his razor-sharp kukri from the scabbard at his side and led the condemned around the corner. Dead Sheep Walking. Naturally, Collins would know how to kill and skin a large animal. Of course. But I didn't need to learn, and went inside to avoid the screams to come.

That night we feasted. Our wooly departed friend made a wonderful entrée, and the Sergeant Major had scrounged vegetables from somewhere, the first fresh produce we had had in months. Whiskey appeared from packs and Rovers and cargo pockets and washed down the huge hunks of meat. Even the weather cooperated on this night, and it got so cool the boys all pulled on liners and fleece pullovers to ward off the sudden cool. Explosions erupted in the distance at regular intervals, always preceded by a crackle over the radio as the EOD lads announced their detonation of the mines and booby traps and explosives they had found.

We were fat and mellow and whiskeyed and quite pleased with ourselves when a long stream of machine gun fire arced just across the road. Tracers laced out and away from us, into the night, red streams burning out quickly in the black. I watched the straight red line, and three or four rounds ricocheted off at right angles.

I was startled, but Collins, several whiskies down by now, was nonplussed. He gazed calmly over the water at the scene.

Ah, someone is going to be unhappy about that. That was a large bone of some kind.

What the *fuck*? How did he know that?

Colin Marks's lads were on security, and Colin ran to the radio to find what had happened. Sure enough, someone had tried to get into their lines, and a gunner had shot the poor guy right through the leg. The ricochets we saw had been bullets bouncing off of his femur.

———◆◆———

There will be unpleasantness in Amarah, Collins said, flat, quiet and confident.

That is why we invaded this country. There are reports of prisoners there, held underground. One of these men escaped and they found him south of here. We are going for peacekeeping purposes, but we must also find out if this is true.

Underground Iraqi prisons. I conjured up an image of a dungeon, handcuffs bolted into the walls, rusting bars, stained concrete walls.

Wait a minute.

Prisoners?

They haven't taken any prisoners, at least none that we have heard of. A coalition POW is the sort of thing the generals would get excited about, and we would surely be there now.

If there had been American or British prisoners, it would have been *on*: we would have left no stone unturned, no house unleveled, no Iraqi soldier unkilled. There would not be one brick on top of another until we found him.

Then it dawned on me: not prisoners from this war. He was talking about prisoners from Desert Storm. *Kuwaiti* prisoners.

That was twelve years ago.

Twelve years in Iraqi prison. Jesus Christ.

15 APRIL 2003 ▶ TAX DAY
QURNAH TO AMARAH, IRAQ.

I did not file my taxes this day.

We formed the entire battalion in a huge column and floored it out of the city and into the countryside, due north. I had completely lost track of the other battalions in the 16th Air Assault. We were totally on our own, north to the fight, looking for trouble.

The country grew more beautiful, more rural and more sinister the farther north we moved.

The trek to Amarah took several hours, great sightseeing on both sides of the road. Palm trees hung over the river which tracked and followed us to our east, and families worked in the fields between their tiny compounds, tucked next to the river, and the road we now drove. The same patterns: fathers and older sons hunched over in the heat, sweating over their crops, while younger boys and girls frolicked and shouted and ran through the dust. Farm animals wandered freely, and shorebirds swooped and darted over the water. It was a lush and beautiful scene, and a reminder that though there was oil under our wheels and nasty Arab politics around us and a Wahabbi theocracy to one side of us and a Shia theocracy to the other, this was Mesopotamia, the cradle of humanity.

The closer we drew to the city, the heavier grew the population density and the worse grew the poverty and the angrier grew the people.

I could never understand why people always clustered in the filth around large cities, anywhere in the world, and with the grinding poverty here I was even more perplexed. I was not naïve enough to believe that the farmers whose land we had just passed through lived idyllic lives, any more than does a farmer in Iowa, but they certainly seemed to have a cleaner and healthier lifestyle.

As we roared closer to Amarah, the cheerful little walled compounds gave way to lean-to huts and shacks and open-walled shelters, teeming with people and surrounded by filth. The smell preceded the view, and that cloying, choking mix of cooking fires and gasoline and diesel fumes and human shit whipped on the 50-mile per hour air through the open sides of our Hummer.

The people here were different. Harder, angrier, tenser, more distrustful. Amarah was the last major city before the Shia land of the Marsh Arabs which stretched south and east, and these people had borne the brunt of Saddam's fury when they had stood up to him in 1991. Sunni thugs had exacted revenge, still reverberating, for the Shia mutiny, still simmering.

This was also about as far as the large American units had gone during Desert Storm, before they had receded back into Kuwait and left a high-water mark of hope which Saddam had quickly erased.

Through his murderous henchman Chemical Ali, Saddam had ruthlessly murdered people in this part of the country by the tens of thousands, and systematically destroyed the way of life for the rest. There was nothing here—no industry, no offices, no farms—and the irrigation which had brought life and livelihood to the north of Amarah had been incrementally destroyed.

These people had stood with us, and we had abandoned them. They remembered, and they stood on the sidewalks and street corners and against buildings, arms crossed, glowering at us.

———•••———

De rigueur for any western army, we set up shop in a soccer stadium.

The entire battalion now formed back up as one tribe and we moved in all together, the first time we had all been in one place since the night before we had crossed the border a month and a hundred years before.

Arriving was a scene from *Blackhawk Down*: Humvees and Rovers and Pinzgauers gathering speed on the surface streets, guards poised for our arrival and throwing open the barriers as we raced through, then slamming them shut behind us as hundreds of people chanted and grasped and screamed and tried to get inside.

The stadium was ringed with concentric circles: concertina and huge earthen berms and guards in mutually supporting posts facing out, and then a ring of humanity, facing in, as the Iraqis stood and paced outside and screamed in at us.

———•••———

We couldn't even shit in peace.

The Irish had dug a magnificent trench with a backhoe, a real sit-down shitter complete with a row of seats spaced evenly along wooden benches. They had covered it with a camouflage net to let us poop in comfort, and even had a little tent flap door to give some modicum of privacy.

But there were no walls, and for some reason the British put the tent right next to the fence. It was quite unnerving to drop your trousers with ten or twelve people watching you, their fingers through the fence like kids at batting practice.

At our first staff meeting, a young officer stood up to report that the people didn't like us shitting out in the open; as Muslims, they found it offensive. Collins stared at him in disbelief for a moment, and then said Well I would invite them not to fucking watch!

The slit trench was moved to the center of camp.

The younger ones, the teenagers and boys, hung on the fence itself, circling the stadium, hemming us in. They yelled in at us: Mistah! Mistah! Good! Hello! Boosh! Boosh! hoping that we would give them some food or water. It was a very unpleasant environment, and everyone avoided going too close to the wire.

It was like looking at a bear pacing in his cage, with that same uneasy feeling that if you put a hand through you would pull back a stump...except we were on the inside, and the threat lay without.

What annoyed me was the obvious dissonance between what these city men wanted and what they did.

Had they put all effort they expended in coming to the stadium to beg from us into working and building their society to what it could be, they would have been able to feed themselves.

Not one male in the cities, of any age, not one, seemed to have any work or any place to go. Their days consisted of standing on the street, complaining about us, and glaring with great macho anger when we drove by. These men had grown up under Saddam, where what they had was given to them, and the thought of actually picking up a broom or a shovel or a clipboard never seemed to have occurred to them.

———••———

Brian had been with ANGLICO attached to a Saudi unit during Desert Storm, his job to advise them in the fight. They had instead skewed his definition of the word *lazy* sharply downward.

He learned from them only two words of Arabic: the words for *maybe* and *tomorrow*.

———••———

They men in the cities were the opposites of their country cousins, who were bent over their Bronze Age agricultural impedimenta.

The women, on the other hand, held the country together.

They were shapeless ghosts, floating along the filthy streets in black robes with not an inch of skin showing. They hid from us. When we saw behind the veils it was quick and furtive, a glimpse behind the curtain: obese crones straight from *Macbeth*, hooked noses, crooked teeth, stooped backs, glares somehow both angry and resigned.

They were never at leisure. Every single woman was at work: carrying a child, carrying a load of food from the city market, carrying an immense basket on her head, sweeping with a pathetic broom made of reeds bound by twine.

The Iraqis were strange inverted images, a photo negative of one another, upside down and backwards: the enormous tense angry exhausted women hidden in black; the men who wore white, went bareheaded, hadn't worked a day in their lives and were lean as jaguars.

It made me angry.

———•••———

The Amarah soccer stadium had been destroyed just as thoroughly and intently as had every other major structure in the country. The stadium itself was still in good shape: cement seats ringing a huge playing surface on which the grass still grew green and thick. Track and field events must have been on the agenda here, also, with pole vault pits and long jump runways next to the pitch and a rubberized track around the perimeter.

But the building also had held dozens of offices, in the same way an NFL stadium in the States would have the team offices attached. All these offices were clustered on one side in a glass-fronted block, three offices high and ten across. Every single inch of the plate glass had been broken, every item inside destroyed, and the broken glass and chunks of cement littered every horizontal surface including the ground far below. The Irish set up communications centers and offices and bunkrooms in these offices, despite the lack of one wall and precipitous potential fall three stories to the concrete below.

From outside the stadium you could watch all the lads walking around at once, thirty rooms' worth of men and gear, blocked out in their strange vertical ant farm.

———•••———

We hadn't seen the operators yet, but knew they were there.

Brian and I were standing below the stadium and an American whom I had never seen before suddenly materialized. I knew immediately that he was either a SEAL or Army Special Forces, because he had The Look all those guys cultivate: long, thick hair; bushy mustache; sunburned, corded arms; washboard stomach and broad shoulders; no rank insignia; about $2000 worth of gear on his person; gorgeous, exotic weapon; top-of-the-line Oakleys worn even—no, *especially*—inside. He carried himself with the cocky air of the BMOC football star that guys from those communities affect after they complete their training, and addressed Brian and me in the same way, ignoring the oak leaves on our flak jackets which showed everyone our rank.

Hey, you the commander? he asked me.

Sir I wanted to prompt him in addressing me, but didn't.

Yeah, I answered warily instead, ignoring the hey-dude-let's-all-be-on-first-name-basis attitude these guys had when dealing with officers.

Uh, my team is downstairs. Can we ask you guys to help us out?

We trailed him down the filthy, narrow stairway to the tarmac outside the stadium, ringed with British vehicles and soldiers. Sure enough, a top-of-the-line Humvee, armored and crammed with gorgeous new comm gear, sat pointed at the front gate. A soldier sat relaxed behind a .50 caliber heavy machine gun, the barrel up in air. The other three team members gave off the same we-are -cooler-than-you-so-don't-start-your-officer-bullshit vibe, all with Oakleys and mustaches like the boss, cultivating nonchalance.

They turned out to be, indeed, Special Forces, from 5th Special Forces Group out of Fort Campbell, Kentucky. I had worked with the Army at Fort Campbell before, and Brian had actually lived with the 5th SF guys during the first Gulf War, so we spoke his language.

He turned out to be OK. His boys were headed back to their safe house in the city, and he simply wanted to make sure some Americans knew where he was in case he stepped into something he couldn't handle. Scull huddled with the SF communications guy and they promised to check in with us hourly, when possible, to keep the link up.

These guys were operating an A Team of ten men in Amarah itself and coordinating with the even blacker Americans: CIA, somewhere deep in the city. They wouldn't even tell *us* where the Agency guys were.

———◆◆———

Men grew more introspective as time drew on. We were drawing into ourselves, like monks: no women, no booze, no TV, no entertainment of any kind, living outdoors, nothing to do but think.

I started to think about balance and mental strength.

Tim Collins had a Triad for Battlefield Survival:

- Ammunition
- Water
- Energy: fitness, food and rest.

I thought of it like this:

- *Physical energy*: strength, endurance, flexibility, resilience
- *Emotional resilience*: ability to bounce back
- *Mental endurance*: focus and concentration
- *Spiritual strength*: commitment to values regardless of the circumstance

Another survival triad, which a fellow Marine wrote to me—just these words in priority order on one piece of paper—while I was at OCS:

- Water.
- Rifle.
- Boots.

———— •••• ————

One day we saw a pack of little kids going to school. *Little* kids: maybe five or six years old.

They were adorable, all of them in uniforms. The girls had free-flowing hair and bright clean white dresses and smocks beneath crisp blue tunics. Their teeth gleamed white and they chattered happily to one another.

I could not—*could not*—get my brain to make the leap from these charming gleaming little sprites to the fat, angry, toothless crones who were their mothers. Were those women once like this? Would these little girls end up like that? I couldn't understand it.

Conde said Hey sir kids going to school today, huh? I said Yeah, thanks to us.

He said No sir, *today*.

I didn't get it until I did.

Muslims. Today was Sunday.

———•••———

Hells Angel—and Marine—George Christie said that if you are going to live in an extreme culture, something different from 9-to-5 society, you will be tested all the time.

He said The Hells Angels, like the Marines, operate between the two poles of power: fear and respect.

———•••———

I have three sons now and I told them once See that guy over there, at the end of the bar, drinking a quiet beer and watching the game alone? That guy is the badass. Not the guy proclaiming how tough and strong and brave he was and is and will be.

Él *que menos habla es el más chingón.*

He who speaks least has the most power.

———•••———

I pushed our teams out and up to the Iranian border.

Five teams, five positions, spread along a Beau Geste picket line looking into Iran.

One team was my combat family, the four of us, set up on a hill with great fields of view in every direction, the highest point of land I could find. We puttered about and set up our little camp.

———•••———

Setup complete, I repaired to my camp chair.

A friend in erudition had sent me Ken Pollack's magisterial *Arabs at War*, a publisher's draft he had somehow laid hands upon and knew I would like.

I flipped it to the chapter on Iraq and skimmed idly a few pages. Until I turned to a map.

The map delineated the Iran-Iraq War, 1980 to 1988. I leaned forward and stared at it.

The center of the fighting, the locus of the pain and suffering inflicted by those two Muslim nations fighting over insufficient Shiism was now populated by ghosts.

And by us.

I looked at the map. I looked up into the mountains in Iran.

I looked back at the map.

My mouth fell open. We were right in the middle of where that war had raged. Those haunted uplands, Yorktown and Corinth and Gettysburg and St. Lo and Anzio and Bastogne and Chosin and Hue City, Katyn and My Lai, Thermopylae and Falkirk and Crecy and Corregidor, all were gathered here, gods and ghosts together where I sat alone.

A villager approached us from over the hill to our rear.

He was a shy man, old, stooped and weathered from a lifetime in the fields, wearing a red kaffiyeh and the ubiquitous white dish-dasha robe of every male in this part of the country. He talked quietly to me, sign language, gesturing back to the adobe huts from which he had come, and I realized that he was not a random villager: he was a farmer, and we were camped on his land.

He seemed calm enough and wasn't telling us to go away, though that's what I would do if four sweaty, filthy, heavily-armed Marines set up shop in my front yard.

He retreated to his little compound, and moments later reemerged over the hill with two others and trekked back up to us. These were obviously his son, a man about 40, and a grandson, roughly 10. Like all the rural male Iraqis they were lean and strong, and the boy was handsome and clear-eyed and scrawny.

I spoke not one word of Arabic; they not a word of English. My bemused team watched as the family communicated with me, using a pantomime to tell us that they wanted us all to come for tea.

Conde and Scull demurred, so I pressed Arreola into chap-erone duty.

As usual, he started to gear up: flak, helmet, rifle, pistol....

Uh, Staff Sergeant... I began.

Sir, you don't know about these people. Could be an ambush. We're in a freaking combat zone, sir.

Staff Sergeant, I said again. Leave it. These are simple people. And it is their country,—hell, *their own land*—for fuck's sake. Bring a weapon, but for god's sake leave the safety on. If they were going to ambush us, they'd have done it already.

All right, sir, he said, exasperated. *Stupid officers.*

We followed our new friends back to the compound, a set of four buildings surrounded by a mud wall in a small bowl in the hills. These were subsistence farmers, no different from the rural poor anywhere people drag an existence out of arid soil. Neatly raked fields lay fallow in the heat, a few spindly stalks sticking out at odd angles here and there.

I got a brief chill. When we walked over the top of the hill and down into the bowl Conde and Scull dropped out of sight on the other side.

Arreola and I were indeed alone, and if a roomful of bad guys was waiting for us no one would know about it until it was too late. My mind's eye saw poor Conde in his Alphas at the hearing, saying to the investigating officer *Yes, sir. They just walked off with those people. Staff Sergeant Arreola even tried to bring a flak and helmet, but Major Coerr acted like that was a stupid idea. Yes, sir, the Major wanted them to go unarmed. No, sir, I don't know why. They only had that one weapon between them. Then Staff Sergeant Scull and I heard the shots...*

———— •••• ————

The elderly man led us to an outbuilding, a one-room mud hut. De rigueur for the Third World, chickens scratched in the dirt and scattered, squawking and irritated, as we walked through.

The men, including the little boy, sat in a circle on a beautiful Persian rug. Arreola and I, city mice, plopped right down on the rug with our boots on, committing a grievous faux pas right off the bat.

The boy brought a large bowl of water and he insisted on washing our hands and feet for us over our vehement protests. Arreola and I, properly cleansed, sat on mats facing them.

Like all people thrown together without a common language, we primarily communicated in analogies and pantomime. The men talked to us in Arabic and we spoke to them in English, and both sides talked louder as if that might help with the communication.

They also spoke French. How in god's name did they know French? Arreola, fluent in Spanish, actually understood them far better than I.

I thought about this little hut, and this little compound.

Just outside the door the Iran-Iraq war had raged for more than eight years. Over *one million men* had been killed in that war ending fifteen years earlier. It had lurched back and forth across the border, within sight of where we sat. Had this old man given a son to that war? Had this middle-aged man fought in it? Did this family fall asleep at night to the sounds of jets overhead and artillery roaring in the distance? Were we the second? Third? Fourth? army that had set up on their land?

A tray appeared in the doorway. Not a person carrying a tray. A tray, hovering a few feet off the ground in disembodied hands. The mother of the family was standing outside, a ghost in black, holding the tray for the men to take, not even able to set foot in the room. I saw only her hands and black cloth before she disappeared behind the wall.

The tea was burning hot and delicious. The middle-aged man served it in tiny cups with huge helpings of sugar. I drank mine in the Arab way, a veteran now, pouring it into the saucer and drinking from that. The large, heavy silver tray (where did these people get a solid silver tray?) had challah bread arrayed in a semicircle, huge flat disks with an egg and oil and salt in the middle of each.

The tray had a bowl of meat in the middle, and Arreola and I dug in. Goat meat, probably...at least I sure hoped it was. I hadn't seen any dogs in a while.

The small door darkened and a baby camel, five feet high and maybe four months old, poked his nose inside, drawn by the smell of the meat. The boy shooed him away.

The men insisted that we drink water at the end of the meal... room temperature water, in a bowl. We came up with reasons why we couldn't do that.

Grandpa then pulled out cigarettes and insisted that we all have a smoke. I had smoked maybe ten cigarettes in my life, but hell, I was from Winston-Salem, and besides, this was foreign relations. I fired one up and made Arreola do the same.

We spent another hour smoking, drinking tea, and conversing in the clumsy way people do when they truly don't know a word of one single sentence of the other's language. For some reason these people knew maybe four words, including the names of George Bush and Jacques Chirac, four more words than Arreola and I knew in Arabic, and that was a starting point.

Tomorrow: hands went up into the air then down again...the sun rising and falling.

Good. America. Sometimes those two words together.

The boy was voluble and happy. I guessed he was 10 or 11 years old, but he turned out to be 14. As was typical in countries without proper nutrition, he was small for his age. He told us in pantomime that under Saddam books were closed...hands open as if in prayer and then snapping closed. That meant that either Saddam had not wanted the Shia villagers to be educated (and perhaps, one day, to stand up to him) or that these kids had had the ultimate snow day, with school out until the war ended.

We of course ended up on everyone's favorite topic: Saddam.

Arreola and I swept our hands around, raised our eyebrows quizzically. Did they perhaps know where he was? No luck.

The middle-aged man leaned forward to me, very intent on looking me right in the eye, and wiped his hands as if ridding himself of something unpleasant.

He then had a question for us. He raised his eyebrows and ran his finger across his throat...*have you people killed Saddam yet?* Arreola and I shook our heads. He was disappointed, shaking his head with the subtext obvious: no? So why the fuck are you guys here?

They pointed to the decorations in the room, pieces of paper torn from magazines. Incongruously, they were quite proud of the photograph of a ski resort in the Alps.

One piece of paper was a yellowed, tattered painting of three men, with the middle one a holy man of some sort, a man with a beard and a gentle expression emerging from a rising sun. Jesus! No, of course it wouldn't be, in a Muslim home. God? Mohammed? Allah? (*Are God and Allah the same person? I should have paid more attention sophomore year...*)

The men repeated over and over: Messie. Messie. Messie. Arreola and I were flummoxed. Was this a picture of Saddam? I went to Duke and Harvard, for god's sake....yet my liberal education failed me.

I finally realized: The *Messiah*. Of course.

Arreola and I finally took our leave. The men were concerned Scull and Conde may have grown faint while waiting for us, so over our protests these hand-to-mouth farmers pressed the rest of the bread into our hands. We walked back over the hill to our little camp and our different world and our different century.

———•••———

Each team got a day off: all the way back to Camp Commando.

The platoon staff gathered us and the three team commanders drew cards. I drew low card: last man. Fine with me. We had been months in the field...each extra day would just make hot showers that much better.

We drove down on a Sunday morning, a six-hour commute from Iran. We roared down the highway, a convoy of five vehicles, my entire team back together: Qurnah, Medinah, Basrah to Safwan, where we would cross the border back into Kuwait.

Saddam was a tyrant but he sure could build a good interstate, and we made good time. The trip north that had taken us four weeks, from the morning we crossed into the war zone up to the Iranian border, was four hours the other way at top speed.

As we headed south continuous convoys of logistics streamed north, towards us, huge flatbeds carrying vehicles and parts and fuel and, mostly, bottled water. I read somewhere that up to 80% of the supply chain in Iraq was water alone, and judging by the uncountable thousands of pallets heading to the war it had to be true. Lots of Army trucks, dark green and too clean, obviously right off the ships and heading to The Show.

Arreola watched the endless trucks grinding north and yelled happily from the back seat Right on, sir! Army! Bring 'em on and let's go home!

———•••———

Safwan was a tiny town on the Iraq side of the border, and like many other shitty towns of the Juarez variety it was important only as a border crossing, with the major north-south highway running right through it. We had not come through Safwan during the invasion, and I wasn't sure what to expect.

Bob Bruce had had a GPS stolen right off his dashboard on a trip through here, so I warned everyone to put important stuff down on the floorboards. We had heard rumors of ambushes and shootings, so we were prepared for anything. We zoomed along now due south, and Safwan Hill hove into view off our right shoulders.

The huge, beautiful highway inexplicably slammed into the city and stopped, our route out of the country suddenly leading through winding streets and intersections. Arreola locked and loaded his weapon and even the laconic Scull looked a little tenser than usual. I directed Conde to keep his speed up and fuck the stop signs; no one would argue with armed Americans.

The rumors were true. The glares and crossed arms which we had only seen far to the north were reflected here. I wondered if Mattis, who had ordered Safwan Hill *a foot shorter* before he took the division across the border, had thereby turned these people against us.

The closer we got to the border the closer the children got to our Hummer, running into the street and singing, chanting, and begging at the windows. Conde had no choice but to slow to a crawl.

Little hands scrabbled inside the vehicle, reaching through the open windows and grabbing at our sleeves. Some even ran between the moving vehicles, falling into our little convoy and wrestling with the latches on our tailgates, trying to open them and steal whatever we had. Arreola and Scull started to yell at the urchins, who seemed to grow bolder as they swarmed the street. This was turning bad.

I radioed back that no one should stop for any reason; if we got surrounded we were in serious trouble. Conde laid on the horn and kept rolling, while Scull screamed at the little faces Fuck off! Back the fuck off, you little fuckers! This wasn't the cheerful greeting in the streets of Qurnah or Medinah or Abu Sakhr or Tawal. This was a grabbing, angry frenzy.

The U.S. Army guards at the border saw us coming. They had seen this before and they waved us through, swinging their arms to hurry us up, slamming the barriers behind us.

We accelerated past them and into Kuwait, and it was suddenly quiet. I pulled everyone to the side of the road for inventory: nothing was missing, but the boys were wide-eyed and shaken.

———◆••———

Ernest Hemingway as he moved with the invasion force into occupied France in 1944 said We all seemed for the moment like minor gods.

———◆••———

We rolled into Commando late in the afternoon.

Walsh volunteered to be the first vehicle watch so the rest of us could go eat. We lined up the five Humvees right in front of the chow hall.

The tiny chow tents of eight weeks before were gone, replaced by a massive circus tent surrounded by concertina wire. Concertina. *Who in the fuck is going to try to take over a chow tent? Seriously?*

The twenty of us stood gaping at it, country cousins in the big city for the first time. We couldn't even figure out how to get inside, and had to wait for a Marine to walk by to follow him.

I only wished there had been a record playing so it could have scratched to a stop.

———◆••———

When we got inside, everyone, *everyone*, maybe 400 people, stopped their conversations, some with forks in midair, and stared at us.

———◆••———

I hadn't realized how we looked. None of us had showered in memory: the last wash we had had was from the fire hydrant we cracked open in Ramaylah. All of us had several weeks' growth of beard. We had sweated through our blouses so many times that white circles of salt were caked around our armpits and across our backs. In the places where flak jackets or cartridge belts rode against our bodies the uniform cloth had been buffed white, giving us a strange, mottled appearance.

Half of my scruffy little team had mustaches to go with the beards, including me. Most of us, including me, wore knives or kukris on our belts. I suddenly realized that none of us, including me, wore any rank. Each man was at least twenty pounds underweight. We smelled like farm animals, though none of us could smell ourselves anymore. All of us had deep suntans, except where our wraparound sunglasses had left white stripes from the corners of our eyes straight back to our ears.

But it was more than our appearance.

As we moved to the stack of trays at the beginning of the chow line, eyes following us, I had the distinct feeling of being the college football hero back visiting his high school, or the local girl who made it big in Hollywood, back to her little hometown.

I was struck with the look in the eyes of these Marines, who had been stuck in the rear while we all went over the border under fire. *Envy.*

Each of us carried himself a little straighter and with a toughened nonchalance that was not affected and that we didn't even notice. Our youngest Lance Corporal was suddenly a hero to these folks who only knew about the war from the radios and computers and CNN.

Sid had been back for briefs a month earlier and told me that these Camp Commando Marines were coming up to him, ten or twelve a day, and begging him to take them over the border with him, *just once*, just so they could say they had been in Iraq.

Looking at them looking at us, it made sense.

They were over here, but they hadn't *been there*.

And we had.

Next

To eat a peach
To safe the storm
A step beyond our peoples' norm
To return myself in all my pieces

Pulled to pieces
Three piece, four
Looking out, beyond your door

Thinking here and being there
Not here, not ere
Ere the long begotten stream of

Strain and strife that young men dream of
Not once never lost our nerve
To swerve
Away from you

To this, to us, to
Me and you and I were then

You knew me then but knew not how

You heard the vow
I wasn't then what I am now

Me and mine pinned, under glass
Dust to dust and
Ash to ash
Not dust but earth
Beyond the sash

Told but once and forward hence
Forced to see the difference

To tell him and them and me and her
To aver
Then to part while
Close at hand
Out of reach, this foreign land
Beyond the sash a step too far
Sash to yard beyond this table
Not all I had
What I was able

———•••———

I didn't even need a map. Conde didn't either. We didn't speak. Conde wordlessly guided us—clean, shaven, hair freshly cut, uniforms washed, rested—from northern Kuwait right back to our camp in Amarah.

I had even made Walsh shave off the Civil War beard, though it was truly magnificent. We were in the military again.

Fuel. A mission order. Do not pass go. Proceed straight to the Iranian border.

The mission order was simple: keep the bad guys out. Oh, and also: keep the bad guys in.

Wait. What? We are right out here in the middle of the Iran-Iraq struggle, literally on the same ground where one million men died over eight years, and you want us to keep them apart?

Yep. Keep the Iranians from coming into this fight. And keep the Ba'ath Party assholes from escaping the other direction.

I knew a perfunctory order when I heard one. Whatever. We rolled out as late afternoon stretched itself across the desert, the mass and weight of the Marine Corps in Commando just this morning fading into memory, us now light and alone, minor gods no longer.

I dispersed my 25 men onto the border itself, facing out, across what should have been the frontage of a reinforced battalion of at least 1000 Marines. Our five little teams were covering a conflicted international border.

Everyone in my little team, my combat family, went quietly about his job, old ladies set in our ways, setting up antennas, throwing out camo nets, brushing teeth and pulling on watch caps and charging radio batteries for the night. The four of us were secure in each other, old hens going wordlessly about our daily routine. We were very quiet, as quiet as we had been since we left California, not depressed but calm and resigned to our lives alone out in the wasteland. We could still taste the hot food and coffee from Commando, now far away into our past.

———•••———

Brian's team joined us.

Brian and I repaired to our campstools with the last of the Bushmills. We looked out at the moon and solved the world's problems and bitched genially about our station in life, and before I knew it I was lying on cold ground and thinking wistfully of our night in a soft cot at Commando. Soft. Warm. Quiet. I wrapped up in my green fleece pullover and fell deep asleep.

In the dark, Scull was shaking me.

I sat up, awake before I was vertical.

Hey, Staff Sergeant. What's up?

Sir, call from Everts. He is taking fire.

What?

What? I got on the hook. Staff Sergeant, Six here. What's going on?

Everts was with me only temporarily, taking over for Sid. He was big, happy kid, very conscientious, and tended to be excitable under the best of conditions.

Sir, shit, they are shooting at us!

Who is shooting at you?

The Iranians!

No fucking way. No way were the Iranians shooting over the border.

Are you sure?

Yes, sir, we took fire from due east!

On the list of Things I Needed Right Now, an international incident, with one of my Marines killing an Iranian national, or, worse, being killed, in cross-border fire, was way down at the bottom. My team, *just us*, could have started a new war. Heavily-armed teenage gods.

Staff Sergeant, back away. Just pull straight back from the border, about a click, set back in, and call me if you need anything. For God's sake, don't shoot back.

I could feel his questions over the handset.

OK, sir. Disappointment flowed around his words.

I went back to sleep.

———•••———

Who would you die for?

What would you die for?

Any Comanche could answer those questions.

———•••———

The boys became glareblind and sunburned and moved at one quarter speed in the oven heat. Iran loomed over us, Iraq pushed us from behind, the Marine Corps ignored us.

We sank slowly into a squalor of porn magazines, Tom Clancy novels, and hip-hop CDs. Packages were driven out to us and dumped unceremoniously on our little teams: more magazines and melted chocolate chip cookies and letters from sweet grannies in a cloud of little old lady perfume. All the letters were warmly supportive of what we were doing. Most were written months before, at the beginning of time, before the war started. I gave up on letters and waited to send e-mails, when we returned to The Rear, which was going to happen Someday Soon.

Sid said they got mail in the bush in Vietnam faster.

———•••———

The pumping station didn't work...so why were we guarding it?

The station was old and decrepit and half-destroyed, like everything else in Iraq. I let the boys take a quick look inside through the windows and stopped them from throwing rocks through the few panes of glass remaining...what was it about teenage boys that they must always break things?

I was concerned about booby traps, fearing that we were the first ones into this facility since the war. I didn't want any surprises. A trap wired to the door didn't care who you were or why you were there...they were equal-opportunity murder.

For some reason this pumping station was surrounded by a monstrous berm, 25 feet high, easily twice as high as the ones we had around our camps in Kuwait. For the life of me, I could not figure out the reason for the berms. Defensive positions? Those they were: they could have defended the Alamo behind there. Keeping floods out? There was indeed a small river nearby. Keeping oil spills in? Iranians out? All of these?

But Staff Sergeant Scull could not have cared less: he had eyes for only one thing. He was as happy as I had seen him: finally, *a hill on which to put the antenna!* The poor guy had been rigging up makeshift antennae for months, sometimes while we moved, so we always had shitty reception and he felt responsible.

The troops crawled up the little mountain on all fours and rigged up our antennae and for the first time in months I could hear everyone crystal-clear, all the way back to Basrah, all the way to Kuwait. The Marines, their jobs finished, cheerfully jumped and surfed their way down the two-story mountain of dirt, little kids, schussing and sliding and leaving brown trails behind them.

I sat the next morning glassy-eyed, *The Hunt for Red October* on my lap, half dozing in the heat.

An engine raced and grew and a vehicle heading south suddenly swerved off the road and barreled toward us. The troops leapt from their camp chairs, weapons in hand, awake now, snapping out of the lethargy which drained all of us, remembering that we were after all in a war zone.

It was a gorgeous, new Nissan SUV, cherry red, clean, sparkling. It was the first clean vehicle we had seen since leaving our Texas oil buddies back in Ramaylah, a hundred years ago. It slammed to a stop in front of us.

Four men got out. Three walked a step slow in deference to the fourth, the man in the front passenger seat.

He was very fat and pale and had cold, sharp, intelligent eyes, polar opposite to the lean, weathered, wide-eyed people with whom we had dealt in the hinterlands.

My troops, analogous to the three other Iraqis, stayed a step back, deferring to me, holding rifles.

I wore filthy shorts, stained with salt from months of sweat, and a T-shirt I had had on for six weeks, the same V of white salt stain on both sides. I had on flip flops and a flak jacket and wraparound sunglasses and a floppy bush cover, also stained with sweat.

Our new Iraqi wore expensive clean leather shoes, a starched, brilliant white spotless Oxford-cloth shirt straining at his belly, sharply creased dress slacks.

Six men—three of mine, three of his—stood frozen as I approached him. We two squared off. Showdown at the OK Pumping Station.

My Marines now spread out in a circle around us and flipped off safeties but kept rifles pointed at the sand. We were all in the same filthy salt-stained T-shirts and shorts and bush hats and were thus identical, but this man realized I was in charge.

I extended my hand.

Stan Coerr, from the U.S. Marines. How are you, sir?

He spoke beautiful, heavily accented English. Like all who learn English as a second language, particularly from the British, he spoke more properly than any of us. He wrapped my hand in a massive paw and identified himself with six Arab names, of which I got Something Something Rasheed Mahi Shiya Something.

He turned out to be the operations officer for the national oil company, educated at University of London with an advanced engineering degree. He was the most educated Iraqi I had met in this entire campaign and by far the fattest and by far the cleanest.

He looked hard at me and unlike his rural countrymen got right to business.

I wish to request and confirm that there will be security here.

I looked at my Marines standing to both sides, all holding rifles. Across the MSR from us, about a mile away, an entire company of British cavalry was newly arrived; we could hear their engines roaring as they patrolled. An entire Marine Division was north and west; a British mechanized division was south and east; an entire Army Corps was already in Baghdad. Security? Why the fuck else would we be here?

Yes, sir, we are here for security.

What is this guy talking about?

No, he said, sharp and hard. This was a man used to being in charge. I wish to request and confirm that security will be here, at all times. I am to rebuild all of the oil here! No looting! If I have looting I cannot rebuild.

I understand. This is why we are here. There will be no looting while my Marines and our British friends are here, but we will not be here for long.

He glowered and looked past me. He swept his arm across the pumping station.

Coalition bombs fall here! Look at inside of station! Look at this damage! Coalition bombs do all of this!

This was, in proper military terminology, bullshit. The damage I had seen inside was of the broken windows and stolen copper wire variety, with none of the cratering and shrapnel marks and twisted chunks of bombs indicative of us. Besides, the whole reason we were fucking here was to *protect* the oil fields. It was second on 43's priority list only to finding Saddam himself.

Looters, Iraqis, his own people, did this.

I marveled for a second at the absurdity of Americans, in Iraq, guarding an Iraqi asset from other Iraqis, and being yelled at by a yet different Iraqi for doing so. Irony can be wounded but never dies.

He continued with his lecture to me. His finger stabbed the air.

I am with Iraqi resistance during the war! I am with opposition party, against Saddam! Intelligence forces hold me for three months, August through October of last year. I am to rebuild here now that there is no more Saddam!

I knew what he meant: the Mukharabat, truly scary guys, had in their Nazi fashion held or killed anyone with any education or leadership skill.

I told him I would do what I could, but ended up talking to his back as he and his men stormed off into the station.

My Marines looked at me...*stop this guy, sir, or shoot him, or what?* I shrugged at them, sighed, and followed him.

We let these guys go through the doors first and we cringed, fully expecting them to coming flying out again in pieces

We turned away and winced, waiting for the explosion. Nothing happened.

The looters had truly raped this place, ripping wires from the walls and taking anything of any value from inside. They had managed to unbolt the brass caps from pressurized flanges on the wellheads...how the hell they had pried those off, particularly with the caps under such pressure, I had no idea. They had even unbolted and stolen the turbines which pressurized everything, leaving lonely twisted bolts on the concrete pads and only a perfect dirty rectangle as a memory of machines. I thought of the Bedouins Brian and I had seen hauling the arc welder into the wasteland. It was shiny, so they took it.

My friend was not happy. He knew his people had done this. He tried to be angry at me but it wasn't working anymore.

He and his men stormed past us without a word and in a cloud of dust they drove away.

And this was the real problem. Once we left...what then?

NONE

When the devil comes, he comes on angel wings.
—Don Winslow

Now back in Amarah the entire Marine ANGLICO platoon had re-aggregated, seventeen teams, a colonel and six Majors, better part of a hundred men. We were moving back to Kuwait. Someday. Very soon.

We were attached to the British brigade but not to our Irish or our Paras, all of whom had rotated back to Kuwait as Tony Blair called them home. I missed them.

ANGLICO was an island unto ourselves in a British camp, surrounded by men who didn't know or really like us, wanting out. There was a British general and his staff and we became a military unit again, sort of, no longer a roving guerrilla band of armed teenagers.

I didn't like it.

We didn't particularly like the other ANGLICO teams, either; we liked the men in them, but we none of us liked the way they were run. Way back in California I had hand-picked the men I wanted and inherited some and stole others: Walsh and Sid and Brian and Scull and Santos and Wilson, Lopez and Cruz and Duperroy, and Arreola, Macis and all of them, men with quirks and an impatience with stupidity, highly intelligent and independent and therefore threatening to weak leaders. I had wanted them and I grabbed them and we had had our rite of passage and we were a tribe and I was the chief.

India was its own world, our own island in the ANGLICO archipelago, and we were loyal primarily to each other. The other teams were cousins. We were brothers.

I set us up far off in a corner, away from the rest of the platoon silliness and staff work and make-work bullshit, five vehicles backed against a wall, a combat tailgate party. Comm was up. One man was on radio watch. Twenty-four of us sat in the sand.

———•••———

We had nothing now but long days under the nets, waiting for whatever brilliant stupid bullshit mission someone could think up, and we played cards and napped and read comic books and told each other the same jokes we had been telling since January. They tried to make us dig fighting holes and I refused.

Spring now in the U.S., summer here. We held a Cinco de Mayo celebration under there, half my team Mexicans, tequila appearing from somewhere and tapatio sauce sent by sweet grannies back home flavoring our MREs and a fierce debate over which state in Mexico is the best. Norteño music trickled from the tiny speakers Scull had rigged off of one of the Humvee batteries and the Spanish flowed over the Arab sand.

There was, truly, nothing to do. No television, no radios, no weight room, nowhere to jog, no computers, no phones. *Nothing.* Twenty-five men, five vehicles, a brick wall, sand.

We were within twelve hours of detaching from the British for good, so we couldn't leave the base, couldn't patrol with the British infantry, couldn't get into the fight with our brother infantry Marines to the north.

The heat was truly oppressive, hitting 126 degrees under the net at one point, draining us, making us woozy and confused. We slept twenty hours a day and were exhausted.

The camo nets were critical for keeping the sun off of us, but they were designed for another purpose: they were infrared blockers, meant to break up the thermal image of a human body when viewed on optics at night. That thermal shielding meant that the nets trapped heat and held it in, on us. Drinking 126 degree water is a bizarre exercise in being thirsty and full at the same time.

Go into the sauna at the gym. Turn the heat to 126. Think of us.

———•••———

Genghis Khan swept out of Mongolia and across the Asian steppes and took cities but never held them. He knew cities bred sickness and disease, though he did not know why. He kept his men at altitude and on the steppes in the scour of wind.

———•••———

Malaria. *Mal aria.* Bad air.

———•••———

We had been weeks in the cities, in the malaria, and we were still in the bad air and now stomach flu slapped us to our knees.

Three ANGLICO Marines were so sick they actually ended up in the hospital on IV fluids. I toughed it out, burning with fever and the Mesopotamian heat and smarting over the loss of Sid.

Sid had been grabbed by the chief, Lieutenant General Conway, senior Marine in theater, who knew who Sid was and how senior he was in the law enforcement world. Conway put Sid in charge of advising him on the entire policing effort in Baghdad. He was today leaving us.

I spent this day in a ball on the ground, lying in the shadow of a Humvee in the 125-degree heat, vomiting into the sand. A helicopter whickered in, flared and landed in a field, and Sid shouldered his pack. I wobbled to my feet, dizzy, graying out, and held him tight and said goodbye to my brother.

Rumors were flying that we would be here for many more months. I lay vomiting and dry heaving in the oven, thinking about the day I walked across the stage in Cambridge to get my Harvard diploma and from that day to this one rolling in the Arabian dirt.

———•••———

Brian got a package from his wife, Carmen, mailed months earlier. Inside was the most important thing a man could have here: a mosquito net to cover him and his cot.

The rest of us chose between waking every hour being eaten alive by mosquitoes and waking every hour, slick with sweat, from pulling our poncho liners up over our heads. I chose each night to sweat and each morning had to turn my poncho liner inside out and let my life force evaporate into the Mesopotamian sun.

———•••———

I was always convinced there was something wrong with Sullivan. This is why I gave him to Sid.

I had thought at first that this was my problem...that he was just a strange guy. He was a huge, NFL-sized specimen, easily 6' 3 and 240 pounds of solid muscle. His biceps were like cantaloupes on greased skids, and he had the butt and hamstrings of a linebacker, the heavily muscled shoulders of the serious lifter. Just a huge, intimidating guy...until he opened his mouth and showed himself a meek, mild man with a soft voice and lisp and confused demeanor.

He was terrified of me: he couldn't even look me in the eye when he spoke to me.

The troops warned me, over and over, that he wasn't right, but I was too smart for their good and knew it all and didn't listen to them.

———•••———

We were ten years old again in the dusk.

Sergeant Santos and I were doing the most basic of all boy things: throwing a ball back and forth. No baseball gloves, not the hey-fire-one-in-here pitcher and catcher thing, just a tennis ball, the two of us in shorts and flip-flops. The temperature had plummeted to 110 or so as the sun set, taking with it the searing direct heat of the day but leaving latent heat to bake up into our feet from concrete and dirt.

The boys lolled about, watching us and talking lazily among themselves.

In front of our vehicles, about twenty yards across an empty field, we had dug a fire pit. Hygiene and sanitation in this bare world demanded that we burn everything. *Everything*: trash, old books, food, empty packages from home, MRE wrappers, ripped shirts, socks, wood, paper, plastic, anything except steel. It was standard procedure for everyone in theater, keeping the vermin down and the stray dogs, which roamed everywhere and were often rabid and which we killed on sight, from our camps. And, of course, there are few things grown men like more than messing with fires, so it served entertainment value as well.

———•••———

The Veterans Administration has started a Burn Pit Registry for those of us who were in Iraq, ready for what we breathed in that toxic smoke to hit, waiting for us to get sick, Agent Orange Redux. I am registered.

———•••———

In her book *The Male Brain*, Louann Brizendine explains male violence.

The male fetus receives a dump of testosterone in utero, his first.

By the age of nine, a boy begins his second dump, testosterone building slowly and in small amounts, in preparation for the largest dump he will have in his lifetime. By age fifteen, testosterone is roaring through his system, and from fifteen to seventeen his total testosterone is the highest it will ever be.

This hormone primes young men for strength, aggression, competition and dominance.

Boys are primed for aggressive and territorial behaviors, she tells us, and the higher the testosterone, the more invigorated and battle-ready the male brain feels.

———•••———

Santos and I finished our little game and I went around behind my vehicle to dig up some chow.

Santos went the other way, over to help with one of the burn details. He and the boys stood around, throwing things in slowly and staring into the fire, mesmerized, the way people do.

Sullivan walked up and tossed in an ammo can.

Dude, don't throw that in there, Santos said.

Sullivan didn't even look at him. Fuck you.

No, I'm serious. The Major said not to throw anything in that won't burn.

Sullivan clenched his jaw and said it again. Fuck you.

Santos turned away, and under his breath said *Asshole.*

Sullivan lashed out, swiveling and tensing and bringing a huge fist from behind his back. He hit Santos as hard as he could, under his right eye.

From fifty feet away I heard Santos scream. What the fuck? What the fuck did you do that for?

I ran with Brian around one side of the Humvee, Arreola running around the other. We converged on Santos, on the ground, shirtless and bewildered, already being attended to by several others. A huge knot was already swelling on his upper cheekbone as we watched.

Several Marines grabbed Sullivan and backed him away, far from the rest of the team.

I held Santos by the lower jaw, *very* gingerly, and looked at his eye. Staff Sergeant, take him to medical.

Aye, aye, sir, Arreola said, anticipating this and already moving.

I turned and yelled at the Marines holding Sullivan. You hang on to him! Don't let him out of your sight!

Brian looked at me, wide-eyed. Holy shit.

Arreola returned within minutes, having deposited Santos with the British medical staff. Those folks were actually happy to see a real patient, having dealt only with diarrhea for weeks as they ministered to teenage boys and young men in their prime of rude male health.

I put my hands on my hips and thought. Staff Sergeant, we gotta take his weapons away and move him out of our team tomorrow.

He looked at me, incredulous. Tomorrow? Sir, we gotta get him out of here right now. Those Marines like Santos a lot. They are going to kill Sullivan. You still want him for another day?

Fuck. He was right.

You're right, Staff Sergeant. I will go talk to the Colonel right now.

I walked through Bob Bruce's team and powwowed with the Brigade staff. The CO quickly authorized the move, and I dumped Sullivan, sans weapons, on Bob.

He put Sullivan in a tent, alone, with a guard out front.

And it was then I remembered what the Marines had tried to tell me about Sullivan, months earlier, at the refinery in Ramaylah, when I had listened but not heard.

So much for my team's reputation.

India was suddenly fuckups, out of control. I couldn't even handle my people. My insistence of taking the misfit toys onto my team was coming back to haunt me. Stan: not as smart as he thought he was. We knew it. That's what happens when you bring in all your own guys. Tried to tell him.

One punch had ruined almost a year of work.

The British medical folks took a quick X-ray and realized Santos was injured beyond their capabilities to handle. Sullivan's fist had crunched into Santos's zygomatic arch, the high cheekbone and socket for the eye. He had fractures throughout the bone, like a dropped vase spiderwebbed with cracks. It was also true that a facial fracture was not the kind of thing you could splint. They drugged him up and let him sleep.

The next morning they let us leave first.

Santos walked in the fading dark under his own power, accompanied by another Marine with his arm around him in case he went downhill, and sat gingerly in the front seat of FCT 38's vehicle. Wilson gave him his own seat, the fluffiest seat we had among us, so the jostling wouldn't be too bad as his splintered facial bones ground together.

We refueled quickly and got moving at first light, bidding farewell to Amarah forever.

After four months of combat success we slunk away in failure.

———••——

We pulled into Shaibah at midday, a little convoy of five filthy, exhausted, broken-down vehicles and five times that in filthy, exhausted, broken-down men. Santos was whisked away, Brian in charge.

The Great ANGLICO Consolidation accelerated, all the teams, hundreds of men, pulling back from positions all over southern Iraq, bidding adieu to their British brothers, and reforming as 3d Air-Naval Gunfire Liaison Company, once again under Marine Corps command, back to the tribe.

———••——

A rumor ignited: the Royal Irish had been flown back to England aboard Richard Branson's 747. I hoped it was true.

———••——

In theory, we would be here for two days and then begin to cycle back to Kuwait. This was it.

Manila was the first platoon to arrive, and the tiny hovel in which the command was housed filled with men and gear.

Vehicles excreted the impedimenta of war. We unpacked every vehicle down to the floorboards. We scrubbed away four months' accumulation of dirt and grease and fluids and fuel and hydraulics and sweat and filth, spilled coffee and weapon oil and food wedged under the seats and mud from multiple provinces. The pretty dark-green Humvees and trucks which had run perfectly, parked in such lovely straight lines at the docks in Long Beach, were now a collection of *Road Warrior* nightmares, skeletons of chassis and spot-welded steel with cannibalized parts and mismatched tires and duct tape and missing doors and bullet holes.

As the Hummers stripped down the mounds of equipment grew, great piles of scuffed packs and clean weapons and MRE cases thrown into the dirt. We took control of the courtyard behind the ANGLICO CP and shamelessly sprayed water by the gallon on everything, the first continuous, pressurized water we had had since January.

The command team had set up solar showers. I let all my Marines go first. I took a very long shower, the last man, so hot my skin turned pink. A few stragglers got in line for the water so I got out, wrapped a towel around my waist, got back in the line and let them have their turn. Then I got back in.

I took another shower, longer than the first, the dirt crusted on me finally giving up and flowing onto the concrete and into the pit filling with the mud that we had worn.

I threw my gear down in the last bare rectangle in the biggest and darkest and air-conditionedest room in the building, lay down on the floor with nothing on top of me as men snored all around at high noon and put my head on my pack and fell instantly asleep.

Like everything else we commandeered in Iraq, the Shaibah airfield had been an Iraqi military installation, an air force base with a huge, beautiful runway and the same collection of administrative and barracks buildings you would find at any air base in the world. We set out to explore, marveling at the feeling of safety and liberation in being in the center of a huge, secure camp. No flak jackets, no helmets, no weapons. We could walk on actual normal city blocks...buildings, street corners, street signs, stoplights and everything, a small town.

Most important of all, this small town had what every American boy needs:

Junk food.

We walked in the falling twilight to the center of town, which had served the Iraqis as it now served us as the social center of the base. A swimming pool, undoubtedly once the officers' club relief from the searing Mesopotamian summer heat, was fallow, empty, dry and cracked. Soldiers and Marines sat around the edge, feet dangling over the concrete hole, and a few even sat on the four steps leading to nothing.

The British had brought up the emporia of Americana: video rental stores, laundry rooms, a tiny library. But we had eyes for only two places: Burger King and Pizza Hut. These were trailers, hauled north from Kuwait, with fully operational kitchens inside, and the smell of hot pizza and frying potatoes wafted gently in the pleasant night air, drawing men from all directions.

Someone had contracted with these companies to provide services to our boys overseas, and you saw those two signs on bases all over the world. The Bangladeshi and Pakistani workers looked uncomfortable in their itchy, hot brightly-colored polyester, but our indifference to the discomfort of others was monumental. Junk food rules the day in camps of hungry, healthy young men with nothing but cash and time.

The twin towers of American Mecca were right there next to the pool, base landmarks doing landmark business. It would have done Dan Monahan's heart good to see the lines of soldiers and Marines, sometimes 200 men long, waiting patiently for their turn at the raised window. A few left orders with their buddies and sat next to the empty pool, joking quietly amongst themselves with their feet dangling ten feet above the bottom.

I was overwhelmed, too much to choose from: a kid on Christmas morning, a man at the Playboy Mansion. I didn't know where to start. After months of nothing but MREs and the horrible British field rations, I suddenly had the artery-clogging cornucopia of America's finest eateries there before me.

I ordered one of everything and ate one bite of each.

———•••———

Shaibah had something else.

Women.

We hadn't seen a western woman, aide from the definitively off-limits Sarah and Daisy, since we left California. Female soldiers walked to and fro in the gloaming, self-conscious and arrogant, the only women for a hundred miles, temporary prom queens. Girls who would have been fives in the U.S.—threes in southern California—had become Bo Derek here. We gaped at them and then ignored them and they us.

———•••———

There was a sense among all of us of laziness, of dropping packs and unloading weapons and relaxing, one foot out the door already even though we were still in Iraq.

We had a welcome-back barbecue behind the India CP. A fire pit roared as chicken and lamb sizzled on what had until that morning been an iron steam grate on a building floor. It smelled wonderful. Whiskey materialized, and warm terrible cheap lovely beer, lubricating our gears as we meshed back together for the first time in months.

As the sun set, there was a hue and cry and a disturbance on the roof looming above us.

Staff Sergeant Luna was from another team, a prankster and a very funny, well-liked leader.

Luna walked slowly to the edge of the CP roof, in the last of the twilight, twenty feet above us, underlit, imperious.

He was wearing a liberated Iraqi officer uniform complete with epaulets.

Marines gathered and yelled, dozens of us, looking up.

With his thick black Saddam mustache (which he had been cultivating assiduously since we went over the border,) his black hair and his dark Latin skin, he was the spitting image of Saddam.

A Marine was at his feet, giggling, holding a flashlight up to illuminate him from below.

Luna stood straight-backed and proud, shoulders back, still, surveying his people.

He very slowly lifted his right hand to greet his followers, the exact pose of every Saddam statue in the country.

The hundred well-lubricated Marines below screamed with laughter and roared approval.

———••———

I reconnected with my buddy Dave Allen, a fighter pilot, my peer in a different platoon.

I had given him one of my Staff Sergeants before the war began and I asked how this man had done and Dave said he did great, as long as the mission was something he wanted to do and as long as it happened during the day.

———••———

Walking back this night to the ANGLICO spaces, I noticed something I hadn't before.

The troops were billeted in what had been classrooms or offices of some kind, just four walls and concrete floors into which they tossed down their packs and sleeping pads. Metallica and Lynyrd Skynyrd boomed from one room; salsa and Spanish ballads from the next; Snoop and 50 Cent—*Fitty*, sir, *Fitty*, my Marines had told white suburban me- from a third.

Each room held maybe six to eight Marines, so one team couldn't all fit together, and the headquarters staff guys had spread out over the preceding weeks. So when our Marines fell in on these spaces, it was every man for himself.

Nothing unusual about that, but I was very surprised that rather than sticking with members of their teams, our Marines broke themselves down by race.

It was a byproduct of the environments in which these kids had grown up, many of them from the ghettos and barrios, the underbelly of a racially divided Los Angeles.

The social scientist in me had always considered the Marine Corps, and the military in general, the most egalitarian large organization in the world, the sort of place where the fact that Colin Powell was black was a matter of pride but otherwise simply not an issue. It was also true that these men, when up in the fight, had ignored racial strata and bonded as brothers.

No one gave a shit who you were: you were either a good Marine, or you were not. You were a valued member of the tribe, or you were not.

You were in the tribe, or you were not.

They were in a way halfway home already, though we were technically still in a war zone. I suppose they were just falling back in with old friends from other platoons, and most of those friends had the same skin color. There was no animosity, no racial tension... it was just the way it was, like kids splitting up in the cafeteria in high school.

I was surprised and it made me somehow sad.

———◆◆◆———

Lieutenant General Jim Conway later became Commandant of the Marine Corps and he told this story.

He had two sons serving in combat as Marine officers. One of them got into a big fight; the other happened to be nearby and was part of the effort to go reinforce those Marines under fire.

As he worked and planned one of his Marines said Sir aren't you worried?

Major Conway said why?

Because, sir, your brother is up there.

And Conway answered they are all my brothers.

VESPERS

And lo it came to be that on the fourteenth of May in the year of our lord two thousand three Lieutenant General James Conway, First Marine Expeditionary Force commander and the highest priest in the land spake from on high, saying yea, verily, send back from Iraq thither to Kuwait thence to the United States thy men.

And we heard The Word and The Word was good and there was much rejoicing.

Malvinas

When it was time to bring
The lads
Home from the Falkland Islands and back to theirs
They came home in two groups

The first group was put aboard the *Queen Elizabeth II* and
    steamed slowly
Taking almost a month to return to the British Isles

During that time they had long talks
Debriefs, in the parlance
What they saw
And did
They talked and drank and argued and fought
With one another

They burned the combat out of their psyches on a floating island
    populated only by those who understood and could tell them
    they were full of shit or
    that they had done nothing wrong

Sometimes both

By the time they arrived back to their island they had worked
The war
Out of their systems and were ready to return to
Peacetime service
To reunite calmly with wives and children
With the world

The second group
Got on a plane in the Falklands and was home

That day
They did not do so well

———•••———

14 MAY 2003 ▶ BASRAH, IRAQ TO CAMP COMMANDO, KUWAIT

MEF passed the order we had waited for:

Send 'em back.

———•••———

We loaded up vehicles in record time and got on the road and did not look back.

The journey to Kuwait, this time, was under an hour from our Basrah base, and we pulled through the ugly, angry town of Safwan without incident. The children and teenagers there, the ones who approached us and threatened us and stole from our Humvees, knew our rules of engagement as well as we did. They knew we weren't going to shoot a kid, so they ran at our moving vehicles with impunity despite the weapons brandished out the windows.

But we were now dozens of vehicles, not the five of us we had been the month before, and we didn't even slow down through the tiny streets of their filthy village. Bob Bruce's guys went ahead of us and they broke the code: they carried big sticks which they swung like clubs at the urchins. The Iraqis hated us anyway...who gave a fuck? The munchkin hordes were startled but realizing the jig was up stayed away from us and we accelerated through their village and did not stop.

———•••———

I thought to what Churchill had once said: *this is not the beginning of the end, perhaps, but the end of the beginning.* I hoped this poor sad beautiful oppressed awful country would recover.

I had done my part and my tribe had stood up and I didn't care anymore.

————•••————

It was a bright and brilliantly sunny morning but as we moved over the border it clouded over rapidly.

We stopped once inside Kuwait to fuel up before the final push as we began home. The Marines stretched and wandered to the side of the highway to pee, and I stood against the Humvee, looking back north into Iraq. Bob Bruce walked up to me and leaned beside me, contemplative like I was.

I just thought of something, he said. Did I just see Iraq for the last time?

I replied firmly that he had, but I wasn't so sure. I could feel an unease, a conviction that given two alternatives, the Marine Corps would pick the one that would screw people the hardest. We were heading back, I could sense it.

I insisted on driving us into the camp, for some strange internal need to finish what I had started. Officers do not drive Humvees, and so I had never actually driven one before. Conde smiled knowingly at me and took up his new seat in the back.

We rolled into Commando in late afternoon, the sun just setting off our right shoulders and illuminating Mutla Ridge towering over the camp. The CO was in such a hurry to get to a meeting at the MEF that he actually had his driver drop him in the lower part of the camp.

The rest of us, dozens of vehicles strong, rolled uphill to the new ANGLICO tents.

Our worn-out vehicles drew stares as we passed the rear echelon Marines who had been stuck, helpless and safe for the entire war with their soft beds and television and hot chow and hot water and Internet and air conditioning, all of it in the wrong country, the poor bastards.

Marines on their way to chow went past us, eyes wide as we debarked, taking in our mustaches and the filthy, faded uniforms hanging off our underweight hips and bony shoulders.

We sent the troops to chow and the officers rolled directly into a meeting with the CO. I felt my stomach twist: if he needed to see us this soon, before we had even put our packs in our tents, it could not be good news.

The CO stood before us, ready to knock the wind out of our sails. I had the feeling you get after your first, of several, final exams in college: accomplished and satisfied, but unable to relax.

He jumped right in. Gents, I went to say goodbye to the British leadership this morning in Shaibah, he said flatly. MEF planners were there. They caught me by surprise. I was hoping they were just happening by, but they had come to find me in particular.

And it wasn't to say goodbye.

My gut twisted for real now, hard.

Mother*fuckers.* I knew it. If we had just gotten back down here a month ago and packed up, instead of inventing things to do on the Iranian border, they would have sent us back by now.

It is looking like they were going to re-task us and send us back north, to work with coalition forces, he continued. I don't have any details. Tell the Marines, but keep it low-key. That's it.

We looked at each other and at him, questions on everyone's lips. How many guys? All of us? Some? Half? When? Who will we work with? What coalition forces? How much longer until we get back home? We trailed off to chow. No one spoke, all of us deflated.

---

15 MAY 2003 ▶ CAMP COMMANDO, KUWAIT
We set off at mid-morning to see Santos, now out of surgery.

SALT India piled into Hummers and rolled out into Kuwait City, all of us staying tight on one another's bumpers. I deferred to Brian, who had taken Santos to the hospital, and thus was the only one who knew how to find it.

After months in the rural outback of postwar Iraq, our driving senses were skewed. Forty miles per hour felt plenty fast to us, and we were all skittish whenever another vehicle came too close, used to wide-open spaces with no other cars on the roads. We were country mice in Kuwait City, and I gaped at the bright yellow Ferraris and candy-apple red Maseratis whining past us at upwards of 100 miles per hour.

I suddenly understood why the Iraqis and Kuwaitis hated each other. The Iraqis thought the Kuwaitis had stolen their oil and turned out a generation of rich, indulged dilettantes splitting their time between Kuwait City and Paris, while the Kuwaitis viewed their oil riches as just desserts after Saddam raped their country and murdered countless thousands of innocent people in 1991. The truth was no doubt somewhere right in the middle, where it always is, and as we trundled along in the headlong rush hour I knew that I was in an entirely different world.

I also saw the road sign that was to be my favorite, ever. At one off-ramp a helpful arrow pointed the visitor to the government agency for carrying out big contracts: *The Ministry of Execution.*

It was fortunate that I had warned everyone to stay tight, because slaloming through Kuwait City rush hour was like trying to find an obscure turnoff in New York City on a Monday morning. We alternated between flooring our poor laboring trucks and slamming to a stop in a never-ending series of traffic jams. Brian took us on a brief detour at one of the endless cloverleafs which split the city into sections, but quickly righted our convoy and led us with aplomb to Kuwait International.

It was the same airport into which we had flown on that bitter cold January night, but looked entirely different in the broad light of day, in the searing heat and from the opposite side. Here the U.S. Army had built a CSH, a Combat Surgical Hospital for the seriously injured on their way to Europe or the United States for follow-on treatment. Here they could do serious surgery: amputations, brain surgery, major trauma care. These were the sorts of repairs on young, mangled bodies that trauma people in Iraq just couldn't handle.

Brian spoke very highly of the surgeons who had worked on Santos. An extremely competent ENT surgeon had insisted that he go into surgery the day he arrived, and she had been non-plussed and professional about what we had thought was a serious injury. Compared to a leg blown off or a chunk of shrapnel in the skull, Santos had indeed gotten away lightly.

My visions of the romantic leaky green tents of the MASH television show were dashed. We parked and entered a maze, a gorgeous, huge complex of some sort of gossamer white fabric inflated by enormous blowers into a series of connected tunnels. It was precisely like the Habitrail hamster cages we all had as kids.

We all exhaled with pleasure when we were hit with the first blast of freezing air inside, and the twenty of us walked endless corridors in the Habitrail searching for our man. We clomped in dirty boots along gleaming, polished wooden decking, and my long-haired, scrawny, mustachioed Marines eyed the pretty, sparkling young nurses as they bustled about and ignored us. Everything was clean, abundant, inviting and cool: it was the opposite of our world.

Santos in our minds' eyes would have one of those Little Drummer Boy bandages around his head, drugged up and immobile, our comrade in arms on death's narrow dark door, in need of cheering up from his brothers.

———— •••• ————

Poor suffering Santos was propped in a standard hospital bed, the top half raised so he could better see the TV, eating a huge bowl of ice cream.

He was clean-shaven, freshly showered and squeaky clean and wearing sweatpants and a T-shirt, bundled under three blankets. We gave him shit for that, but within fifteen minutes we had all started to shiver in the draft. We crowded around his bed, the Marines joking and berating him for his newfound soft life. He was the happiest man among us.

Santos had everything a handsome young Marine Sergeant needed: a remote control for the multiple channels on his TV, a pile of books and magazines, and several very attractive young nurses who asked him every ten minutes or so if he needed anything.

And he had the most important thing of all: a ticket home. They were transferring him to Europe somewhere and then back to California, and it was all thanks to Brian, who had insisted that Santos be treated in the States. I suspected that Brian may have exaggerated his own billet and the clout he carried over Santos, but he was, after all, a full U.S. Navy Commander, and besides it was fine by me. It was stupid to send Santos back to us to heal up, to sit in a tent at Commando in the 125-degree heat and do nothing but wait to get sent back over the border.

With a wink and a nod we said goodbye to our friend. Brian and I lingered and told him that we would most likely head back north into Iraq. Santos immediately sat up straighter and insisted on going with us, but I told him that his war was over.

We piled out of the tent and back into the bake-oven heat of midday, the cool, crisp air vaporizing out of our clothes, already fading into fond memory. Brian vaguely remembered how to find the chow hall, so off we went.

We had a quick enormous lunch, all of us silent and open-mouthed at the fat, sloppy soldiers wandering in and out. It was a shock after months with lean, sunburned combat Marines, and we realized how the rear echelon really lived. It was soft and lovely and easy and we couldn't get out of there fast enough.

EILEEN JOYCE

Everybody takes a beating sometimes.
— Henry Hill, Lucchese family hitman

24 MAY 2003 ▶ DAWN

Our outdoor thermometer measured up to 125 degrees and each day it pegged the minute the sun broke the morning horizon. A scorching dry wind, like a hair dryer on full blast in the face, blew down the Arabian Peninsula and from Iraq across Mutla Ridge to our north, across the camp and out to the Bay of Kuwait to our south.

Any time two or more Marines are gathered together sports competitions break out. This was sports day, a chance for some good healthy competition and a chance for the boys to burn off steam. Most important, like children, if Marines are tired they don't think about being bored. The 3d ANGLICO football team had been practicing in the searing heat for weeks and was ready to take on all comers.

The Marines headed en masse to the football field, ready to cheer on their mates. All of us were dressed in Commando Casual: flip-flops, shorts, no shirts, wraparound sunglasses.

I watched the competition for a bit, then headed back to Hue City, our section of camp, the northernmost part of the base and a good half-mile uphill from the football field. I walked slowly and aimlessly, lost in thought, leaning into the hill, conflicted and angry over machinations of the leaders above me, tuned out.

———◆◆———

I smelled smoke.

———◆◆———

I was born in September 1967, and my parents brought me home to their fourth-floor walkup apartment in Arlington, Virginia. This apartment was on a hill overlooking the large lawn in front of the Iwo Jima Memorial, the lawn on which I would later learn to walk, and it had a large picture window with the statue of my Marines on Suribachi in the low foreground and Washington D.C. in the distance across the river.

When Martin Luther King, Jr. was shot in April 1968 Washington exploded and cracked open, cleaved into anger and fire. I was five months old and my mother would stand before that window at night and rock me in her arms in the orange glow as she watched the city burn.

———•••———

I stopped now in the middle of the road, looking uphill, spinning slowly to find the source of the smell. And there it was, black smoke drifting straight up into the sky, growing, framed against Mutla Ridge, and I did some subconscious trigonometry and realized it was coming from right next to our tents, between us and the tents belonging to our brothers in 2/6.

I sprinted uphill, digging in the soft sand of the road.

I ran through the entrance to our camp and bore up and left, to the upper reaches of the tent city. The smoke was now drifting over and above me, I was running into it, and now I could see bright orange flames, thirty feet high, over the tops of the tents. This was bad.

I heard shouting and saw Marines running in every direction. I turned and looked down at the lower camp, half a mile away, where I could see a stream of lean, sunburned men racing uphill towards the fire, abandoning the field meet and trying to beat the flames to their belongings. Most were barefoot, having been in cheap flip-flops which disintegrated as they ran.

I ran into the melee, shouting orders at the Marines standing outside the perimeter of the fire. Being Marines, they ran into the flames. I joined in with them, all of us trying to fight the fire, but with nothing to use. No water. No fire extinguishers. Nothing. We threw sand on flames where we could get close enough but it was an absurd overmatch.

The fire was truly roaring now, only two tents away from where the ANGLICO tents began, and flames were an orange wall three stories high. I watched in horror as the flames leaped methodically, one tent to another, blown by the hot, dry 30-knot wind coming off the ridgeline above us and blowing toward the sea below us. Embers from burning fabric and wood flew spinning into the air, drifted and swirled and blew downhill, orange spots landing on the downwind tents and igniting them one by one.

There was nothing we could do.

Officers stood in the intersections of the paths through the tent city, shouting orders. I grabbed Sergeant Giannetti and another Marine I didn't recognize, shouting at them to move the Light Armored Vehicle which sat directly in front of our tent, in the fire's path.

Giannetti shouted back to me Sir I can't drive an LAV!

I yelled back, the flames now so close that the roar was drowning us out. I know! Go to the LAV battalion tents and find someone who can! You! I yelled at the other Marine, who was standing wide-eyed, his eyes glued to my face, Go figure out how to release the emergency brake on that thing! If we can't drive it, we can push it. If the jet fuel in that thing ignites we have a much bigger problem!

He and Giannetti ran in separate directions, sprinting through the streets now choked with Marines.

I was hyper-alert, adrenaline pouring into my bloodstream. I could picture myself the previous night, finishing my journal and putting it in a cardboard box under my bed.

———•••———

In Ireland in 1911, Eileen Joyce leapt to her feet in her living room and snatched from the fire a stack of papers her brother James had hurled into it in frustration and fury and disgust, and she thereby saved the only manuscript for *A Portrait of The Artist as a Young Man*.

———•••———

I ran into my tent and dove beneath my bunk. I grabbed the box that was there without needing to even look at it, seizing it by feel, and I ran back out of the tent, running away from the tent city to the twenty foot-high sand berms which enclosed the camp, running sideways out of the fire like a swimmer moving out of a rip current.

I climbed the berm, clutching my box, my legs driving and my running shoes filling with sand. I reached the top and threw the box over to the other side, where the flames wouldn't reach it. Hundreds of other Marines were doing the same thing, all of us on the side of the enormous sand pile, flinging items over the top. Weapons, packs, clothing, belts of ammunition and boots and flak jackets flew over the top of the berm, dark for an instant against the brilliant blue sky before disappearing from sight.

I made two giant leaping, sliding glissades back down the berm and ran back to the tent.

The flames were growing higher and hotter and louder, fed by the bone-dry fabric and wood as it devoured everything before it, running downhill and downwind. It sounded like a freight train.

Bryant Sewall stood over his own bunk, trying to save everything he owned. He looked at me and yelled Here, take this! as he thrust his own duffel bag into my hands. Rather than belt him in the face, as I should have, I slapped the bag away and ran past him. I dove for the equipment of the Marines who were still in the lower camp, helpless, unable to get to the tent in time.

The top of the tent began to smolder, and a hole opened above the bunk next to mine, an orange glowing hole the size of a quarter which expanded to a foot as I watched, amazed. The ceiling went from white cloth to orange hole to bright blue sky in seconds and then disappeared entirely. The entire tent now started to shake, buffeted by the wind of the fire consuming the tent next to ours.

I sprinted back to the berm, up with my unwieldy burden of other Marines' stuff, threw my armload over the top, and surfed back down.

That was it. The flames took everything else. I ran back into the camp and began grabbing and throwing Marines bodily out of the tents. I knew they would stay in there until they collapsed otherwise. They were bent on saving everything as the tents literally exploded into flames around them, collapsing as the wooden frames fell apart, roaring straight up in pieces into the maelstrom as if pulled into the heavens.

I shouted and screamed and used both hands on some of the Marines, propelling them out into the open. Like boxers spun around too many times, dizzy and near heatstroke they didn't know where to run, and some plunged the wrong way, deeper into the flames. Officers and staff NCOs stood shoulder to shoulder, pushing and pointing and yelling at them to get over the berm.

Terry Thomas and I were the last men out.

———•••———

I looked downhill to the main camp and saw sitting idle, unmanned, silent, two parked brand-new fire trucks.

———•••———

The fire simply swept through our tent city, consuming every single thing in its path. It was a flood, a tsunami, an avalanche, a tidal wave, a mudslide, an ocean of flame. My brain spit out similes and analogies and then it shut down, the adrenaline dump receding from my bloodstream, tide going out, leaving me nauseous and dizzy.

The fire was a curling seething living thing, and she hesitated at the road splitting us from the rest of the tents to the south, seeming to stop and think as she burned straight up into the sky.

I stood on top of the berm, upwind of it now, and watched, helpless, as the fire bent slowly downhill, pushed by its own weather system, and slowly dropped burning embers like snow.

It thought some more and then it reached out with an orange arm, a thin horrible tendril of flame 100 feet long, onto the tents below and across the road from us. They, too, exploded in flame and the fire gathered herself and built again on top of the 6th Comm Battalion tents and burned those and built stronger and raced on. I watched the flames roll thick into the sky, heavy black smoke rising hundreds of feet and blowing to the Bay of Kuwait.

The Marines were suddenly exhausted. The searing Arabian heat was bad enough, but the hot wind blowing off the desert and the heat from the fire meant that we had been running in temperatures approaching 150 degrees. The backwash of adrenaline now washing out of our systems left everyone spent. Some fell to their knees. One of our Staff Sergeants was bent over at the waist, vomiting into the sand.

Marines sat, woozy, eyes unfocused and faces an unhealthy bright red. I sat with several and talked and got them on their feet as several hundred men started to regroup.

I went over the berm and walked the perimeter, between the berm and the fence, stepping around the detritus flung there over the past fifteen minutes: shower shoes, camouflage pants, books, letters from girlfriends and wives, weapons, photos, crates of ammunition, flares, shoes, T-shirts, packs, and NBC suits lying in untidy piles as if deposited there by a tornado. The officers and SNCOs got everyone up and organizing gear. There was nothing left to do.

I clambered back up onto the berm to survey the damage. Everything still smoldered but the fire was downhill now, seeming to forget about us and our belongings as she raced downhill, downwind.

Now rounds started to cook off in tents that Marines hadn't gotten to in time, flares and ordnance exploding like a satanic Fourth of July. Bullets exposed to flame don't shoot as they would from a rifle, but simply explode in their brass casings, evil lethal popcorn, and the pop-pop-pop-BANG-pop-BANG of the different-sized rounds cooking off put an exclamation point on a shitty day.

Marines by the hundreds, ANGLICO and infantry and LAV and communications units, the tribe, stood spent and helpless and watched the fire burn.

———•••———

It was skit night.

3d ANGLICO as one sat glum, shivering, confused in the falling twilight, watching halfheartedly as the talent show went on stage.

We had, literally, the clothes on our backs, and some Marines didn't even have that. They had not even worn shirts to the sports day, and with their shower shoes shredded and lost now had to their names a pair of shorts. That was it. The men who had not made it back into the tents had lost every single thing they owned.

Sergeant Delaney, a funny, red-headed Irishman, found a marker and the back of a cardboard MRE box and made up a sign, *a la* the wino on the sidewalk, stating that he Will Liaison For Food.

One wiseacre pulled aside a member of the ad-hoc camp band, ready to perform, and told him they didn't have a hair on their respective asses if they didn't play the Talking Heads' *Burning Down The House.*

The sun fell out of the sky and disappeared, and now, burning hot all day, we were growing cold as the desert gave back her heat and the wind cooled and accelerated. Marines were bare-chested and barefoot and began to shiver. We didn't even know where we would sleep as the camp staff scrambled to figure out what to do with us, several hundred men suddenly homeless.

We ended up in a set of tents in the old abandoned British camp, called Rhino, a good half-mile away. Thoroughly exhausted, ANGLICO straggled in the dark to its new home, many Marines limping barefoot on the rocks, favoring cuts and blisters on their tender feet. We were a stream of refugees, hundreds of men walking in file across the camp to our new home. Every man now had a bunk but no sheets and no pillow, no nothing, but in our fatigue it didn't matter. I found an old, wet towel and threw that over my legs.

I pondered briefly that if I had gone down to watch the field meet with Brian and Sid, I would have lost everything, including the only thing I truly cared about: my journal. My entire war would have remained only in memory, as would this book.

We lay on our strange bare mattresses, refugees, nomads again in the same dry month, sweat drying off bare skin, shivering uncontrollably, and fell immediately asleep.

———•••———

Louis Zamperini said *You must be hardened to life.*

———•••———

We didn't much care about basic things which had been devoured, but we were realizing something much worse: we had lost our war.

Several of my cousins in our sister teams attached to the Desert Rats had videotape of entire firefights, hours of raw footage of heavy combat. One of our Captains, the one who had told me where to go for my tattoo the day before we left a hundred years ago, had held a video camera out the window during their push into Basrah, and recorded the fire and tracers and combat until the tape ran out.

Gone.

We had lost all our film, all our journals, all our footage of what we had done and what we had seen. All the award write-ups we had done on one another: lost. Computers, phones, money, cameras, film, journals, letters, photos: gone.

We had lost *who we had been* in this war. We were different men now, having undergone a violent rite of passage. We were not the same, not the same unit that had assembled in California in January, but the documentation of that change was gone. It lived in us now, inside the teams, and nowhere else.

Brian came as close to being angry with me as I had seen him. He couldn't believe that I had saved his pistol and his flak jacket, but in my frantic haste I had left behind his daypack with everything personal in it. He had lost the kukri the Gurkhas had given him, which I think hurt the most.

It was my fault.

He was angry, and *he was right*: the simple fact was that the Marine Corps obsession with weapons security, begun for every one of us at the hands of our drill instructors, had left a code in my subconscious: always be ready to fight. But I knew the Marine Corps would give us more weapons...and I had saved my own stuff. And JT Withrow's, both within reach in one sweep. Why not Brian's? I didn't have an answer, but I was mad at myself and at the world.

The fire brought out the tribe.

Marines we had never met appeared at our camp, arms full of equipment they had gathered up to give to us. They brought us uniforms, T-shirts, hats, toothpaste, socks, shoes, food. They gave their own gear to us. They literally gave us the shirts off their backs.

They were tribal brothers. We would have done the same for them.

I was never prouder, before or since, to be a United States Marine.

———•••———

The Red Cross, as it always does, came through in spades, actually backing up a truck to our little hovel and delivering whatever they could scrounge up for us. The American Red Cross to this day is the only charity to which I will donate. They are magnificent, in every clime and place.

———•••———

The camp leadership tried to tell us the fire had started from an electrical short. Not one man believed this.

A *hajji* laborer, an Arab, had been seen next to the wiring box at the top of our camp, right where the fire had begun. Dark rumors flew fast and ugly that the fire had been set, retaliation for our infidel presence on Muslim land.

———•••———

More ominously, I remembered a discussion with Brian and Sid, right after we came back into Kuwait weeks before.

They had been inside the barber tent, waiting for their haircuts and idly reading the camp bulletin board.

There on the board had been a notice from the camp commander, stating very clearly that there were to be no open flames, ever, in the camp, *because the tents had been soaked with kerosene.* Kerosene really is a great waterproofing liquid, because it penetrates and coats fabric with a thin film. This is also why it burns so well.

It was a full day before anyone remembered this, but the signs had somehow and I am sure by complete coincidence disappeared since the conflagration. The camp staff claimed no knowledge. The camp commander didn't know what we were talking about. There was a great shrugging of shoulders and furrowing of brows and pointing of fingers but somehow none of them could meet our eyes.

Like our anger at the faceless hajji, our disgust for that faceless idiot who had treated hot, dry cloth with the most flammable liquid imaginable grew in the vacuum of our empty days.

The unit began to tighten.

There is nothing worse for a field unit than to be stuck in garrison, and boredom is worse than fear or fatigue or stress. The boys began to get strange and manifested the classic signs of young men caged up for too long, behaving like prisoners: fights, shouting matches, rumors and innuendo, accusations founded and not, dark mutterings about the stupidity of senior officers.

Weapons discipline went out the window. All of us had learned at the whip hand of Marine drill instructors, every one of whom is completely psychotic about weapons accountability and cleanliness. Setting down a weapon and taking one step away from it is grounds for their corporal punishment, verbal abuse, dire threats of violence and expulsion and exile from the tribe. I had been shocked and amazed when Brian told me that Marines in Desert Storm had simply left weapons on their racks when heading to meetings...but now we were doing the same thing. Marines set rifles and pistols down and just walked away from them for hours at a time.

We just didn't give a fuck.

Our problem was that we were in limbo, able neither to gear up to go back out nor to prepare mentally for going home. We had no equipment, not even uniforms. No ammo, no boots, no communications, no weapons, no navigation or lasers or vehicles or maps.

We could not kill, so we were of no use. The Marine Corps ground on without us.

We were spectators now, all of us waiting on national leadership to get us out of the country.

First Marine Division had come back into Kuwait behind us. Major General Mattis, warrior and leader, the chief, knew what would happen. He started sending people home as fast as he could, trying to get us out of the country before some staff genius realized there was a full-strength combat-hardened division sitting in Kuwait and invented something for us to do.

He was and is our tribal chief and actions like this are why we all love him.

My new favorite guys were the civilian EOD teams.

They were older guys, mid-40s on up, and so when Sid lost his glasses in the fire that was where Brian went to find him another pair: those were the only guys in this camp as old as Sid.

They looked like pirates, beards and long hair, grey ponytails and jeans and work boots and pistols in drop holsters. They wore baseball hats and earrings and didn't give a fuck what anyone thought of them, and they had the most dangerous job I could imagine and thus earned three times what we did.

They drove brand-new SUVs and were always cheerful, and they were as in awe of us as we were of them. They claimed to work for a group called USA Environmental, but all of us knew that was bullshit: they were being paid through some darker mechanism than that. They were specialists, intense when they needed to be and blasé about everything else. I admired them.

———— •••• ————

To keep the Marines pacified, the command structure brought in the USO and with that traveling carnival came two of the sultriest women on the planet: Rebecca Romjin and Alyssa Milano.

The women detonated in our world of weapons and sand and shit and violence and heat and anger and barbed wire. Our troops lined up for hours to see them; the women's job apparently was to sit and look pretty, at which they succeeded admirably, those two the next in the USO Bombshell-In-The-War line stretching back to Marilyn Monroe and Jayne Mansfield and Betty Grable.

The Marines returned to the tents the staff had finally found for us, dreamy-eyed and gooey like girls once were after seeing the

Beatles. Corporal Duperroy wobbled back into the tent and sat with eyes glazed and without speaking for a long time. He finally stuttered that he had touched Alyssa on the shoulder and pronounced that he would never wash that hand again.

All voted this the highlight of the deployment. In this contest Rebecca and Alyssa ran unopposed.

———————•••———————

Then we lost Sid.

We had just gotten him back after his stint in Baghdad. For weeks, though, he had been worrying about abdominal pains, pissing blood. As was normal with men, he ignored it and assumed it would go away. Finally he checked into the medical clinic, who sent him posthaste to the Kuwait City CSH medical Habitrail where we had visited Santos.

Cancer.

Not Sid. Couldn't be. Anyone but Sid. Sid was Superman, veteran of four wars and thirty years in The Hood in Los Angeles. He had been in Vietnam, for Christ's sake. Sid was old enough to be father to any of us and grandfather to some, and he could still run us into the ground. His brutal PT routine (Six miles a day...six days a week! he had announced to me proudly) was a source of awe to all of us, even in the prime physical shape of our lives. He didn't drink or smoke and ate like an Olympic athlete.

They considered him so urgent that the medical people didn't even care where he went, as long as it was somewhere in the First World, with Spain and Germany the two American hospitals which could treat him immediately.

He had told Gator LaSala, who ran into the tent and grabbed all of us from India.

We were in the middle of our daily movie marathon, heavy on the action, sci-fi and sex and light on plot, by which we idled away our days. We had gone through *The Matrix* and were in the midst of mentally undressing and ravaging Angelina Jolie in *Tomb Raider* when he whispered urgently in my ear and led me and the rest of the boys out.

Sid was standing alone on the baking sand, and pulled us into another tent to give us the bad news.

We had the last supper an hour later, in the chow tent with few words passing between us. Montes was waiting in an idling Humvee outside, Sid's gear already packed and loaded. We trailed slowly to the vehicle, all of us miserable, Sid trying to cheer us up.

Then we were there, and he bear-hugged each of us in turn and swung aboard. He disappeared in a cloud of dust.

Not a group now but individuals, alone and each sad, we meandered back to our tent for another night of waiting.

We had returned from the war badly underweight and soft, all our muscle mass gone after months of sporadic eating, days on our feet followed by weeks spent sitting. We were determined to put that mass back on, each of us at least thirty pounds down from where we were when we left California in January.

Next to our tent the Marine Corps had an empty tent with stationary bikes, barbells and weight plates, all of it filthy and ruined after hundreds of Marines' use over the months before we returned.

We didn't care. It was something.

At 0430 every morning we arose and pulled on athletic shorts and ANGLICO sweatshirts, and we walked to the iron in the cool of the desert before daybreak with hoods up, monks on the way to Marine Corps matins, to worship in the canon of sunrise.

—————•••—————

The gym had a shitty old radio that played whatever the armed forces station was in Kuwait City. SSGT Arenas had saved his entire CD collection from the fire, and my entire high school years were in there: Journey, Styx, U2, Def Leppard, The Cars, Bon Jovi. I wore grooves in those disks in that gym.

Lance Corporal Hunter had just turned nineteen and I put the headphones on him one day so he could hear my music from when I was his age. He had no idea what he was listening to. His face was a total blank.

—————•••—————

We all needed ID cards after the fire.

Without an ID card we were each and all totally helpless, like losing your driver's license and then trying to prove who you are using a library card. After days of wavering and hand-wringing, the CO was finally able to wangle us a spot at the ID card center at Camp Arifjan, outside of Kuwait City to the west and a one-hour bus ride for us.

Camp Arifjan was all that was wrong with both our military and our efforts overseas. A massive, sprawling maintenance base, it leapt from the desert, all gleaming new buildings for which any commander in the United States would have killed.

We drove through the gate and all of us just stared, open-mouthed, at the difference between the wartime and peacetime military. Overweight female soldiers sauntered slowly between buildings in the heat, sodas in hand, wearing whatever they felt like. Gorgeous new maintenance bays for Humvees and trucks and even tanks sparkled in the 130-degree heat, vehicles lined up neatly in rows behind them. I had one thought as the brand-new buildings slid past our windows: *this does not look like a place the Americans are going to leave anytime soon.*

We piled out and into the headquarters building, and the Marines collapsed gratefully to the floor in the blasting air conditioning. This building was the first new clean thing we had seen in months, and certainly the coldest. As the Marines sprawled in luxury, the officers went to go sort things out.

We hadn't realized something else that separated a base full of warriors from a base of rear echelon pogues.

Today was Sunday.

Closed.

—•••—

My Marines complained and bitched (not the same thing) bitterly, constantly and accurately about how poorly they were treated by the platoon, the unit, the officers, the MEF, the Marine Corps, the Pentagon, the White House, NATO, the coalition, the allies, the

Arabs: anyone and everyone. The complaining hardened into full-strength bitching and rose to fever pitch as the days slid empty by.

———•••———

I had once asked a prosecutor why women seemed to never leave men who beat them. He answered that if they left, and thereby cut off the man's inevitable begging for forgiveness and buying of gifts and forswearing the action they both knew would start again, those women would lose the one thing that was good in their lives.

———•••———

The Marine Corps pulled itself together and scheduled us to return home.

We were sending one platoon back to the north, to work out of Hillah, the site of the Hanging Gardens of Babylon, one of the Seven Wonders of the World.

Fuck a world wonder, most of us thought.

But not all.

Volunteers were needed, and those bitching loudest were first with their hands in the air. These Marines seemed unable to explain even to themselves why they wanted to go back north.

The money had something to do with it, but there was a sense of pride, of honor, of being different, that none of us could get anywhere else.

They were going to stay with their abusive husbands.

And the rest of us were going home.

———— •••• ————

We found out on the last day in the war that our overweight, incompetent, illiterate buffoon of an executive officer had put in all the rear echelon guys for the Combat Action Ribbon.

The Combat Action Ribbon is next to personal awards for heroism the most coveted of all decorations among Marines, the mark of the warrior, and he did this *despite those men never having set foot in Iraq.*

My boys talked about it at breakfast the morning we left, spinning each other up and telling each other what an injustice this was and getting more and more indignant.

Scull finally reached his limit. He slammed down his fork and looked at me and said Sir I just don't know why I am so loyal to this shitty unit.

———— •••• ————

Omni Air Services had a plane for us at Kuwait International. It was really going to happen.

But as always, the subtheme of everything we did, every movement, every discussion, was one hard-learned by the decades of experience among us: *The Marine Corps is going to find some way to fuck us.*

The Marine Corps never, ever did anything the right way until bullets started to fly. There was always some problem, a hitch, a bad decision of commission or omission, by which Marines ended up sleeping in the rain somewhere unexpected. Even if they tried to do the right things, there would be a problem. So the cheeriness of learning we were actually leaving was tempered and subdued, with the corpus deciding we would believe it when we were standing somewhere else.

———————•••———————

On the night we left the war we held a formation to pass along crucial information on our departure. With square miles of open sand from which to choose our staff chose the spot directly in front of the bank of generators, which roared through the event and no one heard a word.

EXEUNT

Only dead gods are gods forever.
—Jose Saramago

22 JUNE 2003 2200 ▶ KUWAIT INTERNATIONAL AIRPORT KUWAIT CITY

Last Station of the Cross.

A very attractive female Army lieutenant stood before us and our mountain of gear to brief us on what the schedule would be. She was tense and angry and kept to business, all hard edges, with long practice in ignoring thousands of sex-starved men's eyes crawling over her.

They swiped our ID cards and put us through a several hours-long bag check. The officers flopped in the sand to allow the lads to go through first.

The Army people were a flood of dire warnings about consequences of bringing back contraband of any kind: weapons, ammo, switchblades, soil, ordnance.

They were most concerned about men trying to get weapons back into the country; this had been a serious problem during Desert Storm, with guys going to so far as to disassemble AKs and hide the pieces in fuel tanks and engine compartments of aircraft. War trophies were highly prized and they were right to be worried about our trying to get weapons back into the States.

There had been dozens of debates in the preceding week about how—or whether—to get Iraqi weapons out of the country. Most guys, me included, had chickened out and left them in the amnesty cans around Commando, in which you could leave weapons and ammo and bayonets and knives and all contraband without repercussion. But if they found it on you here, the consequences were dire: court-martial, incarceration, months more in Mesopotamia. We all concluded it wasn't worth it.

I had however spirited away a tiny bottle of Iraqi sand and said to myself the Army could go fuck themselves.

For those penitent among us time was fast fading. The confessional was a blue curtain in a corner of the hangar, behind which sat a fat bored soldier. To him sinners could give up contraband weapons and confess and ask the higher powers' forgiveness. He alone could grant you absolution *pro se*. There would be no absolution after this.

———•◆•———

As we were processing out of country that night, the team we left behind was moving back, over the border to Hillah and then to Baghdad.

Carlos Lopez, one of mine, had volunteered to go back into theater. I gave him my very comfortable, broken-in drop holster: I didn't need it, and he did.

———•◆•———

Three months later my doorbell rang in California. UPS handed me a package. No return address.

Inside it was my holster, and a teddy bear for my son.

I reached in for the bear. It was too heavy.

I flipped it over and extracted the Iraqi bayonet Carlos had secreted inside.

It leans now against my photo of that team, those young men at that old time.

---•••---

23 JUNE 2003 0200 ▶ KUWAIT
INTERNATIONAL AIRPORT

We were led from the tent to buses, watched every instant along the way. *Midnight Express*: armed MPs lined up and ensured none of us ran off.

Where in the fuck would we run to, and why? So we could stay here? Who knows what they were afraid of, but it was something nefarious. The buses crawled to the flight line.

Parked wingtip-to-wingtip as we passed were three gorgeous, gleaming new Gulfstream V jets. They had subtle, elegant markings on the side identifying them as belonging to the Kuwaiti emir.

Dave Allen was an airline pilot and issued a long, low wolf whistle and said Right there, gents, that's what one hundred million dollars' worth of airplanes looks like.

Our enlisted Marines who earned $25,000 a year for putting their lives on the line for those Gulfstreams gaped at the jets and we debarked the buses and marched to the only jet we had eyes for: the freedom bird.

---•••---

Flying military charter was like stepping back to the 1950s. The aircraft was parked alone, far out on the tarmac, with a rolling ladder next to it. Security kept an eye under each wing.

At 0230 on June 23, 2003 I walked up the ramp onto a charter 747. I turned and looked the last time at the desert wasteland we had put paid with our lives to protect. Then I turned back and went into my future.

———◆◆◆———

Our route: Kuwait City, Frankfurt, Baltimore, March Air Force Base.

The Marines, who had been jerked around for twelve hours humping hundreds of pounds from place to place and sitting on concrete, collapsed in their seats with joy and exhaustion. The undercurrent kept flowing: *They are going to fuck with us. Somehow something is going to go wrong.* I waited for some officer to come running up the stairs and pull us all off the plane. Knowing our incompetent staff, we were the sort of unit to which that sort of thing would happen. And we had been fucked with for so long that none of us would truly believe we were leaving until we were standing on American soil.

I just didn't feel the elation I expected. I wanted and needed and fucking *deserved* that good, clean feeling of release for which I had waited for six months. It didn't come. Not yet.

———◆◆◆———

Weapons went into the overhead bins.

———◆◆◆———

Omni Air was a charter service: stewardesses were fat, apathetic, cranky, angry at us and each other and themselves and the world. Were they the stewardess JV? Fired by the airlines? Never made it to the airlines in the first place? Was this Stewardess Elba?

The plane was old, cold, loud, dirty. The food was awful, and no coffee at all: if you wanted coffee, they gave you hot water and a package of instant. Seriously? Really?

I didn't expect to treated like someone special just because we were coming out of a combat zone, but I did think we would eat better than we had in the field. I thought wistfully back to the fantastic pilots and the charming, lovely girls on the Delta flight over, who had cried and hugged us when we deplaned because they knew we were going into a war.

I did, however, subscribe to the Sid Heal Theory of Leaving a War: They could strap me spread-eagled to the floor if it meant I was going home.

And, truly, it could have been worse: other guys were flying back in the back of military transports. And since they were being transported by the military they had a further indignity: they had to actually pay for their box lunches.

———•••———

Rhein-Main, Germany. Grass! Trees! You could be outdoors and comfortable *at the same time*!

The bathrooms were spotless, the building strong and functional and pristine and German. Everything here worked. It was the inverse to the Arab world we had left.

They let us out, like zoo animals, inside a fenced compound adjacent to our terminal, long enough to smell, for a moment, Western air.

———•••———

Puer

He leans forward on his elbows and spins his mug slowly
Next to but not on its coaster (beer mat...they call it a beer mat)
The water has condensed on the side of the glass, a cool coating
A very thin layer on the wood (meniscus, he remembers
At least that from high school chemistry, but not much else)

The glass floats and spins smooth above the wood
Any direction

He looks deeply into the glass, right to the bottom
Not the first to look for answers there
He will not find them because there is nothing to find
He has them already
He is young
But he is already full
He is here, right here but his eyes are away
In space but mostly in time

To the place where he is young, he is right here but seeing
Things only the old should know

COMPLINE

Nor ought we to believe that there is much difference between man and man, but to think that the superiority lies with him who is reared in the severest school.

— Thucydides

23 JUNE 2003 ▶ BALTIMORE

At Baltimore-Washington International we set foot on American soil again.

They sent us through customs, which involved taking all of our stuff off the plane, running it through the X-ray machines, and then putting the same bags right back on the same plane.

Then they made a mistake. They allowed us to go into the terminal.

This involved coming up out of the international portal and going through the scanners. So 400 of us left our weapons on the plane and lined up to go through the metal detector, each taking off his boots obediently.

———◆•◆———

We cleared customs and ran for the phones.

———◆•◆———

My grandmother heard my voice and started to cry.

She hadn't greeted family men coming back from war since my grandfather had returned from killing Japs in 1945.

———◆•◆———

And then I spoke to my son.

Jackson informed me in a very grown-up way that he had seen the movie with the orange fish called Little Meemo. But he wanted to go with me, just us two, to the *feeaber* and see it again.

I gripped the phone and started to cry and wondered if he would remember me.

——— •••• ———

We were set loose in the terminal, back among regular humans.

With our sunburns and uniforms it was obvious whence we had just come and a gasp and murmur went up from the crowds of people, regular people, Americans, our people.

We were the first guys back from the war.

Heads swiveled around. Bags were set down.

A few people started to clap. They had seen this only on television and now right here were men who had been there, the first they had seen.

Then more people clapped and it spread and then the entire airport just stopped in its tracks. Thousands of people set down their bags and applauded and cheered.

They cried and so did we.

——— •••• ———

The Marines headed for the beer.

It was nine o'clock in the morning.

We cleaned out every little drink cart and just-opened bar at BWI. Tolerances were low and the boys were swiftly wobbly, and when the word shot through the airport that the plane was waiting for us we collectively shrugged, figured the plane wouldn't leave without us, and ordered booze faster.

Corona with a lime. Ice cold. My first beer since Iraq.

Samuel Adams three minutes later, my second beer since Iraq.

Seven minutes later, my third beer since Iraq.

I stood now, with my fourth beer since Iraq, with Gator LaSala, Sergeant Dirty Steve Salicos and Sergeant Giannetti in a tight circle, toe to toe, and we just looked at each other and did not speak and we drank in silence in the flat morning sun.

———◆◆◆———

A very happy and now very mellow ANGLICO unit filed back down the long twisting Habitrail to our plane.

We wobbled up to the customs and security checkpoint. I was in front.

They stopped us. OK, folks, take off your shoes and empty your pockets please. Any metal objects go in the bin. One at a time through the metal detector.

I, five beers down, said to the security guy You do know that we have rifles and pistols and heavy weapons in the overhead bins *ON THE FUCKING PLANE.*

He didn't care.

There's no fighting in the War Room.

———◆◆◆———

We slept off our beers across the United States and March Air Force Base threw us a homecoming: two fire trucks parked nose-to-nose and sprayed an arch of water for us. It was touching.

The base commander to his credit came to meet us at the bottom of our rolling ladder, and shook hands with each man as he walked off the plane.

We stumbled across the tarmac, jetlagged and drunk and hung over and exhausted and unshaven and happy in late afternoon sun.

We were closely watched to keep us from—what, running for the fence? Trying to escape? Who knew? *Midnight Express* on this end too—and led carefully to the same warehouse where we had sat waiting to go the other direction five months earlier.

A receiving line of little old ladies and VFW-type World War II veterans hugged and held us as we walked through. I choked up as tiny little ladies who came up to my sternum hugged me with wet shining eyes and thought this is America.

———•••———

A police escort took us slowly off the base and put us on the highway with a blast of siren and lights.

We settled into the last hour of our combat deployment to the war in Iraq.

We stared in the gathering dark at traffic that seemed to move so fast after our months of driving on sand. People around us drove and swore and yelled into cell phones and thought about their jobs and their kids and listened to the radio: just a normal evening on the Los Angeles freeways. They were oblivious that feet away sat men who had just done something big but didn't yet know what it meant.

———•••———

Half of our guys were federal, state, or local cops, so all of Los Angeles County law enforcement knew we were coming home.

Halfway through Los Angeles a phalanx joined our bus convoy, dozens of police cars, CHP and Long Beach PD and LAPD and LA Sheriffs, a car on each side of us, and ten or twelve each in front and behind. They took turns zooming ahead to shut down onramps as we passed, leapfrogging past each other, keeping the traffic away from us.

Word had spread across the city and people were gathered on overpasses, unsure who we were but knowing that a couple of school buses with the clout to shut down a rush-hour LA freeway must hold some secret.

That, we did.

———•••———

We went over the Vincent Thomas Bridge out of San Pedro onto Terminal Island and made the final turn into the ANGLICO parking lot, approaching the wired compound crouching as the very very last building alone in a sea of concrete that was once the Long Beach Naval Base, now humble beneath monstrous COSCO Chinese shipping cranes, so tall they had lights lining the crane arms to warn aircraft, enormous *Terminator* behemoths bestriding a row of alien machines beyond sight into the distance.

Signs and banners hung from the fences as we approached, promising hugs and love and sex to the men on the bus with me.

As we started down the access road to the base we could hear from a quarter mile away a roar rise from the parking lot: thousands of people waiting for us. Now we could see them screaming, crying, waving banners, jumping up and down, children running back and forth.

The bus pulled up and all ignored the ignominy of returning from war on a school bus and I was the first one off, and I jogged away at an angle from the bus to get clear of the dozens of men at full sprint behind me. Every wife was leaping into her husband's arms, screaming and weeping and burying her head in men's shoulders in the roar and tumult.

Combat-hardened Marines cried like babies.

Reunions swirled, families with dozens of members greeting their sons and fathers and husbands and brothers.

Every television station in Los Angeles had a camera crew there and they lit the dark like day, recording it all. We had been the first unit out and into the war and now we were the first unit back, and we would headline tonight's 11:00 news.

We trooped inside for beer and food and all of us smiled wider than we had in months. Staff NCOs did what they do and issued dire warnings about weapons accountability and getting names on rosters but they were smiling as they said it and so were we and we all ignored them.

And just like that our deployment was over and then we were free.

24 JUNE 2003 0900 ▶ MY FRONT PORCH,
SAN DIEGO, CALIFORNIA

I sat alone cradling a cup of coffee on my top porch step, up for hours, still on Kuwait time, watching the morning.

My heart was pounding and I had full tears running down my cheeks and dripping onto my shirt.

Then the back door to the car flew open and like a shot my little boy sprinted as fast as his three-year-old legs would carry him up the first stairs and straight to me like a laser.

And he threw his little arms around my neck and held and squeezed and I cried and he cried and neither of us would let go.

———◆◆◆———

Jackson and I that night climbed a ladder to the flat roof of our bungalow. There we stood and looked at the moon.

I asked him why he liked climbing the ladder all that way up instead of just looking at the moon from the yard. He said Because Daddy up here it is closer.

NAMASTE

*All up and down the line, one beheld warriors clustering
in groups of twos and threes as the terror they
had managed to hold at bay throughout the battle
now slipped its bonds and surged among them.*

*Clasping their comrades by the hand, they knelt- not
from reverence alone, but because the strength had fled
from their knees, which could no longer support them.*

This was hesma phobu: fear shedding.

*Many wept. Others shuddered violently. Some
of the men tried to dress their hair but their
hands trembled so badly they could not do it.*
—Steven Pressfield, *Gates of Fire*

Two weeks after I returned from combat I went to visit a tribal elder, Nicholas Warr, a thoughtful, introspective author who had been a Marine officer in the fight for Hue City.

He and I sat and looked at the California sunset while his lovely wife brought treats for my son, who sat near us with his feet not touching the ground.

Nick and I could talk now that I had seen The Elephant.

He said The war will never leave you.

———————•••———————

During the Dust Bowl 1930s, poor families desperate to protect their babies from the swirling dirt had only one option: they covered the cribs with a wet sheet to keep out the dust.

Those sheets quickly became saturated with dirt, which turned to mud on the damp cloth, covering the infants in a dark shroud which the parents dared not lift no matter how the babies shrieked. Those babies became adults and they grew up terrified of the dark.

———————•••———————

First Marine Expeditionary Force put on a parade through downtown Oceanside, harkening back to the way men were greeted returning from World War II.

Lieutenant General Conway led his Marines, tens of thousands of them, through the screaming, cheering crowds.

But he did something no one had seen before.

From the head of the column, his six stars on his collars gleaming in the sunlight, he walked from side to side crossing the street and reached into the crowd and pulled out men who he knew had been in Vietnam, our tribal forebears who had been cast aside after that campaign and who had fought for one another and Corps and tribe and on whose shoulders we stood and stand.

General Conway pulled them each into the parade and the general said to them You are our brothers. March with us. This is the parade you never got.

———•••———

JULY 4, 2003 ▶ EL CAJON, CALIFORNIA

I was one of the first people back from the invasion of Iraq, and I was therefore much in demand from local groups who wanted to hear about this campaign in Mesopotamia.

I was outdoors at a Fourth of July street festival, on a stage behind a microphone on a podium draped with bunting, speaking to a crowd of several hundred people, telling them how magnificent our fighting force was, what I had seen.

I told these people that their Marines and soldiers were in the fight in the desert, winning, doing it right for the people back home, representing the best of who we are as a nation.

Standing far to the back of the crowd was a motorcycle gang, several dozen members of that fearsome tribe. Huge, hairy guys, menacing, beards and bandannas and leather and denim and chains and boots, leaning on their Harleys, inscrutable behind wraparound sunglasses.

As I came off the stage, they came to me as a very large group of very large people.

I took a subconscious step back.

But one of them grabbed me and now I saw the Marine Corps eagle, globe and anchor sewn onto his vest, right next to his Vietnam campaign patch and it was not *his* tribe, it was *mine, ours,* and he embraced me and he wept and so did I and he said Right on, brother. Right on.

CHIRICAHUA APACHE

The war was strange and ugly, stranger and uglier than anyone knew, strange and ugly and fantastic.
—Jack Laurence, *The Cat From Hue*

2004 ▶ ONE YEAR LATER

I was in the gym on Twentynine Palms Marine Base, the home of the desert fighters.

Seventh Marines, to whom I had once belonged.

Seventh Marines: the men Mattis had commanded.

Seventh Marines: the men who saved Sid's life.

I went into the locker room and saw a Staff Sergeant I recognized from my past, a big strong Hispanic guy. I didn't know how I knew him, but he was familiar, one of those faces of men I admired and emulated.

I undressed in silence and worked out and I went into the showers ahead of him and he came in a few minutes later and when he got there naked I saw scars all over his chest and arms, long gouges, bullet wounds, burns across his arms and back.

We dried off in silence and he wrapped a towel around his waist and he looked into my face and recognized me too, and he nodded with respect and I back to him and we did not speak in any way but that which matters.

SEICHE

The war magnified everything, even perceptions of itself.
—Jack Laurence, *The Cat From Hue*

Glenn Walsh is now a very senior leader, a Lieutenant in Los Angeles Sheriff's Department, with dozens of narcotics cops, informants and undercover men working for him all over the city.

He is thirty pounds of muscle bigger than he was in the war, broad and strong, and I hadn't seen him in fifteen years and when I took him to the train station he grabbed me in a bear hug as only a brother would and held me strong and said I love you.

DEBRIEF

*If I were a man I would be on the field of
action. That is where all honor lies.*
—Abigail Adams

Tim O'Brien in his masterpiece *The Things They Carried* said if at the end of a war story you feel uplifted, then you have been made the victim of a very old and terrible crime.

CODA

The war ended, and then it really ended.
—Michael Herr, *Dispatches*

After I returned from the war, I went to a party aboard a boat docked on San Diego Bay.

Everyone congregated at the Sheraton Hotel next to the airport; the marina was behind the Sheraton, and to get on the boat we had to go through the lobby and onto the hotel's waterfront property. The lobby sign advertised some sort of Iraqi-American banquet.

As I approached the huge, heavy glass doors at the front, a group of *very* attractive, *very* stylish women went before me in a swish of expensive dresses and heels.

They were dark-skinned, all of them with manes of thick black hair, and they were speaking rapid-fire Arabic.

Iraqi.

I was off-balance from the war, jumpy at loud noises, far more introspective and emotional than when I had left the United States, *older then than I am now.*

As I approached the door, trailing these women, my brain whickered through memories of their country which I considered now mine as well because if you fight for something is it not yours forever?

I thought of the dead bodies, the smell of the filthy villages, livestock in the streets.

I thought of my American Marine and British Army tribes, united for a cause not our own.

I thought of Shane Childers.

I thought of the Iraqi battalion commander whom we had taken prisoner.

I thought of our 5th Special Forces soldier who was probably still there.

I thought of that world, all hard edges and cold steel, barbed wire and dirt, muscle and foul language and filth and shit and death and tattoos and violence and love.

I thought of standing in the sand drinking whiskey from price-less silver.

Conde, smiling cheerfully despite his fatigue.

Sid and I walking into the ANGLICO CP on the first day of our activation, geared up already for what was to come.

Santos hurt, bruised and broken, his skull shattered, sitting on the hot sand with the confused look of a wounded child.

My Marines, putting their lives on the line for that strange sad country, putting our skills to work to defend people we did not know, putting our lives on hold for the tribe, putting our hands into a crystal vase of pit vipers.

The man in Medinah, tears of joy in his eyes and pouring down his cheeks, who approached our column and insisted that I come to his home for tea and bread.

Walsh leaping from the bridge.

Lopez volunteering to go back north, to keep trying, to keep working and helping people he would never know.

Scull, loyal to a shitty unit.

Children south of Amarah sprinting full speed on skinny legs from their compounds to wave to us as we went by.

Saddam crashing to the ground in Tawal as the entire city screamed with joy.

The little girls we saw on Sunday morning, bright and happy, brown skin and black hair and gleaming white teeth, skipping and chattering their way to school in their uniforms.

I got to the door.

The Iraqi woman closest to me tossed her scarf over her shoulder, leaned into the heavy glass door, pushed it just enough to ease herself through.

She spun, looked at my haircut, glared at me.

And slammed the door in my face.